Kiplinger's

Buying

and Selling

a Home

MAKE THE RIGHT CHOICE IN *ANY* MARKET

From the Editors of
Kiplinger's Personal Finance

 KAPLAN PUBLISHING

This publication is designed to provide accurate and authoritative information in regard to the subject matter covered. It is sold with the understanding that the publisher is not engaged in rendering legal, accounting, or other professional service. If legal advice or other expert assistance is required, the services of a competent professional person should be sought.

President, Kaplan Publishing: Roy Lipner
Vice President and Publisher: Maureen McMahon
Senior Managing Editor: Jack Kiburz
Typesetter: the dotted i
Cover Designer: Design Solutions

Published by Kaplan Publishing,
a division of Kaplan, Inc.

Printed in the United States of America

06 07 08   10 9 8 7 6 5 4 3

Library of Congress Cataloging-in-Publication Data

Buying & selling a home : make the right choice in any market / from the editors of Kiplinger's Personal Finance Magazine.— 8th ed.
    p. cm.
  Includes index.
  ISBN-13: 978-1-4195-3578-9
  ISBN-10: 1-4195-3578-1
  1. House buying. 2. House selling. 3. Home ownership. 4. Real estate business.
I. Kiplinger's personal finance magazine.
HD1379.K52 2006
643′.12—dc22

2005033458

Kaplan Publishing books are available at special quantity discounts to use for sales promotions, employee premiums, or educational purposes. Please call our Special Sales Department to order or for more information at 800-621-9621, ext. 4444, e-mail kaplanpubsales@kaplan.com, or write to Kaplan Publishing, 30 South Wacker Drive, Suite 2500, Chicago, IL 60606-7481.

Contents

What amazing changes have occurred in residential housing markets in the 23 years since the first edition of this book was published.

The interest rate on a 30-year fixed-rate mortgage fell from more than 13 percent in 1983 to less than 6 percent in 2005. A surge of first-time buyers pushed the home ownership rate to more than 68 percent of all households in 2005, according to U.S. Census data. In most of America, home prices surged every year in the decade between 1995 and 2005, making residential real estate a hot investment and diverting capital from the stock market.

New homeowners include not just the traditional young couples and families, but also surprising numbers of single people, especially women. Immigrants, who came to America in record numbers over the past 30 years, have also joined the ranks of homeowners at a gratifying rate, often revitalizing urban neighborhoods in the process.

Big changes have also occurred in where and how Americans are choosing to live. As traffic worsens in most large metropolitan areas, more and more homeowners are rediscovering the joys of living in town, close to shopping, work, and mass-transit lines. This has caused a boom in "in-fill" development—new homes and condos built on vacant lots in older neighborhoods—and "tear-down" development—removing an older home and replacing it with a new one. And even in many new suburban communities, developers are seeing a strong demand for homes laid out in a neotraditional, small-town pattern. These new homes on small lots are often sited within walking distance of stores, offices, and schools, and they face sidewalks and narrow streets around a village green or square, with porches in front and garages (some with apartments above) on alleys behind the house.

While the average new home today is higher priced than ever before, it is also much bigger, more energy efficient, and filled with amenities that were once seen only in luxury homes. And increasingly, "home" doesn't mean a detached house, but a spacious, modern condominium. Many buyers actually prefer the ease of condo living to the maintenance of their own detached home.

There have been a lot of changes in the marketing of homes, too. Discount brokers and buyer's brokers abound, challenging the traditional full-commission broker who is compensated entirely by the seller. The Internet has become a force in real estate, with online Multiple Listing Services offering detailed information and "virtual open houses" of every listing in their region. And thousands of homebuyers are now using the Internet to shop for their financing, often even applying for the mortgage online, through the lender's Web site.

The strong earnings of baby boomers are creating a strong market for upscale trade-up housing. When home prices softened during the recession of 1990–1991, forecasts of long, deep declines in real estate values began to appear in the popular press. We saw no basis for these projections, and our judgment was vindicated by the strong housing market that has followed.

In some parts of the country, the soaring stock market and high-tech bubble of the late 1990s caused crazy speculation in housing, with double-digit annual increases in home prices. This cooled off dramatically during the bear market and recession of 2001–2002, then started up again. According to the National Association of Realtors, half of the homes resold in June 2005 cost more than $219,000; a year before, the figure was $191,000. That's an increase of 14.7 percent in a year, and if you lived on the East or West Coast your home's value probably rose even faster.

These rates of increase are not sustainable, because they have widely outstripped average annual gains in personal income, creating a growing affordability problem for first-time buyers. So it is likely that gains will flatten out—or prices actually decline—in some of the most overheated housing markets over the next few years, especially as interest rates drift up.

In most regions, home ownership will return to its traditional role as one building block of personal wealth, not a vehicle for quick speculative gains. It won't always be one's best-performing asset, compared with stocks or bonds, but that's not a knock on home ownership. It will continue to be a good inflation hedge (matching or slightly exceeding the rate of inflation), an excellent tax shelter (one of the few left), and a handy forced-savings plan, requiring you to add to your equity each time you write a mortgage check. And in case you forgot, an owned home will also be your shelter, some place you know you can stay, without worrying about hikes in rent or termination of the lease.

How This Book Will Help You

This book is really two books in one: Part One, for buyers, and Part Two, for sellers. Whichever you are—buyer, seller, or both at once—carefully read the part addressed to the other party. You will gain insight into the concerns and strategies of all the major players in a transaction, and the knowledge will help you get a better deal for yourself.

Recognizing that the vast majority of real estate transactions are handled by brokers and agents who receive a commission on the sale, *Buying and Selling a Home* tells you the right way to select and deal with these professionals. For the few homeowners who have the time and marketing flair to try their hand at selling without an agent—a very challenging task—we give realistic, step-by-step advice on how to do it.

The book also recognizes that your home is most likely your major investment. It will assist you in investing wisely, both in terms of choosing a house and financing it in a way that best meets your needs. *Buying and Selling a Home* also helps you safeguard your investment and tells you how to use the equity you'll build up to relieve other financial concerns, from remodeling expenses to college tuition. Special solutions to problems senior citizens may face are also covered. Inclusion of a score of worksheets and checklists and references to many more resources will make your going easier.

We hope that *Buying and Selling a Home* helps guide you through the murky and often turbulent waters of real estate deals in America today and tomorrow. Real estate has long been a core subject of *Kiplinger's Personal Finance* magazine, the first magazine of personal finance guidance, so the subjects discussed here will be periodically updated there and on the Kiplinger Web site at http://www.kiplinger.com.

Don't hesitate to write us with your questions or comments. Your ideas will help us strengthen the book in future editions.

Knight Kiplinger

Knight A. Kiplinger
Editor in Chief
Kiplinger's Personal Finance magazine

Part I

For Buyers

To Buy or Not to Buy

Home ownership has long been regarded as one of the key elements of the American dream. The reasons for America's love affair with home ownership are many. Some are financial. Our tax code continues to subsidize heavily the ownership of homes, making it more attractive than renting for most people. Home ownership is also America's favorite forced-savings and investment plan, with an increasing share of the monthly mortgage payment going into the building of equity for future uses—another home, college expenses, or retirement, for example. A home is truly the only investment you can live in, and over the past 50 years or so, it has been an investment that's generally performed well, relative to alternative uses of money.

But much of the motivation behind home ownership is psychological. This country was founded on principles of individual destiny, personal control over one's life and surroundings, and freedom of individual expression. A home of one's own helps fulfill all those promises, making the owner free from rent hikes and landlord's whims, and free to live life as he or she wishes. A home can provide a sense of security and pride. A home gives a feeling of stability and commitment, not to mention autonomy and privacy. It is often the first step a person takes to put down roots in a community.

But like most freedoms, those that come with home ownership also carry heavy responsibilities—not only financial obligations but also the duties of maintenance, record keeping, and planning.

Before you
dive into
the search
for a home,
examine your
motives,
clarify your
wants and
needs, and
focus your
investigation.

The Intangibles

It's no wonder that psychologists rank buying a home high on the list of stress-producing events. Not only is it the biggest purchase most people make in a lifetime, but also it forces a wholesale examination of goals, commitments, and lifestyle. It's an emotional as well as a financial investment.

People buy homes for lots of different reasons. Before you dive into the search for a home, examine your motives, clarify your wants and needs, and focus your investigation.

With so much at stake, don't rush into the market without thoughtful preparation. If you join the ranks of buyers charging about for answers without knowing the right questions, you may—by luck—end up with a house you can live with. Then again, you may spend weeks, even months, looking at houses only to end up feeling thwarted and confused.

Financial Benefits

Treating a home solely as an investment probably is impossible. Financial calculations alone don't give you the perspective you need for such a big decision. Still, a home is a major investment, and the financial aspects of home ownership should not be ignored. Some key financial benefits of home ownership are:

Budgetary Discipline

Accumulating the down payment on a home is often the goal that leads to a family's first real savings program. Later on, paying the mortgage is a strong inducement to creating and sticking with a budget. Depending on your personality and level of discretionary income, this form of enforced savings (and consequent equity buildup) can be an important factor in boosting family net worth. Stripped to its essentials, equity is the difference between what you would get if you sold your home and what you still owe. Equity includes the down payment, all payments against the principal balance, and any appreciation in the market value of your home that occurs after you buy it.

The Power of Leverage

Buying a home offers you the opportunity to magnify the purchasing power of your money through what is called leverage—the use of borrowed money to purchase an asset that is likely to appreciate, magnifying your profit.

Normally, you buy property—whether it's a home or a commercial building—with some of your own funds plus a long-term mortgage. That use of borrowed money enables you to profit from price increases on property you haven't yet paid for.

The larger your loan as a proportion of the home's value, the greater your leverage and potential gain. Say you purchase a $250,000 single-family house with no loan and sell it three years later for $300,000. The $50,000 gain represents a 20 percent return on your $250,000 outlay.

Suppose, on the other hand, that you had invested only $40,000 of your own money and borrowed the

---

QUALITY OF LIFE

Before you take the plunge into home ownership, address questions like these:

- **What does being a homeowner mean to you?** To your spouse or partner?
- **What do you really want in a home, and from a home?**
- **If you have children or plan to someday, how will your choice of a home affect them?** Where you buy determines where children will go to school; what facilities will be nearby for recreation, shopping, and worship; and whether your neighborhood will be "child-friendly."

- **What about proximity and convenience for friends?** Your home's location or design can make it a favorite gathering place for your friends or extended family.
- **How will becoming a homeowner change you and the way you live?** You no doubt have heard stories about the totally unhandy new buyer who ends up renovating his or her home from top to bottom; the successful entrepreneur whose business began in a spare room or basement; or the free spirit who is transformed into a model of financial responsibility by home ownership.

The leverage that is so alluring when real estate values are on the rise can act to magnify losses as well as gains.

other $210,000. When you sell (ignoring for the sake of simplicity the cost of the loan, tax angles, commissions, and other costs), you'll have made $50,000 on your $40,000 investment, a spectacular 125 percent return over the three years of ownership.

Using maximum leverage—with a very small down payment and a very large mortgage—isn't prudent or advantageous for everyone, but most first-time buyers will need all they can get just to open the door.

Appreciation

If your home is worth more when you sell it than when you bought it, that's appreciation. When you sell it you can use the profit as a springboard to a better home. Or you can tap the equity (appreciation buildup) to pay college tuition, buy a vacation place, or take a long-dreamed-of cruise. For many people, the equity in their homes becomes a major source of retirement funds.

Tax Benefits

Homeowners benefit from the tax deductibility of mortgage interest and property taxes. In addition, when you sell your home, $250,000 of profit from the sale is tax-free if you file a single return, and up to $500,000 is tax-free if you file a joint return (see Chapters 3 and 15 for more details on tax benefits for homeowners).

The Risks and Hard Work of Home Ownership

So far, it may sound as if there's no way to lose. But home ownership is not for everyone. There are risks—as well as burdens.

Financial Risks

The value of your home is not guaranteed to go up, and it could go down. The leverage that is so alluring when real estate values are on the rise can act to magnify losses as well as gains. For example, suppose you invest $40,000 in a home valued at $250,000 in a booming economy. Then recession hits your community, you lose your job, and you're forced to sell for $210,000; the $40,000 loss wipes out 100 percent of your investment, and you'll probably have to dig into your pocket to cover commissions and other expenses. Real estate is not a liquid asset. You can lose if you have to sell in a hurry, because of a divorce or job loss, for example.

Some families stretch to the limit to buy homes they can't really afford by relying on interest-only or variable-rate loans to qualify for big mortgages. They may be in for a rude shock when rates rise and payments adjust accordingly. Such a scenario could force them to sell or lead to foreclosure (see Chapters 2 and 10).

You lose, too, if you invest in a home money that could have been invested elsewhere for a better return. If alternative investments—such as stocks or bonds—are rising in value faster than homes in your area, you might do better, in the short run, as a renter-investor rather than as a homeowner.

Even if you buy a home, you may want to hold back some of your cash to invest in income-producing assets rather than pour it all into your new home; this is especially relevant for the trade-up home buyer who has substantial cash from the sale of the previous home.

Homes cost money to maintain. You have to be prepared to pay for routine maintenance (usually with time and money) and for the inevitable replacement of big-ticket items. Average annual maintenance costs are about $1,500, not counting major replacements such as the roof or furnace. Be sure to budget for annual maintenance costs such as painting, cleaning roof gutters, and HVAC servicing, and be prepared for unbudgeted costs such as repair of or replacing air conditioners and major appliances, which can break down without warning.

Reduced Flexibility

Homeowners have less freedom of movement; it's not easy to pack up and move for a change of scenery or a new job. And a hefty mortgage payment may make it hard to maintain savings and investment programs for retirement, vacations, and other things.

Be sure to budget for annual maintenance costs, and be prepared for unbudgeted costs.

Over time, rents tend to increase. But, if you have a fixed-rate mortgage, the basic cost of ownership stays the same.

Rent Versus Buy

In the short run, renting can make more financial sense than buying, in terms of how much shelter you can afford for a given price.

Rents tend to accurately reflect the free-market pricing of housing simply as *shelter.* But the ownership cost of a house or condominium is a combination of both the dwelling's *shelter* value and *investment* expectation.

So at any given moment, you can usually rent an apartment or house for less than the monthly costs that a buyer of that property would pay to carry it through the early years of ownership.

This explains why many young people can't afford to own the very condominium they've been renting with no financial strain, or why a young family might be able to rent a much fancier, more spacious house than they could buy.

That's the short-run picture, but the long-range view is different. Over time, rents tend to rise. But, if you have a fixed-rate mortgage, the basic cost of owning your own home—the monthly payment of principal and interest—stays the same. This relatively stable cost, combined with price appreciation, is what makes home ownership financially attractive in the long run.

Until the "long run" arrives, however, you may have to make some sacrifices as a homeowner. You may have to put up with less space if you have to pay more to own a small home than to rent a larger one. To find a house you can afford, you might have to move to a location farther from your job and favorite haunts; that may result in the need of a second car, extra travel costs, and a change of lifestyle.

Buying a House with Others

While the vast majority of houses are owned either solely by individuals or jointly by married couples, single people living as couples or in groups may want the advantages of home ownership, too. Many lenders are still cool to such arrangements, but willing ones can be found.

The two most usual ways of buying property jointly with relatives or unrelated friends are tenancy-in-common and partnership. A good real estate lawyer can explain these arrangements to you (see also the discussion in Chapter 12 of how to take title).

Owning as part of a group or with an unmarried partner can create problems. When a share of tenancy-in-common ownership changes hands, the lender may declare the whole loan due. For remaining owners who don't want to sell the property, the only recourse is to refinance.

The best strategy for unrelated individuals may be to set up a limited partnership, in which the partnership, not the individual owners, takes the title. In a limited-partnership arrangement, a deceased partner's heirs would acquire the interest in the partnership; the partners could be among the heirs. This precludes problems if one partner goes into bankruptcy or has other legal problems that could cloud the title, because the partnership is separate from any legal hassles of the individual partners.

If you choose to set up a limited partnership, consult with a lawyer experienced in partnerships who can help you draw up the partnership agreement.

A SMART CONTRACT FOR PARTNERS

Make sure your partnership agreement addresses the following points:

- **How the use of the house's space is to be divided.**
- **How ownership will be divided,** which determines who pays how much of the down payment, the monthly payment, and the cost of maintenance and repairs. The contract should describe how any profits or losses from rent or sale of the place will be divided and how tax benefits will be distributed.
- **What constitutes a deciding vote,** and under what circumstances such a vote is considered necessary.
- **Which owner will act as managing partner** and thus be responsible for signing checks and paying routine expenses.
- **How much advance notice a withdrawing partner must give** and how the buyout price will be set.

The legal and financial details associated with ownership by unrelated individuals are just the beginning of your consideration of this issue.

Just as important (perhaps more so) is compatibility of lifestyle and the prospects of a durable friendship among all involved. As for investment value, keep in mind that partnership interests in a commonly owned house are not highly liquid. For any individual to get full value for his or her share, the whole group may have to sell.

There are a lot of obstacles to overcome in such an arrangement, but with careful planning and thoughtfulness among friends, it can work out well both socially and financially.

Assessing Your Resources

Once you have determined that you're serious about buying a home—but before you start looking at houses—gather the information you will need to present to lenders. Review your financial situation to determine what you can pay down and how large a monthly load you can carry.

When you've completed that task, contact a lender to get your figures plugged into mortgage formulas that yield an affordable price range. This kind of preparation—called *prequalifying*—will give you a financial comfort zone within which to shop. You'll know what's easy, what's possible, and what is out of the question.

Keep in mind that prequalifying gives you only a general idea about your borrowing power. Once you start looking in earnest for a home or begin working with a Realtor, you should get *preapproved* by a lender. A preapproval is a lender's firm commitment to giving you a loan, and it tells the seller that you are a serious buyer. It demonstrates your financial strength and shows that you have the ability to go through with a purchase. This information is important to sellers because they do not want to accept an offer that will likely fail if the would-be buyers can't obtain financing. In fact, in a sellers market, most sellers won't pay much attention to your offer unless you have already been okayed for a loan. However, you can even get online preapproval for a mortgage before you start shopping.

HOW TO FIGURE YOUR NET WORTH

What You Own

CASH	$ AMOUNT
Cash on hand	_____
Checking accounts	_____
Savings accounts	_____
Money-market accounts	_____
Life insurance cash value	_____
Money owed you	_____

MARKETABLE SECURITIES	
Stocks	_____
Bonds	_____
Government securities	_____
Mutual funds	_____
Other investments	_____

PERSONAL PROPERTY (RESALE VALUE)	
Automobiles	_____
Household furnishings	_____
Art, antiques, and other collectibles	_____
Clothing, furs	_____
Jewelry	_____
Recreation and hobby equipment	_____
Other possessions	_____

REAL ESTATE (APPRAISED VALUE)	
Homes	_____
Other properties	_____

RETIREMENT FUNDS	
Vested portion of company plans	_____
Vested benefits	_____
IRAs or Keogh plans	_____
Annuities (surrender value)	_____

OTHER ASSETS	
Equity in business	_____
Partnership interests	_____

TOTAL ASSETS	$_____

What You Owe

CURRENT BILLS	$ AMOUNT
Rent	_____
Utilities	_____
Credit card balances	_____
Insurance premiums	_____
Alimony or child support	_____
Other bills	_____

TAXES	
Federal	_____
State	_____
Local	_____
Taxes on investments	_____
Other	_____

MORTGAGES	
Homes	_____
Home equity	_____
Other properties	_____

DEBTS TO INDIVIDUALS	_____

LOANS	
Auto	_____
Education	_____
Other	_____

TOTAL LIABILITIES	$_____

Your Net Worth

TOTAL ASSETS	$_____
MINUS TOTAL LIABILITIES	–_____
EQUALS YOUR NET WORTH	$_____

Figure Your Net Worth

If you don't have a net-worth statement already, it's time to put one together. That inventory of your assets and liabilities will help you to determine the maximum down payment you can make. If money you will need is tied up in illiquid assets such as your current home, land, or collectibles, you must allow yourself plenty of time either to sell or to borrow against them. You can use the worksheet on the previous page to calculate your net worth.

The Down Payment

Now use the worksheet below to find the maximum down payment you could make if you wanted to put all your liquid assets into the purchase of a new home. From your total liquid net worth (including the equity you'll get from the sale of your present home), subtract:

■ **savings** for emergencies, educational expenses, or retirement;

■ **settlement and moving costs;**

FIGURE YOUR DOWN PAYMENT

	$ AMOUNT
NET WORTH (total assets minus liabilities)	_____
Minus funds reserved for college expenses, savings, retirement, emergency needs, etc.	–_____
Minus cash needed to buy the new home	
Sales expenses for current home	–_____
Settlement expenses	–_____
Moving and relocating expenses	–_____
Immediate improvements to new home	–_____
Decorating, furnishing new home	–_____
NET ASSETS AVAILABLE	$_____
Plus gifts from parents, relatives	+_____
TOTAL AVAILABLE CASH FOR DOWN PAYMENT	$_____

■ **and cash** you'll need to improve, decorate, and furnish your new home.

The bottom line will be the sum that you could put down on the new house, if you wished to use it all. The more cash you pay up front, the less you will have to pay month by month on the mortgage, and the lower your total interest costs will be.

Conversely, the less you put down, the greater will be your leverage, tax deductions for mortgage interest, and available funds for other expenses, including decorating and furnishing. Also keep in mind that the money you hold back from your down payment, if invested wisely, might earn you more than the appreciation on your property will add to your equity.

As you figure the amount of your liquid assets, remember that you might not have to put the whole sum into the down payment. Though lenders would ideally like to see you put 20 percent down, many home buyers (particularly first-time buyers) have a difficult time coming up with that much cash. If you put less than 20 percent down, you will be expected to have a higher income relative to long-term debt than someone who puts down 20 percent. And you may be required to purchase private mortgage insurance, which protects the lending institution if you default. But the minimum amount required will ultimately be determined by the lender, the type of mortgage you choose, and whether the loan will be sold in the secondary mortgage market.

Mortgage lenders, of course, prefer a big down payment to a minimal one. That tells the lender that the new homeowner has a major stake in the property and won't be tempted to default on the loan and walk

---

FOR STATE INFORMATION

Contact the **National Council of State Housing Agencies** (444 North Capitol St., N.W., #438, Washington, DC 20001; 202-624-7710) to request the phone number for your state's housing agency, or visit the NCSHA's Web site at http://www.ncsha.org for a listing of state housing finance agencies in your region.

away from the house. The larger the down payment, the less risk of foreclosure and the less chance the lender will suffer any financial loss on the property.

If your calculations indicate that you can't put at least 10 percent down, here are some options:

Check with the FHA or VA. Find out whether you are eligible for a loan guaranteed by the Federal Housing Administration (FHA) or the Department of Veterans Affairs (VA), which require little or no down payment.

Consider a no-down loan or a 97 percent loan. There are mortgages out now that will let you put down as little as 3 percent or will finance 100 percent of the sales price (see Chapter 9). Some will even finance as much as 103 percent for amounts up to $325,000.

Inquire about private mortgage insurance (PMI) to lower down-payment requirements (for a full discussion of PMI, see Chapter 10).

Investigate state and local programs for low- and moderate-income families and for first-time buyers. You may be able to get a lower-rate mortgage with a small down-payment requirement. Check what's available through any lender or real estate agent, or through your state or local housing agency (see the box at left).

Consider buying a less expensive condo or house that needs fixing up.

Use a lease-option contract, which gives you the right to live in the house for a period of time and the right to buy the property for a specified price during an agreed-on period of time (see Chapter 19 for details).

Look for property whose seller is willing to act as the lender. You don't have to meet institutional credit standards and may be able to work out a better deal.

Consider an equity-sharing purchase with a family member who is willing to make the down payment (see Chapter 10).

Try to get help from family or friends. As a rule, you'll be expected to make at least a 3 percent cash down payment in addition to any funds received as a gift toward the purchase. A relative or friend may be willing

---

HOW MUCH CAN YOU PAY MONTHLY?

Income

Add up the following:

Wages, salary, tips	$_____
Interest	_____
Dividends from stocks and mutual funds	_____
Bonuses	_____
Other income	_____
Total Income	$_____

AMOUNT AVAILABLE FOR HOUSING EXPENSES

Do this calculation:

Total Income	$_____
minus **Total Expenses**	−_____
equals **Total Cash Flow or Discretionary Income**	$_____

Divide that by 12 to get **Maximum Available for Monthly Housing Expense** $_____

Expenses
Other Than Housing Costs

Now, add up your expenses:

Income taxes	$_____
Social Security taxes	_____
Other taxes	_____
Food	_____
Life, health, auto insurance	_____
Medical bills not covered by insurance	_____
Automotive loans	_____
Auto expenses (gas, repairs, other)	_____
Other transportation	_____
Other loans	_____
Credit card payments	_____
Child care	_____
Alimony or child support	_____
Education	_____
Clothing	_____
Home furnishings	_____
Recreation and entertainment	_____
Meals out	_____
Vacations	_____
Charity	_____
Miscellaneous	_____
Total Expenses	$_____

to make you a "second-trust loan" (at a competitive market rate, not subsidized) to close the gap between the down payment and the mortgage. But such loans are not allowed by many lenders, and even if acceptable, the lender will scrutinize your finances carefully to make sure you can afford to carry both mortgages.

Most lenders will regard this loan as a gift and will require you and the giver to sign a form saying that the money is a gift and does not need to be repaid; if you and the giver want to treat the gift as a loan later—after the purchase—that's up to you. There may be gift tax and estate considerations involved, so consult a lawyer.

Use a seven- to ten-year balloon loan. This lets you make payments comparable to those for a much longer-term loan, although a lump sum will be due at the end of seven or ten years (see Chapters 9 and 10).

Consider a 40-year mortgage that will stretch your payments over 40 instead of 30 years. Your monthly payments will be less, but you will pay a higher interest rate (see Chapter 10).

Consider a penalty-free IRA withdrawal for a first home. Once in your lifetime you can withdraw up to $10,000 from your IRA, regardless of your age, to help pay for a first home for yourself or a family member (such as a spouse, child, grandchild, parent, or grandparent). You won't get hit with the usual 10 percent early-withdrawal penalty, but the money will be fully taxed in your top bracket (except to the extent that the withdrawal represents nondeductible contributions—money on which you paid federal income before stashing it in the IRA).

Beware of creative mortgage financing, such as the so-called interest-only loan that can leave you vulnerable to sharp increases in your mortgage payments, which will sap your spending and increase the risk of foreclosure. Interest-only loans allow buyers to pay just

> Once in your lifetime you can withdraw up to $10,000 from your IRA, regardless of your age, to help pay for a first home for yourself or a family member.

In deciding how much cash to put down, remember that getting settled in a new home always ends up costing more than you anticipate.

interest and no principal for a few years, but afterward payments rise substantially because the same principal must be paid off over fewer years (see Chapter 10).

How Big a Loan?

How much you can borrow will depend on your income and the size of your down payment. Job stability, credit references, payment histories, and other indications of creditworthiness also are factors. (As stated above, lenders favor down payments that total 20 percent of the home's purchase price. But new mortgage products allow buyers to put down as little as 3 to 5 percent, provided that private mortgage insurance is obtained.)

An old rule of thumb says you can qualify for a loan up to twice your family income. Using that outdated guideline, $100,000 of income should translate to a $200,000 mortgage. Sound too simple? It is. A family with $100,000 of annual earnings, three children, $10,000 in savings, and a new car loan just won't stack up the same way with lenders as a childless couple with the same income, no debts, and a $60,000 stock portfolio.

You'll get closer to reality by applying some of the same tools lenders use to evaluate the creditworthiness of prospective buyers. One common method is to apply a number of ratios to gross monthly income. For example, you may be allowed to devote up to 33 percent of gross (pretax) monthly income to housing expenses (including mortgage, property taxes, insurance, fees, utilities, and maintenance). However, your combined housing expenses and installment-debt obligations may not exceed 38 percent.

Prepare Yourself

Rules and formulas used to evaluate the creditworthiness of borrowers vary depending on the type of loan being sought. But whether you are seeking a conventional loan from a savings and loan or a government-backed (FHA or VA) loan from a mortgage

---

> ## HELP FOR RURAL BUYERS
>
> The U.S. Department of Agriculture's Rural Housing Service (RHS) also has a no-money-down program for moderate-income people seeking to buy in rural areas. For information, ask lenders or contact the Rural Housing Service National Office (U.S.D.A., Room 5037, South Building, 14th St. and Independence Ave., S.W., Washington, DC 20250; 202-720-4323). Tell the RHS where you want to buy a home, and it will give you names of prospective lenders. Or for more information and state-by-state listings, visit the RHS Web site at http://www.rurdev.usda.gov/rhs/index.html.

company, the less you pay down, the more closely your finances will be examined. Lenders will want to know how many people you are supporting and how old they are. Government rules require lenders to estimate your living costs rather than take your word for it.

As you work through the worksheets in this chapter and examine your budget, try to assess the impact home ownership will have on your spending patterns. Will you take fewer vacations? Will you spend less on clothing? Will the cost of commuting to work rise or fall?

Most important, how much will your tax bill go down—and your monthly take-home pay rise—once you begin taking big deductions for mortgage interest, which constitutes most of your monthly mortgage expense early in the term of the loan? Study the next chapter carefully to get a full appreciation of the range and variety of tax breaks you will get from the purchase and ownership of your new home.

How Much Down, How Much Borrowed?

In deciding how much cash to put down, remember that getting settled in a new home always ends up costing more than you anticipate. Hold back some cash for furnishing and unexpected outlays. Add an extra cushion of cash if you're buying an older home that could surprise you with a plumbing or roofing expense.

Should you borrow as much as you can? Small down payments and big mortgages give you the power of leverage (see Chapter 1) as well as available cash for other investments. And when inflation runs as high as or higher than mortgage interest rates, and you are paying back what you borrowed with dollars that are steadily losing their purchasing power, the answer is easy: The bigger the mortgage, the better.

Current tax law still stacks the deck in favor of the largest possible mortgage. Your original mortgage sets the cap for debt on which interest is deductible. (One exception lets you increase this cap by amounts you

---

SHOP ONLINE FOR A MORTGAGE

Mortgage lending is a national business these days, so you can conduct a national search for the best rate. The fastest way to do it is online. (If you don't have access to the Internet, ask your broker to help or make a trip to a computer-equipped friend's house or a large public library.) The following sites can be especially helpful. Each carries up-to-date listings of lenders and rates, as well as general mortgage information, calculators, and other helpful tools for mortgage shoppers.

BankRate Monitor (http://www.bankrate .com). Follows competitive rates in all 50 states and Washington, D.C.; provides credit news and helpful calculators.

E-LOAN® (http://www.eloan.com). E-LOAN offers a full range of mortgages, home equity loans, auto loans, credit cards, education loans, and personal loans. Customers can search for a loan online.

HomePath (http://www.homepath.com). Sponsored by Fannie Mae, offers general information on home and mortgage shopping.

HSH Associates (http://www.hsh.com). Provides mortgage rates, averages by city and state, calculators, and links to lenders.

kiplinger.com (http://www.kiplinger.com). Click on "Personal Finance" then "Rewards Tools" for help in comparing mortgages.

LendingTree (http://www.lendingtree .com). The Web site lists rates from the nation's largest mortgage lenders and brokers, offers consumer information, and allows online mortgage application.

borrow—via refinancing or a second mortgage—for major home improvements. For details, see Chapter 3.) If you make a large down payment but later need the cash, you can tap the money with a home-equity loan or refinance the house. But interest on home-equity loans over $100,000 isn't deductible.

For most first-time buyers, there's no point in weighing the trade-offs. Most will have to borrow to the hilt and scrape hard to come up with the minimum down payment. However, many so-called move-up buyers will come into a substantial sum of money when they sell their old home. Their decision will be tougher: whether to invest the cash in the new home and take out a small mortgage or invest the money elsewhere and borrow a large amount.

Nationally, investment returns on single-family homes over time have been modest compared with returns on such financial investments as stocks and bonds. Home values in some areas will keep pace with inflation and in some areas may do significantly better. Before you buy, try to assess the future of the economy in your home area and the demand for homes of the type, location, and price range of the one you want to own. For example, within a given metropolitan area, some neighborhoods may appreciate very well, while others stagnate. In some areas, luxury-priced houses will go up relatively more in value than starter houses; in others, just the opposite will occur.

If you have unusually good job security, you may want to gamble on a bigger mortgage than someone whose employment is precarious. Job security will affect the kind of mortgage you choose, too. If your job is safe in high-inflation or recessionary times and your earnings will likely keep pace with the cost of living, you'll be more comfortable with an adjustable mortgage than someone who lost ground in the last period of high inflation and high interest rates.

Remember that home equity—unlike financial assets such as bonds, CDs, and dividend-paying stocks—pays no current income, so be cautious about pouring all you have into a new home. For example, if the

> **Remember that home equity pays no current income, so be cautious about pouring all you have into a new home.**

stock market is moving up, your cash will be tied up in a home that is not paying you any income and that may be appreciating less rapidly than good-quality stocks. If you put all your cash into your home and then need some money later, you can borrow it, but you'll be paying at or above the prime lending rate for a home-equity loan, and usually more for a fixed-rate second mortgage.

Clean Up Your Credit Report

Even as you consider your strategy for buying a home, you should be paying attention to your current credit status. Any lender is going to scru-

---

A DO-IT-YOURSELF CREDIT CHECK

Federal law gives you the right to know what's in your credit files. The Fair and Accurate Credit Transactions Act of 2003 (FACT Act) provides that all U.S. residents are entitled to an annual free credit report from each of the credit-reporting agencies. (For your free report, call 877-322-8228, or order online at http://www.annualcreditreport.com.) Before you apply for a mortgage loan, find out whether anything in your record might present a problem. Order a report two or three months before making a loan application to give yourself plenty of time to iron out any wrinkles that you discover.

It's wise to check all three major credit bureaus—Equifax, Trans Union, and Experian—for errors. If you want to order more than the free annual reports, you'll have to pay a small fee. Contact each credit bureau for further details:
- **Equifax** (P.O. Box 740241, Atlanta, GA 30374; 800-685-1111; http://www .econsumer.equifax.com)

- **TransUnion** (TransUnion LLC, P.O. Box 1000, Chester, PA 19022; 800-888-4213; http://www.transunion.com)
- **Experian** (P.O. Box 2104, Allen, TX 75013; 888-397-3742; http://www.experian.com. Use the address and phone number that appear on your credit report to dispute information.)

You may order online or by phone and pay by credit card. If you are ordering by mail, you will need to write a letter including your full name, date of birth, your Social Security number, current employer, and current and previous addresses going back two years.

Mailing letters or filling in forms online can be a hassle. All three credit-reporting agencies offer a merged report that shows your combined credit history. From $29.95 to $39.95, the merged report costs about the same as getting separate reports.

---

tinize your monthly income and outgo at the time you apply for a mortgage. Debts and other obligations reduce the amount of cash you can spend on housing, so try to clear the decks as much as possible before applying for a loan. Pay off as many high-interest consumer loans as possible. If you are planning to buy a new car, boat, or expensive furniture (paying either by cash or credit), postpone the purchases until after you've bought your home.

On the other hand, a good credit record requires that you have used credit in the past. Some cash-only buyers find themselves hampered by their own prudence when it comes time to buy a home. If you've

If you discover an unfavorable report, now is the time to rectify the problem or seek settlement. A lender may view the problem more leniently if the record shows that the matter has been satisfactorily resolved.

If you've been tagged unfairly for nonpayment or slow payment, write a well-documented letter setting forth your understanding of the facts, and file it with the appropriate credit bureaus. If you aren't sure which bureaus have a file on you, find out from the problem creditor.

Better still, get the problem resolved; then request, in writing, that the creditor inform all relevant reporting services that the problem has been fixed—with copies to you. This could take 30 to 90 days.

Errors generated by the credit bureau—such as mixed-up files—need to be corrected there. If using a complaint line or calling the local office doesn't help,

write to the manager of consumer affairs. The bureau should accept documentation proving the account isn't yours.

Report your problems to the U.S. Public Interest Research Group (218 D St., S.E., Washington, DC 20003; 202-546-9707; http://www.uspirg.org or by e-mail at uspirg@pirg.org).

If the problem remains unresolved, you'll probably need to consider hiring a lawyer to clear things up.

When you finally make a loan application, the lender will request a complete update on your file, and you may be charged $100 or so for this credit check. The lender will usually ask the credit agency to reverify your employer, salary, address, and other information. Alert your employer's human resources office to the credit checker's call. If your credit application is turned down, you're entitled to know why.

If you have good credit scores, you could receive a loan at a lower interest rate. And later, if you're late on a payment, the lender will also be less likely to hassle you.

been diligently saving for a down payment and haven't borrowed for a year or more, it's a good idea to create a record of credit activity during the year in which you plan to buy. Stick to small-ticket items, make one or two minimum payments promptly, then pay off the balance.

Typically, your credit file will contain information covering the preceding three years. No adverse credit information, except bankruptcy, can be kept on file for more than seven years. Lenders look for these red flags: late payments, overextension, liens, garnishments, and, the biggest flag of all, bankruptcy.

Your Credit Score

Nearly all mortgage lenders request a mortgage credit score from each of the three big credit bureaus—Experian, Equifax, and Trans Union—to help them determine your current creditworthiness and predict what kind of credit risk you will be in the future. The scores are determined by statistical analysis of the information contained in your credit files at each of the bureaus. Good scores may change the time required to get approval on your mortgage as well as the rate you receive and the way in which your mortgage is managed. If you have good scores, you could receive a loan at a lower interest rate than someone with less favorable scores from the bureaus. And later, if you're late on a payment, the lender will also be less likely to hassle you than someone with questionable scores.

The analysis takes into account about 22 different factors gathered from your credit file at each of the three credit bureaus and specifically looks at such things as how much you are currently in debt, how many places you have applied for credit recently, and what kind of credit you have taken in the past. According to Fair Isaac Corporation, a research company that was one of the original developers of credit scoring, multivariate modeling (modeling that considers a group of variables) synthesizes information by looking at all of your credit history—the bright spots and the shadows. Where the human mind might reject a mortgage application because you once declared bankruptcy, the statistical model will weigh that fact as just one component among the many that it considers.

There are several statistical scoring models available, and each has a different way of determining your score and translating the results. But whatever the methodology, consumers with good credit scores are more likely to repay their debts than consumers with poor credit scores.

Unfortunately, you are not given your credit score even when you request a copy of your credit file. If, however, you are rejected for a mortgage because of your credit score, ask the reason behind your rejection. The statistical models used for scoring will issue reasons for the score you were given—and this information can be passed on to you by the lender. (Fair Isaac Corporation's commonly used credit-scoring product is known as a FICO® score. You may obtain your current FICO score as well as an explanation of the score, your credit-risk factors, and tips on how to improve your score online at http://www.myfico.com for $14.95.)

Obtaining Preapproval with a Lender

Now that you've gotten your financial affairs in order and checked out your credit record, the next step is to contact a lender—mortgage company, savings and loan, bank, or credit union— where you can translate all the data into hard facts about the upper price limit you can handle and the types of mortgages suited to your needs.

The preapproval interview should be free. Because of technological advances, many banks now offer this service over the Internet and by phone, as well as at their offices. You're not obliged to use the lender who conducts the interview. When you're ready to borrow, talk with several lenders. Have tax returns, salary stubs,

> **Whatever the methodology, consumers with good credit scores are more likely to repay their debts than consumers with poor credit scores.**

and other financial data available to enter information online or provide in an interview—along with net worth and monthly cash flow worksheets you've prepared.

Kinds of Loans

F ind out how much mortgage debt you can carry under the most commonly available mortgages. "Conventional mortgages" are transactions between borrowers and institutions operating in the private sector of the economy. They are not insured or guaranteed by the government. Traditionally they feature set monthly payments, fixed interest rates, extended loan terms, and full amortization.

Because the 30-year fixed-rate mortgage is still the benchmark against which other loans are compared, find out what size conventional 30-year loan you qualify for under the guidelines issued by secondary-market mortgage buyers such as Fannie Mae or Freddie Mac. Because these institutions buy only loans that meet their criteria, such mortgages are often referred to as "conforming" loans.

FOR MORE INFORMATION

Knowing and Understanding Your Credit and *Choosing the Mortgage That's Right for You* are free, step-by-step guides from the Fannie Mae Foundation (4000 Wisconsin Ave., N.W., North Tower, Suite One, Washington, DC 20016-2804; 800-611-9566; http://www.fanniemaefoundation.org). You may download them online or receive them by mail via phone, mail, or online order.

A Homebuyers's Guide to Mortgage Fees and Qualifications contains a review of fees first-time buyers face, a worksheet for determining how much they can afford to borrow, and an amortization table (HSH Associates, Financial Publishers, 237 West Parkway, Pompton Plains, NJ 07444; 800-873-2837; http://www.hsh.com/catalog.html#3primer; include $4 for postage and handling).

A Homebuyer's Guide to Mortgage Strategies discusses different mortgage types, selecting the mortgage to meet your time frame and financial needs, biweekly and other payoff methods, worst-case ARM scenarios, and more (also by HSH Associates, above; include $4 for postage and handling).

Find out how much you can borrow under a conforming 30-year fixed-rate mortgage; a one-, three-, five-, seven-, and ten-year adjustable-rate mortgage; and perhaps a 15-year fixed-rate loan as well. Knowing what you can afford to buy with these mortgage types is a useful starting point.

Mortgage information is now readily available online. You can find daily and weekly rate quotes for mortgages and home-equity loans, the requirements for qualifying for special Fannie Mae programs, estimates of closing costs, an analysis of different mortgages, programs available for veterans and for active-duty military personnel, as well as many other helpful bits of information.

If you're planning on getting an FHA-insured or VA-guaranteed mortgage, you may qualify for a bigger loan. However, keep in mind that sellers in a hot market are usually not eager to do business with buyers using this type of financing. They may expect to have plenty of would-be buyers using conventional mortgages, so it's not uncommon for sellers to put the phrase "no FHA and no VA financing" right in the sales contract.

Due to the extra paperwork and appraisal delays these loans often entail, it may take longer to reach settlement, and some sellers won't put up with that. It's a good idea to see whether you can manage a home purchase without resorting to an FHA or VA mortgage.

When interest rates are changing rapidly, shopping for a home can be frustrating. What you can afford may vary week to week. In such a market you can ask the institution preapproving you to provide a list of the various size mortgages for which you qualify at widely varying interest rates. Or you can figure it out yourself using online calculators such as those at kiplinger com.

When interest rates are changing rapidly, shopping for a home can be frustrating. What you can afford may vary week to week.

Get Your Earnest Money Ready

Some people are short on liquid assets but have substantial equity in their homes. This could pose a problem when they have to write a check

If you find that you will be short on earnest money, consider getting a home-equity loan.

for earnest money to submit to a seller along with their purchase contract. Earnest money shows that you're a serious, qualified purchaser. (If the contract is not accepted or the deal later hits a snag through no fault of yours, you'll get the earnest money back, with interest if you specified in your offering contract that the money be held in an interest-bearing escrow account.)

If after assessing your resources you find that you'll be short on earnest money when it comes time to begin house hunting, consider getting a home-equity loan—a line of credit secured by the equity in your current house (see Chapters 3 and 14 for details). But don't succumb to the temptation to use your new equity credit line for unneeded things. As you prepare for the mortgage-application process, you'll want to avoid adding to your current debt.

Home Sweet Tax Shelter

Chapter 3

Your home—probably the biggest investment of your life—can be the best tax shelter you'll ever enjoy.

Uncle Sam is standing by to serve as a generous partner in your investment, ready to subsidize your mortgage payments while you're paying for your house and virtually willing to turn a blind eye to the profit you make when you sell.

Given the favored status of home ownership in America, it is no surprise that deductions for mortgage interest and local property taxes have survived as others have gone the way of the dodo bird. Yes, there is a limit on mortgage-interest write-offs, but it kicks in only when mortgage debt exceeds $1 million.

GOODBYE MORTGAGE DEDUCTION?

Late in 2005, the President's Panel on Tax Reform recommended numerous changes to simplify the income tax system. One recommendation would replace the mortgage-interest deduction as described here with a tax credit equal to 15% of the interest paid on first mortgages of up to $412,000. The reduced cap (from the current $1.1 million) would be phased in over several years. Such a change would benefit lower-income Americans, who usually don't have enough deductions to justify itemizing them, a prerequisite for taking advantage of the current mortgage-interest deduction. The panel also recommended repealing the deduction for interest on second homes and home equity loans. These recommendations face an uphill battle in Congress.

The mortgage-interest deduction can also be nicked by a restriction that applies to taxpayers whose adjusted gross income (AGI) exceeds a certain level, which is adjusted each year. The law wipes out deductions equal to 3 percent of the amount by which AGI exceeds the threshold. If your 2005 AGI was $160,000, for example, the first $422 (3 percent of the $14,050 over the 2005 trigger point of $145,950) of your deductions lose their tax-saving power.

It is impossible to say exactly how this will affect any specific taxpayer, because much depends on AGI and the makeup of your deductions. For that reason—and the fact that, despite the restriction, tax breaks for home ownership remain enormous—the discussion that follows generally assumes that all your mortgage interest will remain deductible.

Buying a home *will* cut your tax bill. But as veteran homeowners can tell you, it will also complicate your tax life.

If you don't itemize deductions now, you're almost sure to begin once you buy a home. After all, the mortgage-interest portion of the first 12 monthly payments on a $200,000, 6 percent, 30-year mortgage is about $11,933. That exceeds the $10,000 standard deduction for married couples filing jointly and the $5,000 deduction for singles for 2005. You'll also get to deduct what you paid in state and local property taxes.

And once you begin itemizing, other expenses that are of no value to nonitemizers—such as state income taxes, charitable contributions, and possibly medical bills—are transformed into tax-saving write-offs.

The deductions for mortgage interest and property taxes just scratch the surface of the tax benefits attached to home ownership. While becoming a homeowner doesn't demand that you memorize the tax

DEDUCTIBLE INTEREST

This table reflects the deductible interest on a $200,000, 30-year fixed-rate mortgage at 6%.

Year	Annual Payments	Principal	Interest
1	$14,389	$ 2,456	$11,933
2	14,389	2,608	11,782
3	14,389	2,768	11,621
4	14,389	2,939	11,450
5	14,389	3,120	11,269
10	14,389	4,209	10,180
15	14,389	5,677	8,712
20	14,389	7,658	6,732
25	14,389	10,329	4,060
30	14,389	13,932	457

law, you do need a general awareness of the rules to take advantage of them.

This chapter is designed as a primer for first-time buyers and a refresher for veteran homeowners in the process of moving.

Deductibility of Mortgage Interest

The opportunity to trade nondeductible rent payments for mostly deductible mortgage payments is a powerful lure enticing you from your rental abode into a home of your own.

Whether you are looking for a first home or planning to move up, the number crunching necessary to determine how much house you can afford demands two calculations: one for actual monthly outlays, the other for the true, after-tax cost.

A SQUEEZE ON DEDUCTIONS

As mentioned, the tax law can restrict the deduction of mortgage interest for taxpayers whose 2005 adjusted gross income (AGI) exceeds $145,950. (AGI is basically your income before deductions and exemptions are subtracted.)

Although this take-away doesn't hit all deductions, mortgage interest and property taxes are among those threatened. But don't assume this diminishes the tax-saving power of a bigger mortgage or higher property-tax bill. Since the law sets a floor for itemized deductions—only those that exceed 3% of your adjusted gross income in excess of $145,950—it takes away the first dollars of your itemized deductions, not the last. Once your deductions pass the floor, every extra dollar of deductible expenses has full tax-saving power.

Even if your AGI makes you vulnerable to the squeeze, you'll probably get to deduct 100% of any increases in mortgage interest and property taxes that come with buying a more expensive home. Say, for example, that AGI of $160,000 costs you $422 (3% of the $14,050 over the 2005 trigger point) of your $30,000 of itemized deductions, so you deduct just $29,578. If buying a new home hiked your interest and property-tax expenses by $5,000, you'd get to add the full $5,000 to your itemized deductions. Only if your AGI rises would the amount of lost deductions increase.

As soon as you purchase a new home with higher deductible expenses, you can direct your employer to begin withholding less from your paychecks.

In the early years of a home mortgage, nearly all of every monthly payment is interest. That's disappointing from one standpoint: It means that you are paying off only a tiny bit of the loan principal. But it's great in terms of tax savings.

Look again at the $200,000, 30-year, 6 percent mortgage cited above. The monthly payment would be about $1,199, and the table on page 30 shows the breakdown between principal repayment and deductible interest in various years.

In the first year, $11,933 of $14,389 in payments— or 83 percent—would be deductible as mortgage interest. Even in the tenth year, almost 81 percent of your payments would be deductible. In fact, only in the unlikely event that you live in the house for 19 years would the scales tip so that less than half of the total paid during the year would be tax-deductible.

Just what the deductions are worth to you depends, of course, on your tax bracket. If you are in the 25 percent bracket, every $1,000 of deductible interest and taxes translates to a $250 subsidy from Uncle Sam. In our $200,000 mortgage example, assume that in addition to the $1,199 monthly mortgage payment you pay $150 a month for local property taxes (which, most likely, your mortgage lender will collect, deposit into an escrow account, and pay out as required). During the first 12 months, you pay a total of $16,189—that's about $1,349 a month.

But $13,733 (your total mortgage payment and local property taxes, less payment of the first year's principal) is deductible. In the 25 percent bracket, that generates tax savings of $3,433 and pulls the after-tax cost to $12,756, or about $1,063 a month.

The tax savings built into the home-buying equation is why you can afford to make higher mortgage payments than your current rent payments without squeezing your budget. As disgruntled renters often complain, there is no similar tax subsidy for tenants. In this example, the after-tax cost of home payments of $1,349 a month are the equivalent of rent between $1,063 and $949 a month, depending on your tax bracket. Of course, owning the house could present you with repair bills a renter doesn't have to worry about, but on the other hand, as an owner you reap all the appreciation on the value of your home.

Adjust Your Withholding

What good is the tax subsidy if you're worrying about coming up with the cash needed each month to make the mortgage payment? Fortunately, you don't have to wait until you file a tax return to cash in on the savings. As soon as you purchase your first home or buy a new house that carries higher deductible expenses, you can direct your employer to begin withholding less from your paychecks. If you are self-employed, it's likely you will be able to scale back your quarterly estimated tax payments beginning with the next one due. In either case, your cash flow can increase almost immediately to help cover the mortgage payments.

The revised W-4 form can be complicated, but basically, to reduce withholding, you must file a revised

---

PROVING YOUR BASIS

Although it's unlikely that you'll have to pay any tax on the profit of your home when you sell, you should still maintain records to ensure accuracy when computing your home's taxable basis. Remember, starting to keep track when you purchase will be a lot easier than trying to reconstruct the basis later on.

As you begin the running tab on your adjusted basis, add these items to the purchase price.

■ **Appraisal and credit-report fees**
■ **Attorney and notary fees**
■ **Recording and title-examination fees**
■ **State and county transfer taxes**

■ **Property-inspection fees**
■ **Title-insurance premiums**
■ **Utility-connection charges**
■ **Amounts owed by the seller that you agree to pay,** such as part of the real estate agent's commission or back taxes and interest
■ **The cost of an option to purchase** under a rent-with-option-to-buy arrangement
■ **Part of the rent payments made prior to closing,** which may be added to the basis if they were applied to the purchase price of the property

> A "point" is a fee—equal to 1 percent of the loan amount—that the mortgage lender charges up front.

W-4 form with your employer. Get a copy of the form and its instructions from your human resources office or local Internal Revenue Service office, or download a copy at http://www.irs.gov.

Record Keeping

Buying a home may be your introduction to the endearing term "tax basis." That's the home's value for tax purposes. Until the 1997 tax bill was enacted, keeping track of this figure was demanding and important. The basis of your home is the figure you'd subtract from the amount you got when you sold the place, and the result determined whether you had a taxable profit that piqued the interest of the IRS.

For most people, tracking of basis is now unnecessary, but it is a good idea just in case you end up staying in your home for many years, especially in areas where home values rise dramatically. The rules exempt from federal taxation $250,000 of profit on the sale of a home for those filing single returns and $500,000 of profit for those who file joint returns.

Even if you aren't concerned about basis, you still need to sort out the tax consequences of the closing costs you pay at settlement (discussed in Chapter 12). Although a few of these expenses may be deducted in the year of the purchase, most are considered part of the cost of acquiring the house so they're included in the basis. First, consider the deductible closing expenses because they have the most immediate financial impact.

Deductibility of Mortgage Points

A "point" is a fee—equal to 1 percent of the loan amount—that the mortgage lender charges up front. If the charge is for use of the borrowed money—as it is when the number of points charged affects the interest rate on the mortgage—rather than for loan-processing costs, the point is considered prepaid interest. As long as the home you build or buy is your principal residence, these points are fully deductible in the year paid.

Assume, for example, that to get a $200,000 mortgage you have to pay the lender three points, or an amount equal to 3 percent of the loan amount. You can write off that $6,000 on the tax return for the year of the purchase. Schedule A provides a special line for the deduction. The deduction effectively serves as a rebate of part of the mortgage costs. In the 25 percent bracket, $6,000 in points translates into $1,500 in tax savings. (Different rules apply to points you pay when you refinance the mortgage on your principal residence.)

A standard piece of advice, in the past, was to write a separate check to pay the points, as proof that the expense wasn't rolled into the mortgage. That was critical because if the points were included in the mortgage amount, you were using borrowed money and therefore were blocked from deducting the full expense right away. But a separate check is no longer necessary. Here's what the IRS now looks for:

■ **Points** paid must be in line with area norms.
■ **The charge** must be based on a percentage of the loan amount and it must be clearly labeled on the settlement statement as *points, discount points,* or *loan origination fee,* for example.
■ **By closing,** you must provide at least enough cash to cover the points. This can include your down payment, escrow deposits, or earnest money.

If you make a $20,000 down payment, for example, you can actually roll points into the mortgage amount and still deduct the points in the year you buy the house. The IRS will assume that points were paid with part of the down payment, rather than with the money you borrowed. You'll get a statement from the lender (IRS Form 1098) showing how much you paid in points to buy your home.

If the Seller Pays Some of Your Points

Buyers can deduct points paid by the seller (the amount will be shown on your settlement sheet) as well

When points are not fully deductible in the year paid, the expense can be deducted instead over the life of the loan.

as those they pay themselves. This also means that when buyers figure their tax basis, they must reduce the stated purchase price by the amount of the deducted seller-paid points.

When the House Isn't Your Home

The right to deduct points fully in the year paid applies only to points paid on a mortgage to buy or improve your principal residence. Different rules apply to points charged for a mortgage used to buy a vacation home or rental property.

When points are not fully deductible in the year paid, the expense can be deducted instead over the life of the loan. On a 30-year mortgage, for example, $\frac{1}{30}$ of the points generally would be deducted each year. In the first and last years, however, an even smaller amount would be deductible, based on the month you bought the house.

An alternative method for figuring the annual deduction gives you somewhat higher write-offs in the early years of a mortgage. It's probably more trouble than it's worth because it involves finding what percentage of the total interest due on the loan is paid yearly and deducting that portion of the points in that year.

Whichever method you use, remember to claim this deduction each year. If you pay off the loan early—because you sell the place, for example, or refinance at an even lower rate—you can deduct all undeducted points at that time.

Deductibility of Closing Costs

If your settlement costs include reimbursing the seller for interest or taxes he or she paid in advance for a period you will actually own the house, you may deduct those amounts as though you paid the bills directly. Such adjustments ought to be spelled out on your settlement sheet.

If the seller made such payments and you do not reimburse him at settlement, the prepayments are considered built into the price you are paying for the house. In that case, you still write off the prepaid interest and taxes as itemized deductions on your return and reduce your basis by the same amount.

Other closing costs and acquisition expenses are generally not deductible. Instead, many such out-of-pocket costs are added to the purchase price to hike your tax basis. Because additions to basis don't produce immediate tax savings, and it's unlikely that your profit will exceed the $250,000/$500,000 allowable limits, you might be tempted to dismiss them. That could be a mistake. You should still keep track of at least major basis-boosting items in case your profit when you eventually sell is greater than the limits—or Uncle Sam changes the rules again.

Other Tax Angles of Owning

It's easy to take advantage of the basic tax benefits— the write-offs for mortgage interest and property taxes. If your mortgage is held by a financial institution, you will receive a statement early each year showing how much deductible interest you paid in the previous year (the IRS gets a copy, too). The statement will also show how much you can deduct for property taxes if you make those payments through an escrow account handled by your lender. Otherwise, copies of tax bills and your canceled checks will provide the information you need to claim that deduction.

Your tax situation is more complicated if your mortgage is held by an individual or you are buying with the help of some sort of "creative financing." The specifics of your arrangement dictate what portion of your payments qualifies as a tax deduction. Special rules also apply to graduated-payment mortgages and other financing plans. The further you stray from conventional financing, the more need you have to consult with a lawyer or accountant to discuss the many tax twists and turns involved in your home-buying pursuits.

If your mortgage is held by a financial institution, you will receive a statement early each year showing how much deductible interest you paid in the previous year.

Local Assessments

In addition to real estate taxes, it is not unusual for local governments to assess homeowners for services or benefits provided during the year. Such bills need to go in your home file because, depending on what the charge is for, the cost may be either a deductible expense or an addition to your basis.

In general, assessments for benefits that tend to increase the value of your property—sidewalks, for example—should be added to the basis of your property. Special charges for repairs or maintenance of local benefits, such as sewers or roads, however, can be deducted as additional local taxes. Fees for specific

---

BASIS-BOOSTING IMPROVEMENTS

- **An addition or conversion of:** unfinished attic, basement, or other space to living area
- **Air-conditioning:** a central system or window units that will be sold with the house
- **Heating and cooling:** attic fan, furnace, furnace humidifier, heat pump, radiators and radiator covers, thermostat, water heater
- **Bathroom:** bathtub, faucets, Jacuzzi, medicine cabinets, mirrors, sauna, shower, shower enclosure, toilet, towel racks
- **Built-in bookcases**
- **Safety features:** burglar- and fire-alarm system, doorbell, intercom, smoke detector, telephone outlets
- **Electrical:** new or upgraded power lines, replacement of fuse box with circuit breakers, additional outlets or switches, floodlights
- **Fireplace:** including chimney, mantel, built-in fireplace screen

- **Weatherproofing:** caulking, insulation, weather stripping
- **Kitchen:** dishwasher, freezer, refrigerator, or stove sold with the house; countertops, cupboards, exhaust fan, garbage disposal
- **Landscaping:** shrubs, trees, underground sprinkler systems
- **Outdoors:** aluminum siding, barbecue pit, birdbath, carport, deck, fences and gates, garage, garage-door opener, gutters, hot tub, lamppost, new roof, paving and resurfacing of a driveway or sidewalks, porch, screen and storm doors, shed, skylight, swimming pool, termite-proofing, walls, waterproofing
- **Plumbing:** new pipes, septic system, solar-heating system, sump pump
- **Rooftop TV antenna and wiring**
- **Washer and dryer** sold with the house
- **Windows:** awnings, screens, shutters, storm windows, weather stripping

services, such as garbage collection, are not deductible and can't be added to the basis.

Improvements and Repairs

Monthly payments are just the beginning of the costs of owning a home. You can count on spending plenty over the years maintaining, repairing, and improving your property. Here, too, Uncle Sam gets involved.

For tax purposes, work around the house is divided between projects considered *repairs* and those constituting capital *improvements* that enhance rather than just maintain your home's value. Before passage of the 1997 tax bill, the distinction was critical, and it may still be important. While the cost of repairs and improvements are nondeductible personal expenses, improvement expenses add to your basis. The reasoning behind the distinction is that although you use and enjoy the improvements, they also are likely to boost the amount a buyer will pay for the place. Since you add 100 percent of the cost of improvements to your basis, every $100 of such expenses ultimately reduces by $100 the potentially taxable profit when you sell.

An improvement is anything that adds value to your home, prolongs its life, or adapts it to new uses. There is no laundry list of what the IRS considers an improvement. However, the box on page 38 provides a checklist of items and projects that can qualify.

Repairs, on the other hand, merely maintain a home's condition. Fixing a gutter or replacing a windowpane are repairs rather than improvements. In some cases, though, the cost of projects that would ordinarily fall into the repair category—such as painting a room—can be added to the basis if the work is done as part of an extensive remodeling or restoration of your home. Also, some major repairs—such as extensive patching of a roof—may qualify as basis-boosting improvements.

As already discussed, while it's unlikely your profit on selling your home will exceed the IRS tax-free maximum ($250,000 for those filing single returns, $500,000 for those filing joint returns), you never know for sure.

An improvement is anything that adds value to your home, prolongs its life, or adapts it to new uses.

You can deduct all interest you pay on up to $1 million of acquisition debt—money you borrow to buy, build, or substantially improve your principal residence or a second home.

So keep records of major work done around the house, including receipts for items that might qualify as improvements. It's better to save papers you might not need than to toss out evidence that could save you money. In addition to receipts and canceled checks or check substitutes, keep notes to remind yourself exactly what was done, when, and by whom.

When toting up the cost of improvements, be sure that you include significant incidental costs. If you pay to have your lot surveyed as part of installing a fence, for example, the cost of the survey can be added to your basis. Although you can count what you paid workers you hired, you are not allowed to add anything for your own time and effort if you do the work yourself.

Deductibility of Interest on Debt Secured by a Home

The tax law divides debt secured by a home—including a second home—into the following two categories:

Acquisition Debt

You can deduct all the interest you pay on up to $1 million of acquisition debt—money you borrow to buy, build, or substantially improve your principal residence or a second home. For the interest to be deductible, the loan must be secured by the house.

Although $1 million is an enormous amount of mortgage debt, the amount on which you can deduct mortgage interest is likely to be far less. Your personal ceiling is set by the size of the original loans that you used to buy or build your main home and second home, plus amounts borrowed for major improvements. As you pay off those loans, the amount of tax-favored acquisition debt declines. (There is an exception to the general definition of acquisition debt. If on October 13, 1987, the mortgage debt on your principal home and a second home exceeded the amount borrowed to buy, build, or substantially improve the homes, you can count that higher amount as acquisition indebtedness.)

Home-Equity Debt

In addition to deducting interest on acquisition debt, homeowners can deduct interest on up to $100,000 of home-equity debt. The interest on such borrowing is fully deductible—whether you tap your equity via refinancing, a second mortgage, or a home-equity line of credit—as long as the loan is secured by your principal residence or a second home.

The interest is deductible almost without regard to how the borrowed money is spent, but there are a few exceptions. If the money is used to invest in tax-exempt bonds or single-premium life insurance, the interest can't be deducted, no matter what kind of loan is involved. Also, if you are subject to the alternative minimum tax (AMT), interest on home-equity debt is not deductible unless the mortgage was taken out before July 1, 1982, and secured by a home used by you or a family member. Interest on acquisition debt is deductible for purposes of calculating the AMT.

Another restriction—which can trip up taxpayers who succumb to campaigns by aggressive lenders who will grant loans for more than 100 percent of a home's value—blocks the deduction of interest if the combination of home-equity debt and acquisition debt exceeds the fair market value of the house. For example, if the balance on your mortgage is $200,000 and your home value is just $210,000, then interest would be deductible on no more than $10,000 of home-equity debt.

Tax-Saving Opportunities

The deductibility of interest on home-equity debt offers great tax-saving opportunities. To the extent that you can replace nondeductible personal borrowing with deductible home-equity borrowing, you can have the government help pay the interest on your debts. This

> **The interest on up to $100,000 of home-equity debt is deductible, almost without regard to how the money is spent.**

makes home-equity lines of credit the debt of choice for millions of homeowners. These loans, secured by your home, offer a line of credit that you can tap simply by writing a check. In addition to preserving the deductibility of interest charged, these loans often carry lower interest rates than unsecured borrowing.

When you buy, the rules on acquisition indebtedness may encourage you to minimize your down payment. Remember that the size of your tax-favored debt is based on your original mortgage—not the price of the house.

The law can also encourage you to borrow rather than pay cash for home improvements. As long as the debt is secured by the home, money going toward an improvement counts as acquisition debt. The tax subsidy of the interest cost could make borrowing cheaper than pulling cash out of an investment to pay for the improvement. You would still count the full cost of the improvement to the basis.

It's important to keep reliable records of your borrowing to back up deductions you claim. If you use a home-equity line, distinguish between borrowing that pays for major home improvements and loans used for other purposes. The amount that goes for improvements is added to your acquisition debt, rather than eating away at your $100,000 home-equity allowance. Also, if you use money borrowed through a home-equity line of credit, or second mortgage for investment or business purposes, you can choose whether to treat the interest as home-equity interest or deduct it as investment or business interest. If, for example, you count it as investment interest—in which case certain restrictions apply—the borrowing would not reduce your $100,000 home-equity allowance.

Refinancing

When you refinance your mortgage—as millions of homeowners have done to take advantage of lower interest rates—there are tax angles to consider.

Deductibility of Points

Points you pay to get the new mortgage are not fully deductible in the year paid, except to the extent that the funds are used for home improvements. Here's an example: A homeowner with a $200,000 mortgage refinances at $240,000 and uses $40,000 to add a sunroom. Assume that two points (2 percent of $240,000, or $4,800) were charged. Because one-sixth of the money went for a home improvement, one-sixth of the points, or $800, may be deducted in the year paid. The rest must be deducted evenly over the life of the loan. On a 30-year mortgage, that would basically mean 1/30 of the remaining $4,000, or $133.33, would be deducted each year. If the house is sold and the mortgage paid off before the end of the term, any remaining portion of the points could be deducted as interest at that time. (If the refinancing is part of the original purchase of your home—say you refinance to pay off a bridge loan or a short-term balloon note—the points can be fully deducted in the year paid.)

The Tax Status of Interest

Refinancing can affect the tax status of the interest you pay on the mortgage. The amount of the new loan qualifying as acquisition debt is limited to the debt outstanding on the old loan, plus any part of the new money used for major improvements. This tale, too, is best told with an illustration:

Assume that several years ago you bought a $150,000 home with $30,000 down and a $120,000 mortgage. The debt is now paid down to $90,000 and you decide to refinance for $150,000. What's the tax status of the new loan?

Interest on $90,000—the remaining balance on the old loan—is sure to be deductible because that amount qualifies as acquisition indebtedness. The treatment of the other $60,000 depends on how the money is used.

Any part spent for major home improvements also earns the status of acquisition debt. Plunge $20,000 of

Points you pay to get the new mortgage are not fully deductible in the year paid, except to the extent that the funds are used for home improvements.

the new loan into a swimming pool, for example, and your acquisition debt jumps from $90,000 to $110,000. Any part of the new loan that does not replace the old mortgage or pay for improvements—$40,000 in this example—is not considered acquisition debt.

That doesn't automatically mean you can't deduct the interest, however. Because the debt is secured by your home, the interest may be deducted as home-equity interest, subject to the $100,000 cap. If the extra funds are used in a business, the interest can be written off as a business expense. If you use the cash for an investment, the interest on that portion of the loan may be deductible as investment interest. If none of those options covers you, however, the interest would be nondeductible personal interest.

Treatment of Prepayment Penalties

Another tax issue rising out of some refinancings is how to treat prepayment penalties. If the lender holding the original loan slaps you with a penalty for paying it off early, the amount is considered interest and is fully deductible in the year you pay it. But what if the lender is willing to cut the amount due to encourage you to pay off the mortgage early? That's not as unlikely as it may appear. In times of soaring interest rates, lenders sometimes offer sweet deals to get out of long-term loans at low, fixed-interest rates. If you're on the receiving end of such an offer, beware. The amount of such a discount is considered taxable income to you.

Define Your Needs, Pick a Neighborhood

Now that you know how much home you can afford, it's time to do some hard thinking about what kind of home you want and need. This chapter and the next—dealing with kinds of housing—will help you narrow the choices.

Buying a piece of real estate is a science. Buying a home is an art. The science is getting the legal and financial parts right. The art is finding a property that you'll be happy living in.

Only you know what you like. Your best preparation for home buying is to clarify your needs, your financial ability, your preferences, and your dislikes. Start with the general—your price range and approximate location—and then move to the specific: neighborhood, age and type of home, and kind of ownership (traditional, condominium, or co-op).

Shopping only within your chosen location can narrow down the range of properties to be inspected. Examining only selected properties within your price range should bring the operation within manageable proportions.

Knowing your financial limits is a good beginning. However, you probably will find 10 or 15 entirely different sorts of homes within your price range. Decide now whether you want to be on the east or west side of town, whether you will accept a cookie-cutter housing development or will go to any length to avoid that, whether you can handle a "fixer-upper" or will need one requiring a minimum of maintenance.

It can't be overstated: Focus on the location and general quality of the property. Don't go chasing an

Start your want list by recalling houses you have liked and jotting down their best features.

exact price or a particular feature, be it a deck, a high-efficiency furnace, or a finished basement. Price can be worked out in negotiation with the seller (given the right general ballpark), and a good-quality home in a good location can be tailored to your specific needs later.

There are two phases to a house-hunting strategy. In the first, you get a feel for different areas and an idea about what's being offered at what price, and you draw up a list of specifications. In the second phase, you search for the house that meets all or most of those specifications.

Make a List of Needs and Wants

Most buyers are in search of something they cannot describe. They may be trying, often unknowingly, to replicate a childhood home, if it was a happy one. This doesn't mean that they are looking for the same red-brick house with privet hedge, but rather that they are seeking a feeling, an ambience. It could be a sense of spaciousness, warmth, airiness, the amount of daylight, the quality of the light, coziness, the abundance of nooks and crannies, a parklike backyard.

If you're looking for a home with the help of an experienced agent, he or she should be able to help you define your needs and wants. But if you're too vague, a really good agent may decide not to waste time on you, and you could end up with someone who is more of a hindrance than a help, someone with endless patience, but no direction.

Start your want list by recalling houses you have liked and jotting down their best features. You'll find further inspiration in the checklist on the opposite page. That list, combined with the price range you have already determined, will give you a sieve through which to sift the dozens of ads you will read in conducting your search. Keep in mind, though, that the final choice of a home almost always requires compromise.

WHICH FEATURES ARE IMPORTANT TO YOU?

Check off the features that you must have in your next home and those you'd like to have, by degree of priority.

	MUSTS	WANTS (rank them) High	Medium	Low
Commuting time				
Less than one hour	_____	_____		
Less than half hour	_____	_____		
Setting				
Suburban	_____	_____		
Urban	_____	_____		
Rural	_____	_____		
Specific neighborhood	_____	_____		
Specific school district	_____	_____		
Public transportation	_____	_____		
Zoning laws				
(Allowing or prohibiting	_____	_____		
on-street parking, pets,	_____	_____		
in-law suites, and so on)	_____	_____		
Specific architectural style				
One story	_____	_____		
Two stories	_____	_____		
Split-level	_____	_____		
Yard	_____	_____		
Specific number of				
Bedrooms	_____	_____		
Baths	_____	_____		
Bath in master bedroom	_____	_____		
Eat-in kitchen	_____	_____		
Separate dining room	_____	_____		
Basement	_____	_____		
Expandability	_____	_____		
Fixer-upper	_____	_____		
Energy efficiency	_____	_____		
Fireplace	_____	_____		
Garage	_____	_____		
Other	_____	_____		

Consider things that other buyers might object to. Heavy traffic on the street might not bother you, but it could make resale tougher.

Make a "Don't Want" List, Too

Finding a home with all the desired features is only half the challenge. The property must also be free from objectionable features.

Objections, which constitute your don't-want list, fall into two major categories: personal prejudice and economic fear. And there's plenty of overlap between the two.

Now is the time for you to do some systematic soul-searching. Go back through your past again, and this time think of all the homes you have not liked, whether you lived in them or merely visited them. Include all the houses and apartments that for one reason or another made a negative impression on you.

If they gave you a "I wouldn't want to live here" feeling, now is the time to identify what prompted that feeling for you. Make a list of the things you didn't like (see the checklist on the next page).

Also consider things that other buyers might object to. Heavy traffic on the street might not bother you, but it could make resale tougher.

Other buyers might also balk at buying your house if it's overimproved. A home may have great entertaining space, a swimming pool, and extensive landscaping—all features that are normally attractive to upscale buyers. But if the house is the only upgraded home in an area of ordinary homes, it will not be attractive to the typical high-income buyer. That makes it an interesting white elephant, and it could be a terrific bargain for you if you can negotiate the price down to reflect the home's wrong location, but such bargains can be deceptive: sweet on the buying end and sour on the selling end.

After you have your list of things you don't want in a home, assign them weights. Decide which objections are negotiable and which aren't. You might, for example, accept a house with a western garden when you really wanted a southern one, but you would not take a heavily trafficked street instead of a cul-de-sac.

If you're buying a home with a spouse or a partner, compare your don't-want lists. Frequently, the person

YOUR LIST OF DISLIKES

Knowing what you don't want is as important to successful house hunting as knowing what you do want. Use this checklist as a starting point for identifying your personal objections, and add to it.

- ❑ Windowless inside rooms, such as kitchens or bathrooms
- ❑ Small bathrooms (or too few)
- ❑ Exposure that doesn't suit (northern, too cold; southern, too warm)
- ❑ Too little daylight (or too little shade)
- ❑ Frame, block, or other type of construction
- ❑ Casement windows (or double-hung windows)
- ❑ Dormers
- ❑ Type of siding (wood, vinyl, asphalt shingle, false brick)
- ❑ Awkward floor plan (too open, too subdivided, too inefficient)
- ❑ Insufficient cupboard, closet, or storage space
- ❑ Basement laundry
- ❑ Too many stairs
- ❑ House doesn't fit with its surroundings
- ❑ Character of neighborhood (too many kids, too many retirees)
- ❑ Scary neighborhood
- ❑ Homeowners' association (or lack of one)
- ❑ Tiny yard (or too big of a yard to care for)
- ❑ Too far out of town
- ❑ Too close to the road
- ❑ Proximity to a commercial zone (or lack of proximity to one)
- ❑ Location on dead-end street, cul-de-sac, or flag lot (access gained through neighbor's property)
- ❑ Heavy traffic
- ❑ Street with no trees (or street with overgrown trees)
- ❑ Whatever else you can't live with:

_____

_____

_____

_____

_____

_____

_____

_____

_____

If you can't afford what you want where you want it, sacrifice something inside the house rather than sacrificing the location.

with the strongest objections is the silent partner of the team. The more vocal one may take the lead in putting together the "want" list, but when it comes to crunch time, it is often the silent one who produces a veto, often for an objection not previously voiced—or even thought about.

Besides harming the house-hunting process, these out-of-the-blue vetoes can put terrific strains on a relationship. Agents, mortgage loan officers, and escrow agents never cease to be amazed that a couple may know all about each other's tastes in food, vacations, cars, clothes, and entertainment yet not be aware of strongly held prejudices and opinions about what makes a home. Since rental living is so often a matter of expediency or convenience, it doesn't offer a good comparison to home shopping with someone.

Objections are much more elusive than demands because they don't get thought about or talked about as much. But if you know yours, and know each one's relative importance, you will be ahead in your search for a home.

Choosing a Neighborhood

You've probably heard the old cliché that the three major determinants of housing value are: (1) location, (2) location, and (3) location. Like many clichés, it's basically true. If you can't afford what you want where you want it, sacrifice something inside the house rather than sacrificing the location. You can add a second bathroom or install hardwood floors to bring a house up to your standards, but you can't improve the neighborhood single-handedly. Better to take one that needs work in a good neighborhood than to take one at the same price (or even a bit lower) that's all dolled up but in a marginal location.

What's more, price doesn't guarantee a fine location. Just because a builder puts a $500,000 house on a particular site doesn't mean the market will justify that price. Some builders can't resist gambling on a cheap piece of land, often to regret it.

Obviously, everyone can't live behind the country club overlooking the seventh fairway—nor would many buyers want to. What's good about a location, like many other features of a home, depends on your own taste. Confirmed city dwellers won't be put off by a restaurant or corner deli on the block. But suburbanites might find the same low-key establishments intrusive.

Looking at the Neighborhood

Much of the value of a home rests in its surrounding economic and social environment—its neighborhood.

In general, the more defined a neighborhood, the more likely that homes there will maintain their value. You are looking for more than just a cluster of homogeneous properties. A few blocks of carefully tended homes otherwise surrounded by blight isn't a viable neighborhood. Typically, it takes at least a dozen blocks, marked off by recognizable boundaries, for a neighborhood to sustain its character. The boundary might be a park, a highway, a campus, a river, a county line, a string of stores—anything that interrupts the pattern. One highly visible boundary gives residents a sense of belonging within it. Several such dividing lines make the neighborhood identification even stronger.

> **WHAT IS LOCATION, ANYWAY?**
>
> Depending on the market, "location" can be a city, a town, or a county. Location also is a neighborhood. It may be a home on a particular plot of land. Consider all three levels of location in choosing your home.
>
> - **Pick a town** or community with a character and style that match your own.
> - **Then go and scout out** the town's best neighborhood you can afford.
> - **Finally, zero in on the best home** on the best lot within that neighborhood. Remember, it doesn't have to be the most expensive.

In the 1970s and 1980s, some city planners, developers, and financiers embraced a new concept of single-family-lot subdivisions called planned unit developments, or PUDs. PUDs promote greater use, higher-density plans offering a variety of housing types for community designs that incorporate bands of open space separating neighborhoods from retail and commercial users. Schools, religious centers, and shopping centers are located within each community. The towns of Reston, Virginia, and Celebration, Florida, are large-scale models of the PUD concept.

Be wary of the overimproved house in a neighborhood of lesser homes.

Small towns and villages are the inspiration for one of the newest types of planned development—the traditional neighborhood development, or TND. The idea is to integrate residential, retail, office, and civic use of the land in a way that enhances a sense of community. Each development has a mixed-use core area that includes a major civic space and large, open public areas. There is a mix of residential designs—often on the same street—and roads and parks are laid out to encourage walking.

In addition to being located in the right neighborhood, a home must not clash with its surroundings. A poor fit imposes a harsh penalty on any home's value. Picture any million-dollar home in the poshest neighborhood of your city. Now, mentally move it to the worst slum you can imagine and guess what it would be worth.

Next pick a setting in between—say, a nice middle-class community. If you have an appraiser's eye for value, you will recognize that bringing that mansion from the slums where it is unsalable to a midway location won't restore even half its value. What's true for a transplanted mansion is just as true for a $400,000 house in a $150,000 neighborhood.

Be especially wary of the overimproved house in a neighborhood of lesser homes; even if you love it, it may be hard to find others who feel just as you do when the time comes to sell.

The Price of Caprice

Some homes command premium prices because of the special cachet of their neighborhoods. Even the plainest, smallest home in Beacon Hill in Boston, Nob Hill in San Francisco, Beverly Hills in Los Angeles, or Georgetown in Washington, D.C., commands a high price on a per-square-foot basis. Professional appraisers call such premiums "caprice value."

In any city, some neighborhoods enjoy inflated values because they're considered fashionable. By comparison, other neighborhoods with strong schools or other highly desirable features may be undervalued because they aren't "in." A buyer who is indifferent to fashion can find good values in neighborhoods that offer desirable amenities and services—and end up with a lot more house for the money.

Deliberately choosing to pay caprice value can be worth it if social prestige is important. If you want to buy a home with a socially desirable address, make sure the high price is in line with the market. Get an appraisal. Properties in prestige areas sometimes attract speculators who hope to make exorbitant profits off unwary buyers, especially wealthy newcomers from out of town. And not all residents of such neighborhoods are above doing a little "fishing" for gullible buyers. Go into it knowing why you're paying extra and make sure you're comfortable with it.

Tips for Relocation

If you're looking for a new home in an area where you already live, you'll have a good sense of the strengths and weaknesses of various parts of town, and you can do your neighborhood scouting on your own, without an agent. But if you're coming from out of town, you'll need help, especially if you're relocating on short notice.

Try to find acquaintances or friends of friends in the area you're moving to, and get their opinions of neighborhoods.

If you're being relocated to a branch office of your current employer, talk to your new colleagues and secure the services (at your employer's cost) of a relocation firm that works with real estate agents in your new area. Long-distance house hunting is very difficult, but it can be smoothed by the services of professionals.

Try to schedule several lengthy house-hunting trips, allowing enough time to drive around the whole area and get a feel for neighborhoods.

Long-distance house hunting is very difficult, but it can be smoothed by the services of relocation professionals in the new area.

Inquire about the quality of neighborhood schools, even if you aren't a parent.

Start your research by getting a detailed map. It should indicate schools, fire departments, parks, lakes, and shopping areas. Once you begin house hunting, use the map to familiarize yourself with the area and to get a general feel for the proximity of individual homes to schools, stores, and the like.

Ask the local real estate board or title company for prices of homes in the desired neighborhoods and jot them down to give yourself a base for comparison shopping.

Assess the look and feel of a community as you walk and drive around its neighborhoods. It can't be quantified, but it's important. Trees, shrubs, cul-de-sacs, curved streets, and landscaping around small retail stores are good signs. But unless you already live there, you need to probe deeper.

Inquire about the quality of neighborhood schools, even if you aren't a parent. Schools affect the taxes you pay on your property. And good schools increase property values for parents and nonparents alike. Parents may want to schedule a meeting with the neighborhood school's principal.

Do at least one rush-hour practice commute. Make it on a weekday at the time you normally would be en route. Use the public transportation system if that would be your usual mode. How often do buses or subways run during morning and evening rush hours? What is the weekend and off-peak schedule? If you are depending on buses or trains to get to work or for other commuting, try to determine whether there are proposals to reroute or drop the line you would be using.

Shop the stores. Is parking adequate during hours of peak demand? Can you buy aspirin and sodas nearby, or will you have to hop in the car to meet unexpected family requests? Note the kind of stores and the quality of the merchandise. Merchants have to be responsive to

QUESTIONS TO ASK ABOUT SCHOOLS

- What schools are nearby?
- How many elementary schools are operating?
- What is the average class size in grades one through six?
- How do most children get to school?
- Are before- and after-school care available?
- How do students in the town or county rate on standardized tests?
- What enrichment courses are offered?
- How are special needs met?
- What do recent high school graduates do following graduation?

For online information about schools in the area you're considering, go to www.homefair.com and click on The School Report®.

subtle changes in the socioeconomic level of their patrons. They buy what they perceive their customers want. The range of products from staples to "luxury" items in a supermarket might tell you something about whether it's a neighborhood you'd feel comfortable in.

Consider your travel patterns. Figure what roads you might have to travel to deliver your children to day-care centers or school. Is there a convenient place for you to stop after work to pick up groceries, or will buying bread and milk entail a lengthy side trip? Does the surrounding community offer recreation and entertainment that suits your interests, or will you face frequent long drives for a movie, concert, or athletic event?

Don't overlook the obvious. Make sure you choose a place you'll enjoy living in six months after moving in. If you like it, then in the future, when you're ready to sell, prospective buyers will like it, too.

Read up on the local politics and history. It will offer possible clues to the future. The chamber of commerce, the town hall, and the local library are other

Find out what plans the municipality or developers have for use of undeveloped land.

good sources for background. They also may have information on population and income trends. County and city governments also can provide critical information on taxes and zoning regulations. Subscribe to a local newspaper.

If time permits, attend a community meeting. A political fundraiser, a PTA meeting, a zoning hearing, or church or synagogue service will enable you to meet some of the residents. Find out what plans the municipality or developers have for use of undeveloped land.

Weigh the Negatives

A town or neighborhood can decline, or take off toward renewal, before home-sales figures reflect it. Before you take a fancy to a home, rule out locations where negative factors outweigh positives.

Crime

Is crime in the area increasing, decreasing, or staying about the same? Pass up casual conversations here and go to the police precinct station for records of robberies, break-ins, vandalism, assaults, and drug-related problems. Parents will want to know how safe their children will be going to and from school and playing in the neighborhood. Or log onto http://www.homefair .com and click on "Relocation Crime Lab®" for information about types of crimes per 100,000 people committed in your location and a comparison of its crime rates with other locations in the United States.

Traffic

Heavy traffic is a major drawback in any residential area. It generates noise and pollution. Of course, being on a busy street is less a problem for highrise condo dwellers than for families in detached one- and two-story homes. Even so, a unit on the quiet side of the building certainly is more desirable than one where you can hear the steady roar of automobiles.

Visual "Pollution"

Look for public-utility substations and transformers, radio or television broadcasting towers, gas stations, auto dealerships, salvage yards, overnight parking for commercial auto fleets, bus stops, and ball fields where night games are played.

Smells and Sounds

Does the commuting pattern create air pollution or smog in the area? What about food-processing or chemical plants? Even something as delightful in small doses as the smell of bread wafting from a bakery is a nuisance when you can never escape it. Visit the area during the day and at night, and on weekdays as well as weekends. Does it lie in the flight pattern for airplanes? Is it too close to a bus stop, fire station, or school?

Overcrowding

Are roads, parks, stores, and pools too crowded? Are there too many cars parked on streets and in driveways? Is there any sign that homes are being used as rooming houses or broken into multiple units?

Early Warning Signs

Full-blown blight is usually easy to spot. What you need to be alert to are the earliest signs of neglect or decay. A neighborhood that appears slightly down-at-the-heels may not reveal any other signs of decline . . . yet. Perhaps nothing is broken, littered, or really shabby. You still should try to find out why the level of maintenance has slipped. Is the ratio of owners to renters shifting? Are such municipal services as sidewalk and road repairs being postponed or reduced?

How Is the Neighborhood Organized?

Once you find a home you like, give the land it sits on more than a perfunctory once-over. Step back and notice the overall pattern of blocks and streets in the neighborhood. Most subdivi-

> **Be alert for early signs of decay. A neighborhood that appears slightly down-at-the-heels may not reveal any other signs of decline...yet.**

Give some thought to whether you will enjoy living on a lot before you fall in love with the house there.

sions are laid out in blocks and lots. A section of land is blocked off and divided into lots. Use a map to determine the layout of the community that has piqued your interest.

According to the Urban Land Institute, suburban developments after World War II continued using the grid pattern of streets—the design that was predominant and is still evident in America's older cities and towns. After the 1960s, however, most developments favored curvilinear street patterns, which essentially follow a hierarchy of streets—from major arteries out to secondary streets that end in cul-de-sacs.

The curvilinear pattern lends a more rural look, with small parks dotted throughout residential neighborhoods. But the disadvantage of this street pattern is that often the streets lead you nowhere, so you may spend extra time driving to get to the store or work.

In more recent years, some developers have been returning to the grid pattern because it's reminiscent of small village life and accommodates the trend toward smaller lots. Which pattern works best in a particular geographic area depends on the topography and the various amenities planned for the community. What you should look for when viewing a neighborhood from street level is whether the streets are safe for vehicles and pedestrians, are laid out in an efficient and livable way, and whether the land has been put to good use.

Examine the Lot

Give some thought to whether you will enjoy living on a lot before you fall in love with the house there. Your answer will depend, to some degree, on how you feel about the following:

■ **Do you spend a lot of time outdoors?**

■ **How much privacy do you want?**

■ **Will you maintain the grounds yourself,** or will you hire someone for such routine chores as mowing the lawn and trimming hedges?

■ **Do you want to be involved with landscaping,** or would you prefer an established yard with mature trees and shrubs?

Then, consider the physical dimensions and composition of the lot itself, including:

Shape

Look for a basically rectangular or square lot with adequate road frontage and enough land behind the house. Lots with unusual shapes can make it harder for you to sell your home.

Size

A lot that falls pretty much within the average for the neighborhood probably is the best bet. Bigger isn't necessarily better. Many couples don't have time for large-scale groundskeeping, and help is expensive and hard to find. Acreage that can't be subdivided can keep a property on the market.

Slope

The contour of a lot determines not only what was already built on it but also what could be added after you move in. A home built on a steep hillside may preclude the addition of two extra bedrooms that might be needed later by a growing family.

Drainage

Slope and the ability of the soil to absorb water combine to determine where and how fast water drains from the lot. Low areas that hold water can mean trouble inside and outside the house. Muddy spots are a nuisance, particularly just outside the back door. They may be only a symptom, however, of the real problem inside. A wet basement goes beyond the nuisance level. Drying it out permanently will likely be expensive. It may even be impossible.

Get a feel for a house's drainage problems by checking whether the building is on a rise or in a low spot, and simply asking yourself where rain is going to go

> **Low areas that hold water can mean trouble inside and outside the house. You want an obvious slope away from your foundation on all sides.**

after it falls on the roof. You want an obvious slope away from your foundation on all sides. If you are worried about what you see, go back for a look during and just after a hard rain. Also check local flood information—often available through mortgage lenders. You must get federal flood insurance through a commercial insurance agent if you live in a flood-prone area.

Soil Composition

Look for a good layer of topsoil that will support a healthy lawn and border plantings. Is there an established vegetable or flower garden? An inexpensive soil analysis can provide you with answers about soil quality. Some lots are scraped bare in construction and may need extensive preparation for a top-notch garden. Soil composition also affects settling of a house. Unstable soil conditions can make settling a never-ending process, leading to cracked walls and other eyesores, even damaging foundations and other structural components in the home. Contaminated soil can raise health anxieties or even cause illness.

Many Kinds of Homes

Chapter 5

Population density, topography, climate, history, and ethnic heritage all can have an impact on your choice of housing.

If you choose a particular school district in a small county, for example, you may have to rule out buying a condominium, town house, or cooperative apartment. You'll have to buy the single-family detached dwelling best suited to your needs.

Are you thinking about buying a manufactured home? Local zoning laws may dictate where you can live and limit your choices.

Large metropolitan areas usually offer a mix of homes. But in expensive locales, the middle-budget home buyer may be forced to choose between a small, close-in condo and a detached home far from work.

Here's a brief rundown of the possibilities, with some pros and cons to jog your thinking:

Single-Family Detached Houses

The single-family detached house is the essence of home ownership, with all its joys and headaches. You have four walls to call your own, and usually a yard or garden, too. These offer privacy, but they also present the burden of upkeep (painting, planting, mowing, raking leaves off the lawn in fall and shoveling snow from sidewalks in winter, and so on) that would be less or nonexistent in a condominium, town house, or apartment.

The big decision in detached housing is whether to buy an older home or something new.

If you want a house with character— perhaps even a history of its own— consider an older home.

The Older Home

If you want a house with character—perhaps even a history of its own—consider an older home. Middle-aged houses often reflect the love and care that have been lavished on them through such owner-added touches as crown moldings, carved fireplace mantels, and built-in bookcases. Often older homes are also found in neighborhoods that present a more varied environment—using a broader range of architectural styles, as well as a range of colors and texture of materials. Mature trees, established lawns, and years of gardening often add much to the feel of a community.

The older home may also be better built. Though not always true, you're more likely to find slate roofs, copper gutters, chimney flashing, hardwood floors, and plaster walls in an older home than in a new one in the same price range. And property taxes may be lower or rise more slowly because the community is settled—streets, sewers, and utilities are all in place.

With older homes, however, come older floor plans that may not fit into today's lifestyles. Traffic flow may not be convenient, master bedrooms may be small, closets almost nonexistent, and kitchens and baths outdated. You can consider remodeling to modernize, but this will add significantly to the cost. Get estimates before you make a purchase offer, but don't be surprised if the eventual work ends up costing considerably more. And if you think remodeling costs will make the house the most expensive home in the neighborhood, keep looking or you may lose money in the long run.

Your repair bills will most likely be higher than they would be if you buy a new home—at least in the beginning years of ownership. And remember that old homes are unpredictable—you never know when the roof, furnace, or water heater will need to be replaced.

The New Home

If you'd rather have a more maintenance-free existence with all the most modern designs, head for the new housing developments, where you should find the latest in floor-plan designs and kitchen and bath amenities, as well as improved storage and closet space. Most new homes also come with wall-to-wall carpeting and installed appliances and fixtures.

Does this reduce your cost of decorating over an older home? Not necessarily, if you're buying a home that's considerably larger than your current residence.

One distinct advantage in buying a new home is that the major mechanical systems (plumbing, wiring, heating, and cooling) and the structural members should last a long time. If the home was well designed and the builder competent, your mortgage payment and utility bills should be the only housing expenses, at least in the early years. And your utility bills should be lower than in an older home of comparable size.

If you're buying in a new (and fairly large) development, chances are that you'll find recreational facilities such as swimming pools, exercise clubs, tennis courts, and bike and walking trails.

Sound too good to be true? Well, there are some negatives. Often the new communities are built on the fringes of suburbia, so you may have a lengthy commute to work and to weekend activities in the city.

Many new developments have a cookie-cutter look. Your choices for the exterior may be limited to whether you have black or gray shutters, a brick facade or vinyl siding, or a front- or side-load garage. Some people like the consistency this lends to a neighborhood; others want their house to have at least some unique features. If you're in the latter group, you may have a difficult time finding a new home without considering a house from the next section—a custom-built one.

Also, if you buy into a development early on, expect a lot of construction traffic, noise, dirt, and mud.

> **WHAT PAYS OFF?**
>
> The most popular remodeling projects—kitchens, adding space, and baths—do the most to enhance your home's value. Depending on the housing market in your area, kitchens generally recoup from 40% to more than 100% of their cost when you sell. Bathrooms do just as well, with a second one adding more value than a third. Also offering good returns: upgrading to master suites and making renovations that blend the house and yard with larger windows or doors leading to decks and patios.

Ask owners how long it took to complete their home and whether it was delivered when promised.

And plan on doing a lot of landscaping; new developments tend to have a rather barren look.

Depending on the quality of the workmanship of a new home, you may find problems beginning to appear after several months. It may be because the builder cut some corners or used poor materials, or it might simply be bad luck. In any event, this is an area you'll need to keep an eye on. Make sure the builder does the repairs before time runs out—usually at the end of the first year.

If the House Is Still on the Drawing Board

Buying a not-yet-built house isn't like buying an existing one—it's harder. You reap advantages similar to those you get buying a new house; ditto the disadvantages. But, depending on market conditions and the builder, you may be able to tailor plans so you help design your dream house.

BUY BASED ON REPUTATION. The key point to remember: You're not buying a piece of land and a house; you're buying a builder. More to the point, you're buying a builder's reputation.

Make the usual checks with the Better Business Bureau and the local builders association. Look at the model homes, but keep in mind that you're looking at the builder's best effort, loaded with eye-catching "decorator options," such as molding, custom lighting, and special finishes.

For a more realistic picture, go to a comparable subdivision also put up by the same builder. Walk through the neighborhood or attend a homeowners association meeting, and visit with homeowners; ask what they think of the builder's quality and service. The latter is especially important because new houses routinely require follow-up repairs that are the builder's responsibility. You'll want to know:

- **Did the builder respond to complaints?**
- **Were repairs done well?**
- **Did problems recur?**
- **Would owners buy another home from this builder?**

AN EXTENDED WARRANTY?

Find out whether the home will be covered by an extended warranty plan such as Home Buyers Warranty. If so, check that your contract notes coverage. Such plans cover repairs for certain major construction defects and usually last for ten years. Builders pay the premiums for these plans, which remain in effect until expiration even if you sell the house (for more on this, see Chapter 8).

Ask owners how long it took to complete their home and whether it was delivered when promised. Ask the builder what happens to unsold homes. Houses that are discounted to sell quickly can affect the value of the entire subdivision.

CHECK OUT THE NEIGHBORHOOD. Once satisfied with the builder, look at the neighborhood. What will happen to those big fields to the west or that blank area to the south? Will it become home to more houses like yours? Or a gas station or factory? When it comes to information about future development, look beyond the sales agent for verification. Check the master plan filed with the local planning department. And visit other land-owning builders to find out what they have in store for nearby lots.

TIME YOUR OFFER. Timing affects the price. You may find a slower market in fall and winter. You probably won't get a discount, but you may be able to negotiate for options like a deck or upgraded carpet. Consider at what point in the construction cycle to buy. Prices may be lower when you buy a house that's built early on. In booming markets, house prices can jump in $10,000 increments as development is completed. Buy too early, however, and you'll live in a construction site for several years. If you wait you may get further from the main road to the development. There's also less risk when you buy later. You can monitor the quality of houses and watch how the neighborhood shapes up.

When new construction is slow and not in great demand, you can often negotiate the price of upgrades. Otherwise, be prepared to pay extra for everything.

HAMMER OUT THE CONTRACT. You put a contract on a to-be-built house just as you would on an existing one, but you face many more decisions before you can sign on the dotted line. For starters, if the market is active, you may need to put a deposit on the lot immediately. Typically the deposit is 5 percent, but you may be able to bargain it down. Also, insert a clause in the contract to protect your right to regain the deposit if the deal falls through—because of problems with financing, for example.

Sit down with the selling agent and hammer out the details. You pick the model and the options you want to add. If there is a model built, you can point to things you want. Otherwise, you'll be using illustrations, brochures, and samples of materials.

Prepare to pay extra for everything—from kitchen cabinets made of cherry rather than oak to better carpeting, humidifiers, intercoms, fireplaces, decks, and a finished basement. When new construction is slow and not in great demand, you can often negotiate the price of upgrades. But if you're in a seller's market, be prepared to pay the listed price.

Consider how you'll pay for each option. If the cost is lumped into the mortgage, it's easier to afford but more expensive in the long run because it's amortized over two or three decades.

You may be told you must have certain things installed, even though you don't want them or don't like the quality. Carpet is a good example. Lenders may require carpeting before a house can be sold. Fine, but you think the basic carpeting stinks and don't like the optional colors any better. If you're told that the choices you see are the only ones available, keep pushing. Insist on getting something you want to live with, especially if your offer is not contingent on the sale of another house—a status that puts you in a powerful negotiating position. One solution is to draft a letter of agreement to the lender indicating that you will place carpet of your choosing in the house within a specified time after the closing date.

In most states, contracts favor the builder. You probably won't be able to get the builder to guarantee delivery on a specified date. You can, however, add a clause to your contract demanding that your house be built to the quality standards of the model.

STUDY SETTLEMENT DETAILS. You'll be given a list of disclosures about the subdivision. It must include such information as the location of any airports within a given radius of the house.

You'll also get a copy of the development's homeowners association bylaws. As local governments have shifted the costs of maintaining services to residents, they have required new developments to assume more responsibility for road maintenance, garbage collection, and recreation facilities. Homeowners associations may be relatively inactive, but they have power over how you live. They can assess you for emergency expenses and put a lien on your property if you don't pay your dues. Have a lawyer review the bylaws—as well as everything else in the contract—before you sign.

Condominium Ownership

The term "condominium" refers to a legal form of ownership, not a particular type of property. Under such a plan, the owners of individual dwelling units in a housing development also own undivided proportional interests in such common facilities as the grounds, hallways, elevators, and recreation areas.

Condos give owners virtually the same financial advantages as do single-family houses. The federal income-tax breaks are identical:

- **Mortgage interest and property taxes** on your home are deductible.
- **You probably won't have to pay any tax** on any profit you make when you sell. Up to $250,000 of profit on the sale of a condo is tax-free for those filing single returns, and $500,000 escapes federal taxation for those who file joint returns.

> Condos give owners virtually the same financial advantages as do single-family houses.

On the downside, when the housing market goes into a tailspin, condo prices are usually the first to suffer and the last to recover.

Condos typically offer a trade-off: less cost for less space. Instead of having your own backyard, you may share one with 200 or so other residents. In place of your own full basement or attic for storage, you get a storage bin in the basement. You may have to share coin-operated washers and dryers. And you can't keep a bike and workbench in your parking space.

On the other hand, less space is precisely what many buyers are looking for. They want the enjoyment of an indoor swimming pool that's an elevator ride away, or ready access to a tennis partner on Saturday mornings. They don't want to rake leaves and mow the lawn.

A condo—whether it's a garden apartment, a town house or a highrise—locks you into community living. While cost may be your first priority, a condominium's facilities and the lifestyle it mandates—particularly interaction with your fellow owners—should be ranked not too far behind. You may get a bargain on the place and still end up with buyer's remorse if your neighbors are noisy or otherwise objectionable. You will be subject to rules adopted by other owners. Certain activities and hobbies may be restricted or even banned. Pets may be forbidden, especially cats and dogs.

MANY KINDS OF CONDOS

Just about any kind of development you can think of comes in condominium form: converted older apartment houses, townhouse complexes, elegant old mansions divided into luxury apartments, commercial lofts and office buildings, apartments fitted into former schools or farm silos, and virtually self-contained villages of freestanding houses, complete with tennis courts, golf courses, pools, and community houses.

Questions to Ask

Before you shop, learn as much about condominium ownership as possible. Line up a good lawyer who understands condos. Then investigate and question, question, question.

WHAT'S THE AREA LIKE? You want your unit to be a good investment as well as a good place to live.

Generally, look for residential areas with good-quality apartment buildings and homes in the middle to upper price range. Assess convenience to public transportation, stores, schools, hospitals, and parks.

Find out whether units have been appreciating. Compare recent selling prices with original purchase prices. How much of that appreciation occurred in the months or year after the development sold out? How much is occurring now? Information on sales is available from county land-transfer records.

Try to visualize what the neighborhood might look like in 5, 10, or 15 years. What are the zoning rules covering nearby unbuilt areas? Could the view be obstructed by a future highrise? Could a highway be constructed nearby?

IS IT FINANCIALLY SOUND? What debts does the condo association owe, and to whom? Are there adequate funds in reserve to handle routine maintenance as well as replacement of expensive items, such as boilers and roofs? Has the association tended to rely on special assessments for emergency needs?

WILL YOU FIT IN? Do you desire compatibility with other tenants, in terms of lifestyle, occupation, age, or any other characteristic? How are problems resolved? Will you be expected to vote on every little detail—like what color to paint the halls—or will routine decisions be made by the elected board?

WHAT'S THE VACANCY RATE IN THE REGION? An oversupply of condo units in an area can depress prices generally. Too many vacant units in a particular building can not only depress prices but also, among other things, reduce the funds available to the condo association for maintenance and repairs and increase the pressure on the developer or current owners to rent rather than sell.

HOW MANY UNITS ARE RENTED? Some units usually are rented out by investors, others by owners who have

Try to visualize what the neighborhood might look like in 5, 10, or 15 years.

Ironically, you may find it best not to buy if the condo does not impose enough controls.

moved away temporarily. In resort areas, most of the units in a project may be on rental during the vacation season, but that's a special case. A high proportion of renters is undesirable, so much so that the FHA won't insure condo loans in projects with less than a 51 percent owner-occupancy rate (although local HUD offices can increase that number depending on market conditions). Other lenders will hesitate, too. Renters, it's charged, are less concerned than owner-occupants with preserving the building and grounds, and investors are less likely than homeowners to upgrade and renovate their units.

IS THERE A HEAVY SALES TURNOVER? You expect turnover in a resort project. But heavy turnover in a year-round residential community can create an uncomfortable feeling of impermanence; increase the wear and tear on elevators, hallways, and other common elements; weaken security controls; and discourage compliance with rules.

WHO OWNS THE COMMON FACILITIES? Developers sometimes hang on to such facilities—laundry room, parking areas, pool, and other recreational facilities—for the income from rental fees. Avoid a project in which important amenities are not owned by the condominium owners. Otherwise, you become a captive user, exposed to uncontrollable fee increases and inconveniences.

ARE THE FACILITIES ADEQUATE? Inspect the pool, tennis courts, parking area, and other facilities at times of peak usage. A pool that's big enough for a 200-unit building occupied mainly by working couples and singles could be an overcrowded mess with the same number of apartments filled largely by families with children. Free parking may be limited or unavailable. You may have to pay to use a party room or gym.

WHAT ARE THE RESTRICTIONS? There are sure to be some, so read the declaration or master deed, the bylaws, and the house rules before you sign a contract. Ironically, you may find it best not to buy if the condo does not impose enough controls.

WHAT HAPPENS IF FUNDS ARE STOLEN OR MISHANDLED? Will owners be adequately insured? Are funds in an insured account? If not, what would happen if investment losses occurred? Ask for evidence of liability insurance, property insurance, and fidelity bond.

Where to Find the Answers

Answers to many of the important questions about condos can be found in the following documents, which you should examine before you buy a condo. Some states require developers to give potential buyers a prospectus with relevant facts about the offering. No matter how onerous the job, you and your lawyer should take the time to evaluate all this material before you buy. If your state doesn't require delivery of documents before you sign a contract, insist on your right to obtain and examine them.

MASTER DEED. Also called an enabling declaration, a plan of condominium ownership, or a declaration of condominium, the master deed is the key document. When the master deed is recorded, it legally establishes the project as a condominium. Among other things, the master deed authorizes residents to form an operating association and describes individual units and commonly owned areas.

BYLAWS. These spell out the association's authority and responsibilities, authorize the making of a budget and the collection of various charges, and prescribe parliamentary procedures. They may empower the association to hire professional managers or contain other special provisions. If the condo master deed doesn't do so, the bylaws may set forth insurance requirements and authorize liens against property owners who fail to pay monthly charges.

The contract may provide for a cooling-off period during which you can back out. If not, insert a clause to that effect.

HOUSE RULES. These state what owners can and can't do. Restrictions on pets, children, decorations, use of facilities, and such are among them. House rules may be incorporated in the bylaws or they may be set out in a separate document.

SALES CONTRACT OR PURCHASE AGREEMENT. While basically similar to other real estate contracts, there are a couple of differences. When you sign a condo contract, you probably acknowledge receipt of the other documents just described. The contract may provide for a cooling-off period during which you can back out. If not, insert a clause to that effect.

Likewise, make sure the contract sets out when and how you'll get out of the deal if you fail to get the financing you want.

If the project isn't yet completed, ask for written assurance that it will be—and as promised.

Ensure your right to an inspection prior to settlement, and make sure your deposit is placed in an escrow account.

OTHER PAPERS. No less important, these could include a copy of the operating budget, a schedule of current and proposed assessments, a financial statement for the owners association, any leases or contracts, a plan or drawing of the project and your unit, and an engineer's report if one was done.

Determine how much money has been set aside for emergency outlays. (The board should set owners' condo fees high enough to create a reserve fund for replacements and major repairs.) Ask the board treasurer for copies of recent budget reports, and obtain an engineer's summary of the physical condition of the building, including projections for major repairs.

Find out what assessments were made during the past five years in addition to the regular condo fee. While some associations deliberately choose to operate with minimal reserves, relying instead on special assessments, good management is generally associated with a healthy reserve.

Getting to Know Them

If you've never lived in a condo, you may be astonished to discover just how much power is held by the board of directors. As mentioned, the board has the power to put a lien on your unit if you don't pay your monthly fee or are late with the money for a special assessment. It may have license to spend tens of thousands of dollars on a repair or improvement without the prior approval of other owners.

Elected by condo owners, the board is much like a miniature government with ultimate authority to run the condominium, even if it turns day-to-day operating details over to a resident manager or an outside management company.

Request information on the background of each member, and attend at least one board meeting. If you are serious about condo ownership, plan on participating in a certain amount of organizational activity just to protect your interests.

Financing

You may be asked to make a larger down payment on a condo than on a comparable single-family property. But otherwise, getting a mortgage for a condo is no different from getting one on a single-family house.

Down payments can be 5 percent or less, but FHA-insured mortgages may not be available to prospective owners of condo projects less than a year old.

Cooperative Apartments

The "stockholder in 202-F" may sound like someone with a seat on a securities exchange, but if you live in a cooperative apartment, that's how you might describe your neighbor.

Unlike condominium ownership, which gives you title to a particular unit and an undivided interest in the common areas, buying a co-op entitles you to a share in a corporation. Stock ownership or certificate membership in the corporation, in turn, gives you the right to live in a particular unit. You become a tenant-

If you are serious about condo ownership, plan on participating in a certain amount of organizational activity just to protect your interests.

stockholder. Typically, the corporation owns and manages the co-op, pays the property taxes, and finances the project with a "blanket" mortgage.

In most states your collateral is considered personal property rather than real property. However, if your cooperative complies with certain Internal Revenue Code requirements, that portion of your assessment going to pay real estate taxes and interest on any blanket mortgage should be tax-deductible on your personal income taxes, along with interest on any share loan.

Because a tenant is a fellow shareholder in the whole building, current co-op tenants tend to be choosy about prospective owners. It's common for a co-op board to interview prospects and require them to submit personal references as well as financial statements. Most co-op boards zealously protect the lifestyle of their tenant-stockholders, going so far as to reject those they believe could be noisy, reclusive, sloppy, or inclined to throw large, boisterous parties. But they can go only so far. Boards are prohibited by federal law and many state statutes from rejecting or discouraging a prospective buyer on the basis of race, gender, creed, or national origin.

Financing a Co-op Unit

Unlike the collateral (property) that secures a traditional mortgage, collateral for a "share loan" includes stock in a corporation. When you own a co-op, you do not actually own the rooms that comprise your unit. You own the shares in the overall ownership of the building(s). The National Cooperative Bank, through its subsidiary, NCB, FSB, is one of the largest single share-loan originators.

NCB, FSB will evaluate your creditworthiness using the same Fannie Mae underwriting guidelines

---

CO-OP ASSOCIATIONS

The National Association of Housing Cooperatives (1707 H St., NW, Suite 202, Washington, DC 20006; 202-737-0797; http://www.coophousing.org) can provide a list of publications.

National Cooperative Business Association (1401 New York Ave., N.W., Suite 1100, Washington, DC, 20005; 202-638-1374; http://www.ncba.org)

CO-OP FINANCING INFORMATION

National Cooperative Bank, through its subsidiary NCB, FSB, provides co-op unit financing (also referred to as share loan financing) nationwide. In addition, NCB offers home equity lines of credit to co-ops, a product usually not offered outside of the New York metropolitan region. For more information about co-op financing in the New York City metro area, call 212-808-0887 or 800-668-9417; in the Washington, D.C., metro area, call 202-336-7637 or 800-955-9622, x7637; and elsewhere in the country call 866-622-6446.

For a free copy of *A Consumer's Guide to Buying a Co-op,* contact NCB's Marketing Communications Department at 800-955-9622, x7742, or view it online at http://www .ncbhomeloans.com.

---

that are applied to a mortgage for a single-family home or a condo unit.

Required Reading

The following are common cooperative-housing documents you need to study before you buy:

ARTICLES OF INCORPORATION. A cooperative is incorporated under state law, and the corporation's purpose, powers, and obligations are described in the Articles of Incorporation.

AUDITED FINANCIAL STATEMENTS. Make sure that you receive statements for at least the past year. You can use these to check the co-op's reserves, maintenance records, income sources, and so on.

BYLAWS. These spell out the duties and responsibilities of shareholders, officers, and directors, and probably specify how many units may be rented out to non-shareholders.

Besides collecting money for taxes and debt, adequate sums must be set aside to replace structural elements and major components.

STOCK, SHARES, OR MEMBERSHIP CERTIFICATES. Shares or membership certificates are your proof of ownership in the corporation.

PROPRIETARY LEASE OR OCCUPANCY AGREEMENT. The lease sets up the terms and conditions by which you occupy your co-op unit. It obligates you to pay your pro rata share of the corporation's expenses, including real estate taxes, operating costs, and debt. Rules on using your unit, subleasing, and maintenance also are found in the agreement.

RECOGNITION AGREEMENT. A share-loan lender and the co-op corporation enter into this agreement in order to document the lender's rights as well as the corporation's responsibilities and obligations to the lender. A corporation may enter into recognition agreements with more than one lender.

REGULATORY AGREEMENT. This document is issued by the lender or government agency that has provided the blanket mortgage. It sets out requirements for such things as reserves, reporting, and budget approval. Like condos, co-ops must establish reserve funds to pay taxes and debts, as well as to replace structural elements and repair systems. A general operating reserve must be established for other contingencies and for resale problems. Income for these funds typically comes from the tenant-stockholders, commercial use such as parking, and income earned on the reserve funds.

SECURITY AGREEMENT. In this document, the share-loan borrower assigns the proprietary lease (or occupancy agreement) and pledges his or her stock, shares, or membership certificate to the lender in return for a loan.

The Right Questions
Be sure to get answers to the following questions:

IS IT FINANCIALLY SOUND? Is there adequate income in the co-op to meet expenses? Income has three primary sources: tenant-stockholders, commercial use—for example, rental income from parking—and interest or dividends earned on reserve funds. Expenses include debt repayment, real estate and income taxes, building maintenance and operations, and reserve-fund payins for replacements and capital improvements.

A cooperative financed with an FHA-insured blanket mortgage is required to have reserve funds that meet the agency's criteria. Besides collecting money for taxes and debt, a cooperative must have adequate sums set aside to replace structural elements and major components, such as heating, cooling, plumbing, and electrical systems. In addition, a general operating reserve must be established for other contingencies and for resale problems. These reserves are established under the co-op's regulatory agreements, and documents should be available to prospective owners.

NCB/Fannie Mae's project-approval standards give lenders the tools they need to evaluate co-op projects. Typically, they require, among other things, that each project have an adequate cash flow and that monthly assessments be structured to handle operating expenses and build sufficient reserves.

WHAT IS THE AGE AND CONDITION OF THE BUILDING? The answer sets the stage for the kind of financial experience you'll have once you're a tenant-stockholder. Is there an engineering report on the condition of the property? If you discover the galvanized plumbing in the building is nearing the end of its anticipated 40-year life span, you know it will have to be replaced, not repaired. How does the board plan to pay for the job? From the reserve fund? With a special assessment? By refinancing the mortgage?

HOW WILL YOU FIT IN? How old is the average shareowner? What is the financial status and philosophy of the majority? Up-and-coming professionals in their

How does the co-op board plan to pay for repairs? From the reserve fund? With a special assessment? By refinancing the mortgage?

> **If a building is dominated by tenants rather than owners, it changes the nature of cooperative living.**

early 40s may have a very different money-management philosophy than retired or soon-to-be retired people.

Likewise, if you can afford to buy into a particular cooperative only by living in the smallest unit, you may be at odds with affluent neighbors who insist on a uniformed doorman—regardless of cost.

WHAT IS THE COMPOSITION OF THE BOARD AND ITS FINANCIAL PHILOSOPHY? Is there some consensus among board members on how to conduct the corporation's affairs? Do their views on important issues reflect those of other tenant-stockholders? Do they jibe with yours?

ARE YOU PREPARED TO PARTICIPATE IN COOPERATIVE LIVING? Many of the problems of condo and cooperative living are similar. How willing are you to be involved in meetings and group efforts?

HOW MANY UNITS ARE RENTED? What do the bylaws permit? Conceivably, a majority of a co-op's units could be occupied by tenants or "nominees" of partnerships, trusts, estates, and corporations rather than by shareowners who have joined together as "cooperative homeowners." If a building is dominated by tenants rather than owners, it changes the nature of cooperative living. It also may have tax and resale consequences for individual tenant-stockholders.

MAY YOU SUBLET YOUR APARTMENT? Some cooperatives forbid it. Others allow it but may impose a one-time sublet fee or an additional monthly maintenance surcharge.

Manufactured Homes

Manufactured housing has come a long way since the days of its earlier cousin—mobile homes. In fact, one of the reasons for the name change is that these homes are no longer very mobile. Built in factories and assembled in the plant or on site, manufactured homes make ownership possible for many families and individuals who would otherwise be priced out of the market. On a per-square-foot basis, manufactured homes cost about a third as much to build as site-built homes.

Rent or Buy the Land?

Before you buy, decide whether you will place the home on land you own or on land you rent or lease. The decision is important because if you later regret your choice of a homesite, the only practical solution may be to sell. It also has tax implications.

The majority of buyers put their manufactured homes on land they own. Your best approach is to select a lot before you buy the home. While zoning restrictions that keep manufactured homes out of residential neighborhoods still exist in some areas, many states have passed legislation that prevents such zoning discrimination. Check local zoning ordinances before making plans to situate your new home.

There are numerous well-designed, attractive subdivisions to choose from; you may be able to find land in a ready-made community, complete with swimming pool, recreation center, and nearby schools and shopping. A good subdivision developer can help you select a lot suited to the home you have in mind.

If you plan to rent the land on which your home will be situated, you should understand that the management in many manufactured-home communities may have restrictive rules by which you must abide. Also, residents tend to keep an eye on each other—so you must like living in a close-knit community.

If you move into an established community, you will rent a piece of property and have your home installed at your expense. A lease may or may not be involved. There are generally rules and regulations, and you should ask for them in writing. In most cases you will rent your space from month to month or year to year, but longer-term leases are now offered in many states.

In a new development, the management may also be the dealer, and you can get into the community only

> **Check local zoning ordinances before making plans to situate your new home.**

by buying a home from the dealer. This arrangement isn't entirely self-serving. It allows management to enforce strict standards for homes that go into the community. When you select a lot, you also pick a home from among models approved by the management. You will be shown a complete catalog and price information, and in some developments management will encourage you to go to the factory to custom-design your model.

New developments and those still under construction are often promoted on the basis of nonexistent amenities such as swimming pools, shuffleboard courts, and recreation halls. Once settled in, you may discover—to your dismay—that the landlord lets the pool wait while funds and space are devoted to developing homesites. What's more, you may have been required to pay an entrance fee of several hundred dollars—a practice now banned in some states.

Keep in mind that leasing land rather than buying puts you in a vulnerable situation. You will own a valu-

---

SELECTING A HOMESITE

Whether you intend to buy or rent a homesite, here are some considerations:

- **Visit several developments.** Stay a few days if you can, to sample the neighborhood and meet residents.
- **Familiarize yourself with each community's rules and regulations.** In condominium developments, for example, residents own part of the common facilities plus their own units and lots.
- **Try to determine how much turnover there is.**
- **Find out how most residents view their community.** Is your lifestyle compatible with that of potential neighbors?

- **Check on security, fire protection, and trash collection.**
- **Remember that the character of a rental community can change** much more rapidly than that of a community of landowners. As a tenant, there may be little you can do if a community is sold or if the management becomes lax.
- **Study the purchase contract or lease, bylaws,** rules and regulations, and all other pertinent documents.
- **Do not commit yourself to a lot** or a home until you've consulted with a lawyer.
- **Don't sign anything you don't understand.**

able piece of property located on someone else's land. In a dispute with the landowner you may have no recourse but to sell or move. Moving even a single-section home is costly. Including necessary dismantling and reassembly, you can pay thousands of dollars to move a luxury multisection home less than 50 miles. Because of the expense and damage that can result from vibration and road shock, you could be forced to sell, possibly at a loss, and be faced with the prospect of buying another home elsewhere.

Questions of Quality

You might pay around $32,000 for a single-section unit, from $55,000 to $100,000 for a multisection. The purchase price usually includes some furniture, major appliances, draperies, carpeting, and delivery from the manufacturer to a homesite.

"Single-section" or "single-wide" units may give you up to 1,600 square feet of living space. You can join two or more single sections together to form a multisection home. At first glance, the most luxurious multisection models—featuring wood or vinyl siding, pitched roofs, cathedral ceilings, fireplaces, bay windows, drywall interiors, and the like—can be hard to distinguish from their conventional site-built counterparts.

WHAT'S REQUIRED. Manufactured homes are not subject to local building codes. Units built after June 14, 1976, are covered by the National Manufactured Home Construction and Safety Standards Act and must display a permanent label saying that the manufacturer has conformed with the standards.

The standards do not apply to units made before then, nor to multifamily manufactured homes or modular units for the handicapped, which are covered by local building codes. All manufactured homes are built to federal Department of Housing and Urban Development (HUD) code. HUD has overall responsibility for enforcement, but inspections are conducted by approved state or private agencies.

At first glance, the most luxurious multisection models can be hard to distinguish from their conventional site-built counterparts.

In 1992, Hurricane Andrew destroyed thousands of homes in south Florida, including about 9,000 manufactured homes. Soon after, HUD issued final standards for builders focused on improving the ability of manufactured homes to withstand high winds in the hurricane-prone coastal regions. If you purchase a new manufactured home that you plan to locate on the southeastern coast or near the Gulf of Mexico, check the "Data Plate" (see the box below) to ensure that the home is constructed for the location where you intend to site it.

Single-section manufactured homes are more prone to wind damage from hurricanes, tornadoes, and severe thunderstorms than many site-built homes—even when properly tied down. Multisection units are more stable than single-section, particularly when properly tied or attached to a permanent foundation. A significant number of structural problems have been traced to improper installation of units on their sites, which HUD does not regulate. For that reason, installation should be done only by trained personnel.

QUALITY IN MANUFACTURED HOMES

Signs of good construction include:

- **a floor that is level and firm,**
- **windows and doors that open and close smoothly,**
- **walls that do not give excessively when pushed,**
- **a firm ceiling, and**
- **at least three axles if the unit is 60 feet long or more.**

Also, look for an 8½-by-11-inch Data Plate sheet or certification label, located near the 2-by-4-inch aluminum-label main electrical panel. It indicates that the home conforms with Department of Housing and Urban Development (HUD) standards. The plate gives:

- **the name and address of the home's manufacturer,**
- **the serial number,**
- **model and date of manufacture,**
- **thermal insulation, and**
- **the wind and snow loads for which the unit is designed, as well as other key information.**

The home should come with important information relating to such things as heating and appliance operating efficiency.

States set their own standards and regulations governing proper installation. Check with your local building-inspection offices (or your state's Manufactured Housing Association) on details and procedures to ensure that your home is properly installed.

Financing the Purchase

You should be able to finance your home with a mortgage if the unit is permanently set up on land you own (or on land you are buying along with the unit, in what is known as a single real estate transaction). Fannie Mae and Freddie Mac buy qualified manufactured-home loans originated by banks, savings and loans, and mortgage bankers.

Manufactured houses are eligible for government-backed FHA and VA loans. In California, you may be able to title your manufactured home as real estate even if you don't own the land on which it is installed. Some lenders in that state have made mortgage loans on such homes when the borrower has had a long-term lease on the land.

> ### CHECK YOUR WARRANTIES
>
> Once you've bought your unit, you may get warranties from the retailer, transporter, installer, and appliance manufacturer. Note what each warranty covers and doesn't cover. How long does each last? Who will actually do any necessary work under the warranty? Where will it be done?

But most manufactured homes are financed like motor vehicles—with personal property (or so-called chattel) loans—and dealers and park and subdivision developers still arrange most financing. Most lenders will want a minimum down payment of 5 percent and will have loan terms ranging from 15 to 30 years. Interest rates are higher than on real estate loans—by as much as two or three percentage points—than on FHA, VA, or Freddie Mac– or Fannie Mae–qualified loans.

Another growing trend for homebuyers is to finance their home and land together as real property using conventional mortgage financing obtained through a traditional mortgage lender. Fannie Mae and Freddie Mac, the primary secondary market sources for mortgage loans in the United States, encourage this trend through their guidelines for accepting real estate

---

MORE ABOUT MANUFACTURED HOMES

How to Buy a Manufactured Home, by the Manufactured Housing Institute, in cooperation with the Federal Trade Commission's Office of Consumer and Business Education, may be viewed online (http://www.manufacturedhousing .org) or ordered (2101 Wilson Blvd., Suite 610, Arlington, VA 22201; 703-558-0400). It includes information on:

- **warranties and other consumer protections**
- **home selection and placement**
- **site preparation**
- **transportation and installation**
- **and home inspection**

mortgage loans for 20- and 30-year terms secured by manufactured homes.

Interest on debt you take on to buy or renovate a manufactured home (or home and land together) is fully deductible for federal tax purposes, as long as it is secured by the house and you use the house as your principal residence or as your second home.

When you find a unit you like and know how much you want to borrow, ask lenders about rates and terms. A few phone calls could save you big bucks.

Manufactured-home loans are subject to the federal Truth in Lending law—and if land is involved, the Real Estate Settlement Procedures Act (RESPA)— which means you must be informed in writing of the finance cost expressed as an annual percentage rate (APR). If you're quoted an unusually low figure, it's probably an "add-on" or "discount" rate, neither of which reflects the true cost. Always insist on being told the APR, and have the APR inserted in any purchase contract. With add-on loans, interest is added to the amount borrowed before payments begin. If an interest-rebate formula called the "Rule of 78s" is used on pre-payment or refinancing, you could actually owe more than you borrowed even after making payments for several years.

The FHA Title I program is available for financing manufactured homes. This program insures loans on either manufactured homes, manufactured home lots, or a combination of the two. Maximum loan amounts are $48,600 for the home only and $64,800 for the home and lot. In high-cost areas, these amounts may be increased by as much as 85 percent. Loan terms are 20 years for single-section units and 25 years for multiple-section homes.

The VA guarantee for manufactured homes is $20,000 or 40 percent of the loan, whichever is smaller. (This means you can finance a house and lot costing much more than that.) A 5 percent down payment will be required. Loan terms are just over 20 years for single-wide units, just over 23 for double-wides, and just over 25 for double-wides and lots.

House-Hunting Strategies

Chapter 6

Once you've gone through the steps outlined in previous chapters—assessing your resources, getting preapproval for a mortgage, defining needs and wants—you're ready for serious house hunting.

Adapt your strategy to the mood and economic realities in your targeted location and price range. The housing market usually depends on the economy—local, regional, and national. But within the best and worst markets, there are recurring seasonal differences. Try to shop when other buyers aren't out in force.

Across the country, demand surges in April and May. It's understandable that sellers generally don't feel pressured then to cut a deal right away. Some will feel differently by June; more will be eager to sell by the time the late-summer doldrums hit.

September, October, and November generally usher in a brisker pace. But from Thanksgiving through the winter, holiday activities and cold weather combine to slow activity. Buyers should find sellers more interested in dealing—an advantage offset by the smaller number of houses for sale.

Naturally, the seasonal ebb and flow of market activity varies. Ski areas and beach resorts have their own market cycles, as do other specialized markets and different climatic regions. A seven-year analysis of prices and sales activity in Texas, for example, showed that July, August, and September were the best months for selling a home in that state; by contrast, the first quarter—January, February, and March—was usually a buyer's market. Learn the local pattern and, if possible, use it to your advantage.

When things are cold for sellers, time is on your side. You can be more deliberate and drive a harder bargain.

The Buyer's Market

In a buyer's market, there are lots of houses for sale relative to the number of serious lookers. Houses sit on the market, and sellers often cut asking prices and even assist buyers with cut-rate financing.

When things are cold for sellers, time is on your side. You can be more deliberate and drive a harder bargain. You can get a house appraised before you submit an offer and ask the seller to pay all or part of the cost. You can spend more time checking out comparable properties. You can even load your offer with contingency clauses that help you—inspection, financing at a specified interest rate, seller's help with mortgage points, even the condition that you be able to sell your current home before closing on this purchase—and still get it accepted.

In a buyer's market, a diligent house hunter can do reasonably well without a real estate agent. You generally don't have access to new listings in the local multiple listing service (MLS) database (the real estate trade's computerized clearinghouse of properties for sale), but you might not miss much, especially if you have Internet access (see page 96). Most Realtors advertise listings on their Web sites, and most houses will remain on the market long enough to be advertised and shown, many more than once.

The Seller's Market

When asking prices are firm or rising and new listings are snapped up as soon as they show up in the MLS, it's a seller's market. You'll notice more for-sale-by-owner properties, too. In a sizzling market, good houses are often sold before being advertised or keyed into the MLS computer. Often within hours, multiple contracts are submitted on the same property, and buyers vie with each other by bidding more than the asking price.

If you want to buy in this climate, be ready—financially and emotionally—to move fast when you spot something that meets your needs.

Sellers won't pay much attention to timid or unprepared buyers or those who load their offering contract with lots of protective contingencies. The would-be buyer who must have the contract reviewed by a not-yet-selected lawyer and the buyer with insufficient earnest money who wants the seller to take a personal note for a few days won't get serious consideration from owners of desirable properties.

Have a lawyer and home inspector on standby. If you haven't selected them, do so now. Get names from friends, lenders, a title company, and real estate agents. If you are buying a condominium, co-op, or farm, find a lawyer and inspector who specialize in such transactions.

Save time by becoming familiar with the contract you intend to use. Have contingencies you plan to insert drawn up by your lawyer in advance, but remember, a "clean" contract—one not littered with lots of escape clauses—will be treated with more respect by the seller.

Financial Readiness

Be prepared to write a check for the earnest money—this usually accompanies your offer as evidence of your intentions, good faith, and ability to close the deal. If necessary, cash in certificates of deposit and stocks and move the money to your checking or money-market account. Consider establishing a home-equity line of credit on your current home well before you begin looking for your next home (see the discussions of home-equity loans in Chapters 3 and 14).

In a hot market, one thing that could set your offer above other bids would be your ability to go to settlement fast. You may lose out if your contract is contingent on the sale of the house where you presently reside. Obtaining preapproval for a mortgage is a must in a hot market, so do it as soon as you decide that you are serious about buying a new home.

The Search for Houses

In a hot seller's market, use every tool at your disposal to spot good prospects. It is not enough to watch the

> **Consider establishing a home-equity line of credit on your current home well before you begin looking for your next home.**

Use the scouting services of at least one aggressive, experienced agent who knows your targeted area.

newspapers every day for advertisements of houses just put on the market or to wait around for weekend open houses. Many fine offerings will be sold by word of mouth, without ever being advertised in the paper or entered in the multiple listing service.

Some of these unpublicized sales will be "by owner," with no agent involved. Others will be transactions started and completed within one real estate firm, where one agent's new listing is sold to a buyer assisted by another agent in the same office.

For these reasons, use the scouting services of at least one aggressive, experienced agent who knows your targeted neighborhood. In some cases, it may be useful to have several agents in different firms helping you simultaneously. (But keep in mind that when agents are competing to sell you a home, they are under tremendous pressure to get you to buy. Helping you find the best property may take second priority.)

Use your own energy and ingenuity. Ask friends who live in or near your ideal neighborhood to let you know if they hear anything that suggests a house might be coming on the market soon. It could be news of a company move, a split marriage, retirement, or the death of an elderly person living alone.

Searching on Your Own

Smart house hunters will approach the owners of houses they admire, even if the house is not for sale. If you are interested in a particular neighborhood, you might consider distributing letters there asking people to call you if they might be thinking about selling. Sometimes the owner has never thought of selling but is surprised to hear what his house might be worth; suddenly, you've got an interested seller.

If you're looking at houses with an agent, he or she can make contacts for you and work with both interested parties to make a deal, earning a commission in the process (see page 104 for tips on handling the "sale by owner" purchase). Go solo, though, and you'll have to do that yourself, and much more. For one, you have

---

USING THE OBITS

As ghoulish as it may sound, some house hunters watch the obituaries and look up the address of the deceased to see where he or she lived; after a suitable period of time, they write or phone an heir listed in the story and inquire respectfully whether the house will be for sale.

---

to know the comparables—the selling prices and descriptions of similar homes that recently changed hands in the neighborhood where you are looking. You can get a ballpark idea by attending open houses in the area. But check asking prices against actual sale prices in local newspapers or at the county courthouse.

Suppose one of your contacts does show an interest in selling to you—what then?

- **Once you agree to talk business,** do it in writing, even if you're sitting across the table from each other.
- **Start with things the seller wants to know,** such as how financially qualified you are, how much earnest money you'd be willing to offer, and when you could go to settlement.
- **Keep the offering price off center stage** until you can get agreement on as many other contract details as possible.
- **If the owner is interested but unprepared** and leaning towards calling an agent for advice, ask for the chance to tour the house, obtain an appraisal, and make an offer.
- **Point out that a private transaction,** without an agent's commission, could net substantially more. The savings could be split in some proportion between you, benefiting both.
- **You could also suggest sharing the cost of a professional appraisal**—for the owner's protection and your own—in order to get negotiations under way.

If that approach doesn't work, perhaps the owner has no idea what the house is worth or how to conduct negotiations. At that point, you may be wise to advise

**If you
want help,
contact agents
with proven
reputations
in the
neighborhood
and price
range in which
you're looking.**

the owner to ask an agent to represent him. If he does so, here's your strategy: Suggest the seller add a clause to the listing contract specifying that he may, for a specified period of time, sell to you and you alone (you must be named in the listing contract) without paying a commission. The unsure seller gets the advice and counsel he needs and the possibility of an immediate sale. The agent gets the possibility of a listing and a commission if the deal with you falls through. If the deal does go through, you benefit from a seller who is better prepared to work with you—and you get the house you want.

Shopping with a Real Estate Agent

Most people don't venture into the housing market without the help of an agent scouting out new listings, accompanying them on tours of open houses, and offering advice.

By and large, house hunting on your own puts you at a disadvantage. Unless you're very knowledgeable about the market in a given area, you will miss the help and access to the MLS computer listings of houses for sale that an agent can supply.

Because most houses for sale are listed with realty agents, when you call to inquire about an advertised house or go to an open house, you are going to encounter agents at every turn. If you identify yourself by name—for example, by signing the registry book at an open house—you'll soon start getting calls from agents offering to help you find your dream house. At this point, it's "choose or be chosen." If you want help, take the initiative and do the selecting by contacting agents with proven reputations in the neighborhood and price range in which you're looking. If you don't, be firm and avoid entanglements until you're ready.

How Agents Work

There are two basic roles in the real estate business: broker and agent (or sales associate). A broker is licensed

> ## WHO WORKS FOR WHOM?
>
> Many states and the District of Columbia require agents to disclose the legal and financial arrangements they make with the sellers, for whom they work, to buyers they help. Even so, unwary buyers continue telling agents too much about their strategies and intentions—all of which agents are duty-bound to tell sellers.

by the state to conduct a real estate business and to negotiate transactions for a fee. An agent is a broker's representative and is usually an independent contractor rather than an employee. He or she is permitted to sell real estate under the supervision of a licensed broker. Both brokers and their representatives are properly called agents because they act as agents for their clients.

Contrary to public impression, not all brokers and agents are Realtors. A Realtor (capital R—it's a trade name) and a Realtor-Associate (who works for a Realtor) are members of the National Association of Realtors, a trade and lobby organization.

Since most real estate agents are compensated by sellers through a commission based on the sales price of the house, why would an agent who didn't make a listing want to help you find and buy a home listed by another agent? Because the sales commission is split between the seller's listing broker and the so-called selling broker who brings in the buyer. The brokers in turn pay their respective agents a portion of their proceeds. Real estate agents make money from finding both houses to sell and people to buy them, so a well-qualified, serious house hunter represents a paycheck to the agent—but only if the sale goes through. Unless "your" agent submits a successful offer, there will be no compensation for all the hours spent accompanying you through houses.

Unless you hire your own agent (a so-called buyer's broker; see page 98), an agent always works for a seller and is paid by a seller. This is true even when an agent spends hours and hours working with you, the buyer.

Experience, experience, experience are the watchwords for picking an agent.

It is true even if "your" agent has never met the owners of the home you ultimately buy. For both buyers and agents, this awkward situation is a gamble. The agent gambles that in return for his time you will be loyal enough to buy a home through him. You gamble that your loyalty will reward you with service and produce a suitable property.

How to Pick an Agent

If location, location, location are the watchwords for picking a property, experience, experience, experience are the watchwords for picking an agent.

Too many buyers don't pick their agent—they acquire one at an open house or by responding to an ad. Many select one who is a friend, relative, or neighbor. You could be lucky; such an agent might turn out to be skilled, experienced, and resourceful. On the other hand, you could end up with an amateur.

Obtain the names of brokers and agents active in the area where you want to buy. The classified ads are a good place to start. Brokers with agents that list and sell homes in a particular neighborhood will advertise regularly. Ask friends, associates, lenders, and attorneys for recommendations. And by all means, consider using a buyer's broker (see the full discussion that begins on page 98).

Check the broker's reputation in the community. In the case of an agent, find out who his or her managing broker is, then check out the broker's reputation and that of the firm. Ask the local real estate board or state real estate commission whether there have been complaints or problems reported. Talk to clients they've worked with in the past.

Call two or three recommended brokerage firms. Talk to the managing broker. Let her know what kind of buyer you are, what kind of house you're looking for, and the general price range you are working with.

PROSPECTIVE AGENT'S PROFILE

Name of firm _____

Phone number_____

Managing broker_____

Recommended agent _____

Number of years selling real estate full-time _____

Names of previous firms_____

Continuing Education

❏ GRI (Graduate, Realtors Institute)

❏ CRS (Certified Residential Specialist)

❏ CRB (Certified Real Estate Broker)

❏ CRE (Counselor of Real Estate)

❏ Other

Number of listings_____
(acquired in the past year and comparable to the house you want)

What does the agent know about your targeted community?

_____

In general, what services will the agent and firm provide?

_____

_____

How will disputes be handled?

_____

During your meeting, does the agent pay attention to your concerns?_____

Would you enjoy working with this person?_____

Miscellaneous notes_____

_____

_____

If this is your first foray into the housing market, you may want an agent who is intuitive and patient. If you're a much-transferred corporate executive, you may want an agent who specializes in listing exclusive homes.

Once you've chatted with the managing broker, ask for the names of two agents she thinks could best meet your needs.

Interview the agents. Use the worksheet on the preceding page as a guide.

WEB SITES FOR BUYERS AND SELLERS

The Internet has made it easier than ever to house hunt, especially if you're planning to relocate out of state. More and more agents (as well as owners selling homes on their own) are posting listings on the Internet. The listings customarily include prices, features, photos, and, in some cases, statistical information about the neighborhood. Here are a few sites to consider:

Homegain (http://www.homegain.com) lets you search for homes listed for sale across the nation. It will help you find a local real estate agent and determine the value of your home.

The Homestore Network™ (http://www.homestore.com) is the largest and most comprehensive family of Web sites devoted exclusively to home and real estate–related content. Among the sites it operates, the following are particularly helpful for home buyers and sellers (you can access the sites from Homestore's Web site or by going directly to the sites):

REALTOR.com (http://www.realtor.com), the official Web site of the National Association of Realtors, features more than 2 million existing homes for sale, neighborhood information, and directories of real estate agent and broker services.

Homebuilder.com (http://www.newhomesearch.com), the official new homesite of the National Association of Home Builders, lets you search for new homes by builders in major metropolitan areas nationwide.

The School Report (http://www.theschoolreport.com) lets you do a free search of SAT scores, student-teacher ratios, and numbers of computers per classroom for more than 12,000 public-school districts.

"For Sale by Owner" Web sites, such as forsalebyowner.com, fsbonetwork.com, allthelistings.com, sellyourhomeyourself.com, and fsbofreedom.com, list homes that are currently for sale by the owners.

Select one or two finalists. If you conducted phone interviews initially, arrange to meet each of them face-to-face in their office. If you conducted interviews in person, have follow-up phone conversations. Be candid about the degree of service you're expecting and whether you'll be looking at houses with other agents.

Use the worksheets in Chapter 4 to develop must-have, would-like, and don't-want lists. Use these to give agents a sense of how much deviation from the ideal you'll tolerate and in what areas. Will you want them to screen new listings or show you everything remotely similar to your target house?

> ## THE SMART APPROACH
>
> Savvy buyers keep their lips zipped when it comes to strategy and price bids. They study the art of real estate negotiation to better represent themselves, and they retain a lawyer to review the contract and settlement papers impartially.

Protocol for Working with an Agent

If an agent takes you to a house and tours it with you the first time you see it, you should submit your contract offer through him or her. If you don't, that agent may still be entitled to a share of the sales commission from the seller should you buy the house.

On the other hand, if an agent merely mentions that a particular house is for sale, but you first tour it by yourself or with another agent, the first agent will probably not have any claim to part of the commission. That's why agents don't give house hunters the address of a listing when they call. Instead, an agent will offer to meet you and drive you to the house for a tour.

Should you ever use more than one agent to help you with a house hunt? Yes, if the house you're looking for is very unusual in some way and you don't want to risk missing the few possible listings, or to extend your reach in a hot market—when houses move very quickly, you may need more eyes and ears and scouring energy than one agent can supply. Good listings are often sold within one firm, with the seller's commission being shared by the listing agent and a colleague in the same firm who brought in the buyer. Because the listing won't show up in the MLS database, if you don't have

If you are looking for advice from your agent, consider hiring a buyer's broker to get you through the process.

a relationship with an agent at that firm, you wouldn't ever hear about the house in time to see it or bid on it.

If you intend to work with more than one agent, tell each one you'll reward hustle by accompanying him or her immediately to see the new listing—providing that agent is the first one to call and tell you about it. Then remain loyal to that agent for all dealings relating to that particular house.

Pretty soon, you'll start getting calls from several agents within minutes or hours of each other, each trying to be the first to tell you that something good has just shown up in the MLS or, even better, that a new listing has just come into the firm and won't go into the computer for another 24 hours—a typical period after which the firm is obligated to enter the new listing for other agents to see. (Privacy-minded sellers may ask their agent to keep the listing unadvertised and strictly "in house" for a while, with no notice placed in the MLS database.)

Be aware that this approach can sometimes cause problems, because all agents have access to the MLS. If two (or more!) agents call you about the same house there can be misunderstandings about which agent notified you first.

Using a Buyer's Broker

The special fiduciary relationship between seller and agent should cause buyers to wonder whether they can trust the agent who is helping them find a house. How can an agent who is going to be paid by the seller, and whose pay will be based on how high the sales price is, negotiate in your best interest? This concern about conflict of interest in residential real estate sales—dual agency, as it is called—is why buyer brokerage is a growing business.

To command an agent's undivided loyalties, hire your own. When you do that, you enter into a "single agency" contractual relationship with an agent.

There are several ways that a buyer's agent representing you can be paid. The most common way is the same way other real estate agents are paid: the sales commission is split between the listing broker and the broker of a buyer's agent. The difference is in the contract, which states that the buyer's agent's portion of the commission is paid "on behalf of the buyer" and comes from the proceeds of the transaction, so you won't incur any additional costs for the broker's services. Buyer's brokers can also be paid a set fee or by the hour.

There are three or four advantages you get when your agent is contractually obligated to you:

■ **You expand your options.** A buyer's broker can help you buy a property not currently being listed for sale—without seeking to get the owner to list it.

■ **You get help negotiating the deal.** A broker you employ and pay is obligated to help you find a home that meets your needs, at the best possible price and terms. Your agent can openly suggest a smaller down payment, different financing terms, use of a contract that meets your needs, and an opening offer far below the list price.

QUESTIONS TO ASK A BUYER'S BROKER

Ask these questions when interviewing a prospective buyer's broker. The compensation plan you agree on with him or her should be spelled out in the brokerage contract.

■ **What kinds of services and advice will the broker provide?**

■ **Will you pay the agent:** an hourly rate, a set fee, or a percentage of the purchase price?

■ **Will there be an incentive commission?** This applies if the agent negotiates a price lower than the asking price— say, 10 percent of the savings.

■ **Will you pay an initial retainer?** If yes, how much and will it be applied against the total fee due?

■ **Is there a minimum fee?** If yes, how much?

■ **Is there a cap on total cost?** If yes, how much? This is especially important if you are paying by the hour.

■ **How will conflicts of interest be handled?**

■ **What will happen if you buy a property shortly after the brokerage agreement ends?** Will the broker get a commission? If so, under what conditions?

■ **How will disagreements be handled?** For example, both parties could agree to submit to binding arbitration, using a neutral third party.

■ **You know who to trust.** Because you establish a contractual relationship with the buyer's agent by signing a buyer's agency agreement, the agent is legally accountable to you and not to any seller.

■ **You can also remain anonymous if it suits your purposes.** A buyer's broker can act as an agent for an undisclosed principal.

Unfortunately, things rarely stay so neat and clean. Some agents who call themselves buyer's brokers engage in such activities as fee splitting. In this case, your agent will be paid by the seller. Because compensation is tied to the sale price of the home, it raises the very conflict-of-interest issue most buyers were seeking to avoid by hiring a buyer's broker. If you use an agent operating this way, hash out and address your concerns in writing in any contract that you sign.

FINDING A BUYER'S BROKER

Ask your local board of Realtors and large real estate firms for names of buyer's brokers. Professors of real estate at local colleges and universities may also be willing to help you.

The Buyer's Agent Inc.
(2010 Exeter Rd., Memphis, TN 38138; 800-766-8728; http://www.forbuyers.com) represents real estate buyers on either a fee or commission basis. This franchiser has 70 franchises in 37 states. Call or write for the number of the office in your area.

Buyers Resource Real Estate
(P.O. Box 1290, New London, NH 03257; 800-500-3569; http://www.buyersresource .com) has several dozen offices nationwide. Most transactions are conducted on a commission basis. If Buyers Resource does not have a franchise in your area, it can probably still put you in touch with a buyer's agent through the Home Referral Network (same phone number).

The National Association of Exclusive Buyer Agents
(NAEBA, National Headquarters, 191 Clarksville Rd., Princeton Junction, NJ 08550; 800-786-1570; http://www.naeba .com) can provide you with information on the role of exclusive buyer's agents and the names of agents in your area. The members of this consumer-advocacy and professional training organization must sign an affidavit stating that not only the agent, but also the agent's office, represents only buyers in real estate transactions.

The Dual Agent

The relationship between the real estate agent and the buyer and seller has been called into question since the buyer's broker idea took hold. How should a large real estate firm handle representing both parties— or should it be handling both sides at all? Dual agency is the outgrowth of this controversy. A dual agent serves both the buyer and the seller—acting as an intermediary between both parties. In this role, however, the agent cannot advise you on negotiating tactics; nor can he or she pass along any information that could be considered confidential. And remember that the agent's payment is based on the selling price of the home, so there is still the incentive to get the highest possible price.

Though the dual agent may serve neither side very well, it is legal when disclosed. Most states require agents to inform their clients of whom they are representing. Attitudes toward dual agency vary, so you need to ask your agent/broker how he or she handles this issue. Some appoint different agents to the buyer and the seller, while others have adopted the policy of representing only the sellers on the properties that they list and the buyers on properties listed with other brokers. Still other firms allow agents to represent both the buyer and the seller.

Where does this leave the consumer? If you feel confident of your negotiating skills and knowledge of the real estate market, the dual agent may be okay for you. But if you are looking for advice from your agent, consider hiring a buyer's broker to get you through the process.

Pick the Right Firm

Before you sign a contract, check the reputation and experience of the firm and agent. Does the firm handle sales and buyer's brokerage under the same roof? How does it avoid conflict of interest? What are the firm's disclosure rules? Once you're satisfied, set up a meeting with the broker to discuss your needs. You shouldn't have to pay for this initial consultation. Before they'll

A dual agent serves both the buyer and the seller— acting as an intermediary between both parties.

start work, some buyer's brokers may require a non-refundable fee, which will vary depending on the difficulty of the search and the overall compensation plan.

Who Pays Whom?

When you buy a house with a buyer's broker whom you are paying separately, the seller's agent should be willing to cut the 6 percent sales commission. If the total cost of two separate fees—one paid by you to your buyer's broker and one paid by the seller to the listing broker—is held to an amount equivalent to the 6 percent commission the seller expects to pay anyway, your agent should have no difficulty persuading a seller to accept your offer.

Here's an example: Say the owner lists her property for $208,000 and agrees to pay a 6 percent commission. If the house sells for $200,000, and commission is $12,000, the seller will get $188,000. In a conventional transaction, the $12,000 commission would be divided between the listing broker and the cooperating or selling broker, with each getting 3 percent of the sale price.

Now suppose the owner receives an offer from a buyer represented by his own agent. The owner is told that the purchaser will pay his own agent and she accepts an offer of $194,000 for her home. Result: The seller still nets $188,000—after paying $6,000 to the listing broker. The listing broker goes along with the deal because he gets the 3 percent commission he was likely to earn anyway. The buyer pays $194,000 plus the agreed-upon fee to his broker.

Alternatively, the buyer could offer a higher price to the seller and stipulate in his offering contract that the seller will pay the buyer's agent and his own listing agent. The buyer could specify the amount to be paid to his agent.

You can ask your lender to fold your buyer's broker fee into the mortgage loan; most lenders will agree to this. However, lenders making loans guaranteed by the VA are not permitted to do so.

Perusing the Ads

Whatever kind of market you're hunting in, get acquainted with the classified real estate ads in print and on the Internet, because many newspapers also offer free online access to their current issues. Also check the Internet real estate sites listed in the box on page 96. They can help you get a feel for various neighborhoods. A few weeks of discriminating reading will give you an indication of price ranges and acquaint you with brokerage firms concentrating their efforts in a particular area. Print and online ads can also uncover homes being sold by owners and builders as well as the weekend array of open houses.

The classified section is particularly useful in a slow market. You could keep current on offerings, price reductions, and published sale prices. If you know how long a property has been advertised, what its starting price was, and how many real estate firms have offered it, you have an advantage when you negotiate an offer.

A successful ad tries to entice you to a property. It tells you only about features that might attract you. It withholds details that might discourage you. Before you start calling agents to inquire about an advertised property, pull out your checklists of wants and don't-wants. Have it handy when you call and cut through the ad's smoke screen with a few key questions. That way, you'll avoid a long conversation about how you could buy the property with seller financing, only to realize that you hung up without learning how many bedrooms it had.

After a while, you'll get the hang of all those cryptic abbreviations in the print ads, like "2b, 1ba, lctm, owc, q.pos." You'll decode it as: two bedrooms, one bath, low cash to mortgage, owner will carry mortgage, quick possession. You won't have that problem on the Internet, because the ads are more detailed and words are spelled out.

You'll also get acquainted with all the clever euphemisms that agents use in their ads. "Handyman's special" and "lots of potential" often mean the house is falling in. "Just awaits your loving touch" means a total

A successful ad tries to entice you to a property. It tells you only about features that might attract you. It withholds details that might discourage you.

redecorating is needed. "Charming dollhouse" means the rooms are tiny. "Convenient to everything" can signal a busy corner near the bus route. "Low upkeep" might mean it has no yard at all. And so on, limited only by the agent's gift for poetic license.

Don't overlook new developments and apartment condominium conversions. You won't be pointed to these properties by most agents, unless they specialize in condos or the builder has promised to compensate agents for bringing buyers in.

Condos and cooperatives will usually be listed in the same classified section as detached houses but under their own listings. The new-house market tends to be advertised separately from the classifieds, in large display ads in newspapers' weekend real estate sections.

Handling the "Sale by Owner"

Don't overlook the "sale by owner" ads in the newspaper classifieds and on the Web sites. They could result in sticky, awkward negotiations, but good deals are to be had if you are determined and knowledgeable, and get the advice of a good lawyer. You could hire an agent to negotiate on your behalf.

If you stumble on the perfect for-sale-by-owner house while working with an agent you haven't hired, you have some options:

- **You could abandon your agent and deal directly with the seller,** with no compensation to the agent. After all, the agent knew all along that he or she would get paid only if you bought a listed house you first saw with the agent; that's the risk of the business.
- **You could deal directly with the seller but pay the agent a modest fee** for the time and effort expended on you. But you're not legally obligated to do so.
- **You could try to persuade the seller to accept your agent and pay the agent a 3 percent commission** (or a sum you can agree on). The agent would then help the seller with negotiations and mortgage arrangements, and work to get you both to settlement without a hitch. The agent could end up getting the

same commission (some part of the 3 percent, shared with the broker's firm) he or she would have earned from a regular listing.

Why would a seller agree to this? After all, hasn't he listed the house himself, arranged for advertising, prepared fact sheets, and held open houses at least partly to avoid paying someone a 6 percent commission? His reaction to your suggestion will likely depend heavily on how much he needs a willing buyer. An eager seller might be willing to pay "your" agent 3 percent, getting some service for the price.

In fact, many "sale by owner" sellers put the phrase "brokers welcome at 3 percent" in their ads. They don't want to pay a full commission, but they don't want agents to boycott their property, either.

If the seller refuses to consider compensating the agent, you're left with options one or two.

Sketch out floor plans on your first visit, or even better, take along a video or digital camera to record the tour.

Touring the House

If you have the luxury of deliberation, make several visits to any house you're seriously considering. If things are so frenzied that you're likely to lose out if you follow that route, get the most out of every minute you're in the house. Consider yourself a reporter and detective, there to gather as much information as possible about the house and the sellers.

You probably know your wants and don't-wants list well enough that you won't need to take a checklist with you, but by all means take a notepad and tape measure. At most open houses you will find an information sheet about the house. The most complete spell out such things as square footage of lot and house, room sizes, property taxes, average monthly utility bills, and the ages of appliances and major mechanical systems, as well as the number of bedrooms and baths, and other basic data.

If, at first glance, this looks like a house you'll want to pursue, sketch out floor plans on your first visit; they'll help you envision the house hours or days later.

Sellers and their agents are required by law to warn buyers of "material" defects in a property that would not be apparent during a routine inspection.

Even better, take along a video or digital camera to record the tour.

You'll want a professional inspection made later if you decide to buy, but you can make some tentative judgments on your own:

- **Take a close look** at the furnace, electrical box (fuses or circuit breakers), and appliances. Do they appear to be in good shape?
- **How about the roof,** gutters, and exterior finish?
- **Does the house have storm windows,** or will you have to add them at your own cost?
- **If the floor plan doesn't suit you,** can you rearrange space or add on?
- **Are you looking at older houses** with the intention of remodeling or expanding? If so, have an architect or contractor standing by to accompany you on a second visit. The judgment of these professionals on the ease and probable cost of renovation should play a major role in how much you offer.

Scope Out the Sellers

Find out as much as possible about the sellers, starting with the first visit. Everything you learn will make you a better informed, and therefore more capable, negotiator should you decide to make an offer.

Conversely, do not give away strategic information to the seller or the seller's agent or broker. You are at a disadvantage if the seller discovers you have sold your current home and are anxious to find a replacement. The same is true if you have a soon-to-expire lease or are shopping from out of town.

It's hard not to be forthcoming in a pleasant conversation, but resist showing your hand. Put on your best poker face and give noncommittal answers.

If you would rather remain anonymous until your offer is presented, don't give your name to agents at open houses and don't sign visitor registers. And ask the agent who is helping you look to refrain from identifying you to sellers until an offer is submitted.

Seller motivation will determine how the house is priced to sell in the first place and how receptive to price cutting the seller may be later on. But the seller, and the seller's agent and subagents, may be coy or less than candid because everything you learn will make you a tougher adversary in the negotiation that follows. Try to ferret out answers to the questions in the box below. If you can, talk with the seller's neighbors in a nonthreatening way that doesn't invade their personal privacy. You might ask whether any houses have been sold in the neighborhood recently, and so forth. Then, try to steer the conversation toward the sellers and the house you want to buy.

What Sellers Must Tell You

Sellers and their agents are required by law to warn buyers of material defects in a property that would not be apparent during a routine inspection. Each state puts a different twist on the definition of "material," but generally it means physical defects that would change your assessment of the property's value. Bad septic systems, cracked foundations, or leaky basements are obvious material defects.

WHAT YOU NEED TO KNOW ABOUT YOUR SELLERS

Here are some things you'll want to know about sellers whose home you're interested in—although they certainly don't have to tell you:

- **Are the sellers truly "motivated,"** as the agents say, or are they just trying to find out how much they could get for their house?
- **Are they scheduled to go to settlement on a new house?**
- **Why are they selling?** (a job transfer, divorce, retirement, financial setback, need for more or less space, health problem, children off at college, death of spouse, dissatisfaction with the house or neighborhood?)
- **How long have the sellers lived here?** (You can learn this, and also how much they paid for the house, from public land records.)
- **When do they want to settle?**
- **Do the sellers need to stay in the house after settlement?** If yes, for how long?
- **Would they consider helping you with the purchase**—by taking back a second trust, for example?

Sellers should tell you about known structural deficiencies or building-code violations. A homeowner selling a house in the middle of a long, dry summer could be held responsible later by the courts if he or she doesn't tell prospective buyers that the basement usually leaks in the spring. That's a hidden defect even a responsible buyer could not discover. And sellers can probably be held responsible for defects that are covered up. Say the walls of a basement showed water damage and the seller covered them with paneling prior to putting the house up for sale. Sellers in states that still subscribe to the "buyer beware" philosophy may have less liability for easily detectable defects—so-called patent defects—unless they make misleading comments about them.

But the trend—in recent court cases, new state statutes, and pressure from the National Association of Realtors—is to hold home sellers to tougher standards. In about half the states, written seller-disclosure forms are now required, and some real estate firms elsewhere won't show a home without one. The California disclosure law requires sellers to provide a prospective buyer with a statement indicating, among other things, known

FOR MORE INFORMATION

If you think you've been discriminated against, contact a lawyer or any of the following agencies:

National Fair Housing Alliance
(1212 New York Ave., N.W., Suite 525, Washington, DC 20005; 202-898-1661; http://www.nationalfairhousing.org), through its local offices, conducts "testing." Someone will pose as a buyer or renter to see whether he or she experiences the same type of discrimination as you did. This information can prove very helpful if you take your case to court.

The HUD Housing Discrimination Hotline (800-669-9777; http://www.hud.gov/complaints) provides information on fair housing and will investigate individual complaints of discrimination.

The U.S. Department of Justice
(202-514-4713; http://www.usdoj.gov/crt/crt-home.html) will investigate cases that indicate a pattern or practice of discrimination, such as cases of suspected discrimination by large property owners or a city housing authority. The Justice Department shares information with HUD.

defects or malfunctions in walls, ceilings, floors, insulation, windows, foundations, electrical and plumbing systems, and other structural components. Sellers must also disclose deaths that occurred on the property within three years, neighborhood nuisances such as a dog that barks every night, and potential natural hazards from floods, earthquakes, fires, and other problems.

An agent can't know everything about a particular property, of course. But honest ones should tell you about problems they're aware of, and agents can be held accountable for giving buyers misinformation about things they should have known.

If You Encounter Discrimination

Members of racial and ethnic minority groups often encounter overt or subtle discrimination when they go looking for a home to buy. A black family may be steered away from a neighborhood being told "you probably can't afford to buy there." A seller may refuse to sell her home to an Hispanic family because she believes her neighbor would be angry. A Jewish homebuyer may be told that an owner "just took the house off the market," when in fact it's still available. A borrower may be turned down because "we don't make loans under $50,000."

Discrimination may be wrong, but unfortunately it's not always illegal. The federal Fair Housing Law (Title VIII of the Civil Rights Act of 1968, as amended in 1974 and 1989) broadly prohibits discrimination in the rental, sale, and financing of housing.

However, the law has a big loophole: It doesn't cover private individuals who own no more than three single-family dwellings, providing: (1) a broker is not involved in the sale or rental; (2) there is no discriminatory advertising; and (3) the owner has not sold more than one house (in which he or she was not the most recent resident) during any two-year period.

Real estate professionals—who handle the bulk of the nation's housing transactions—are covered by the law. Agents and mortgage lenders may not:

> **Discrimination may be wrong, but unfortunately it's not always illegal.**

- **Refuse to sell, rent, deal, or negotiate** with you because of your race, color, religion, sex, or national origin, or because you are disabled or have children under 18.
- **Deny that housing is available** for inspection, sale, or rent when it really is available.
- **Persuade owners to sell or rent** their homes by telling them that minority groups are moving into the neighborhood—a practice called blockbusting.
- **Set different terms or conditions** for mortgage financing based on race, creed, religion, sex, national origin, disability, or pregnancy.

What You Can Do

If you suspect discrimination by a real estate agent or a seller using an agent, keep a record of meetings and phone calls. Note the person's name, title (if you know it), meeting place, date, and time. Write down what happened and what was said. Save all receipts, applications, business cards, and other such documents.

Then confront the person and demand an explanation. If you don't get a satisfactory answer and your suspicions persist, write a letter about the agent to the agent's employer-broker and send a similar letter to your state's department of real estate. Complain in writing to the fair-housing enforcement agency in the city, county, or state where you are house hunting (see the listing in the box on page 108). The state or local agency is required to begin proceedings within 30 days and proceed with "reasonable promptness." You might contact the National Fair Housing Alliance for the number of a fair-housing group near you. Other options include filing a complaint with the Department of Housing and Urban Development (HUD) within a year of your encounter, or hiring a lawyer to take your complaint directly to a state or local court within 180 days or to federal district court within two years.

Making an Offer

You know what you can afford. Now decide just what you're willing to pay for the home you want. There are several ways to do this; some are more realistic in slow markets, but all require you to gather certain information.

Get an analysis of comparable properties, or "comps," from your assisting agent. You should find several on the list. No two will be exactly alike, but they should be similar enough to serve as a useful tool in setting an offering price. Look at sale dates. Under normal conditions, a comparable should have sold no more than six months earlier. Note locations. A similar home in a different neighborhood may not be comparable at all. An identical house on a prime lot may be worth a lot more. Compare the features of each property. Comparables should be roughly the same age and condition. Elements such as lot size, number of rooms and baths, and total living space should be close.

Finally, scrutinize terms and conditions. Properties sold with seller financing, for example, can't be readily compared with those sold using conventional 30-year mortgages. A sale in which the seller took back a second mortgage at a below-market interest rate was really one in which the price was cut. You'll have to discount the price to use it for comparative purposes.

How Much Is the House Worth?

If you know the neighborhood, have studied sale prices of comparable homes, and have an adequate sense of your seller's motivations, you may be com-

When might paying for an appraisal be wise? When a property is unusual in a way that makes finding good comparable properties difficult.

fortable making an offer. But if you aren't—and if time permits—consider an appraisal.

When might paying for an appraisal be wise? When a property is unusual in a way that makes finding good comparable properties difficult. Or when a house has been for sale much longer than others in its price range. In fact, any circumstance that makes putting a value on a home hard makes it a candidate.

If you opt for an appraisal, find out what it will cost and how long it will take. Demand for appraisals from homebuyers and refinancers, combined with newly implemented licensing requirements, could leave you waiting too long for a valuation. In a few states where demand has been heated, appraisers have set up what is called tiered pricing. Under this system, buyers pay from $250 to $500, with $350 being the national average for a standard residential property. Turnaround times for appraisal reports are typically a few days to two weeks.

Finding an Appraiser

Pick a licensed appraiser who specializes in residential properties in your area. Ask local mortgage lenders for names of appraisers they use on a regular basis. Check the status of their licenses, work experience, training, credentials, and education. Appraiser organizations, in which appraisers claim membership, should be able to tell you whether an individual is a member in good standing and has the credentials claimed. They may also be willing to give you names of other licensed members working in your area, so long as you don't ask them to recommend anyone—something they can't do. You may also call your state's appraisal board (check the blue pages in your phone book) to check credentials, or contact the appraisal subcommittee of the Federal Financial Institutions Examination Council (202-293-6250; http://www.asc.gov).

In most cases, you will not want to contract for and pay for an appraisal yourself, because you're going to

---

GET A PROFESSIONAL

Contact one of the organizations listed below to get a list of professional real estate appraisers in your area.

- **American Society of Appraisers**
  (ASA; 555 Herndon Parkway, Suite 125, Herndon, VA 20170; 800-272-8258; http://www.appraisers.org)
- **Appraisal Institute**
  (AI; Union Tower, 550 W. Van Buren St., Suite 1000, Chicago, IL 60607; 312-335-4100; http://www.appraisalinstitute.org)
- **National Association of Real Estate Appraisers**
  (NAREA; 1224 North Nokomis N.E., Alexandria, MN 56308; 320-763-7626; http://www.iami.org/narea.cfm)

---

be required to pay for a lender-ordered appraisal before your mortgage can be approved, anyway. And examining the sale prices of comparable homes should give you a good idea of the value of a property.

An experienced local real estate agent should be able to tell you what the house is worth based on his or her knowledge of the current market and the comps. Make sure your agent shows you the comps so you can see for yourself the recent sale prices of similar homes. When looking at comps check that:

- **The sale has occurred within one to six months**—the more recent, the better.
- **The house is quite similar to the one you wish to buy**—in terms of age, size, and the type and number of rooms.
- **The homes in the comps are in the same neighborhood** or within six to ten blocks of the house that you want.

You should also check the Internet sites listed in the box on page 96.

Whether you get an early appraisal or not, you have the right to see a copy of the lender-ordered one. You must request this in writing when you apply for the loan.

Rank the elements of a deal according to your own wants and needs: price, financing, date of possession, extras.

Establish Your Priorities

Price is always important, but it may not be the primary factor. Rank the elements of a deal according to your own wants and needs: price, financing, date of possession, extras. Put your priorities down on paper and keep them to yourself. They will be an important tool in evaluating any counteroffer you receive from the seller.

Consider how you might accommodate the seller—at the right price. For example, suppose the owner doesn't want to repaint before moving. What price reduction or added feature would make that hassle tolerable for you?

Need Seller Financing?

Seller financing, whereby sellers become the mortgage holder for their buyers, has tended to be popular at certain times and for certain reasons: when market mortgage rates are high and sellers have to help buyers if they want to make deals at all, and when many buyers fail to meet the stiff down-payment and loan-qualifying hurdles imposed by commercial mortgage lenders. In the latter instance, the hardest hit are first-time buyers, the self-employed, those who need to spend more than a third of their monthly income for housing, and families with heavy credit card and car-payment obligations. Sellers may also be motivated by the prospect of getting a better return by holding mortgage paper on the homes they sell than by putting their cash in certificates of deposits or money-market funds, not to mention expanding the number of prospects willing to buy their home and the possibility of deferring taxes on the gain.

If your down payment and first mortgage won't be enough to swing the deal, you'll need seller financing.

Because seller-assisted financing would tie you and the sellers together long past the purchase transaction, it's only natural for them to take a strong interest in your financial resources, job stability, and personal life. Be prepared to supply considerable detail; as your prospective creditor, they're entitled to know.

Your need for seller financing greatly reduces your ability to negotiate the purchase price of the house. Concentrate your efforts on the other terms of your offer. The sellers will demand a price high enough to compensate for the risk of becoming a lender and accepting installment payments rather than up-front cash at closing.

If you think you'll need seller financing, turn to the discussion of "creative financing" in Chapter 10. Bone up on the details before you make an offer.

Hire Your Own Representative

This is a good time to get expert help, if you haven't already done so. A buyer's broker or a real estate lawyer you pay will represent your interests, deciphering the contract form, suggesting contingency clauses, and negotiating with the seller or seller's agent.

Get names of experienced lawyers from friends, associates, bankers, title-insurance officers, and the local bar association. When interviewing, ask for an advance estimate of the fee. Find out what role he or she usually plays, and determine the charge for reviewing a contract, for being present at settlement, and so on.

Do you expect more? Do you want assistance in drawing up a contract? During negotiations? Now is the time to get this settled.

Hone Negotiating Skills

Buyers often are seriously handicapped by their lack of negotiating experience. Many don't realize that they can bargain on every element of the deal, and agents don't always tell them that they can. So don't forget that you are initiating the bargaining when you make your offer to the seller.

Remember, good negotiating has more to do with knowing exactly what you want from a deal than it does with playing the role of tough bargainer.

> **Good negotiating has more to do with knowing exactly what you want from a deal than it does with playing the role of tough bargainer.**

Keep a log of the negotiating process, using the worksheet on page 118. Make note of repairs and replacements that are needed or soon will be. Write down the negative features of the property.

Put It in Writing

Do your negotiating in writing. Don't reveal your strategy, and don't make oral offers. You want to buy the house, but you don't want to hand over your money until you're sure the seller is legally capable of conveying a good title and meeting other conditions. The seller, in turn, doesn't want to deliver the deed until you've paid for the property. Now what? You (or your representative) present the seller with a written contract setting out the commitments and promises that you and the seller need to agree on and fulfill in order to make the sale. A well-drawn contract should protect all parties.

You can have your lawyer or buyer's agent draw up a purchase contract. Naturally, a contract used by a real estate agent acting on behalf of the seller is written to meet the needs of sellers, not buyers. It may lack important clauses and contingencies that protect you, such as a requirement that your offer be accepted within a specified time or become void, or a statement that the contract becomes binding on you only after it has been reviewed by your lawyer and after a professional home inspection satisfactory to you has been completed.

If you are working with an agent who is acting as subagent to the listing broker, you probably will be asked to use the firm's preprinted contract form. Although you are under no obligation to do so, you can start there and then amend and modify it to meet your objectives. Contingencies typed or written in the margins or on the back of preprinted forms should be initialed by you before the contract is submitted to the seller. The same goes for other changes to the body of the contract.

NEGOTIATION

If you're going to be doing your own negotiating, *Not One Dollar More! How to Save $3,000 to $30,000 Buying Your Next Home* (2nd Ed.) by Joseph Eamon Cummins (John Wiley & Sons; $16.95) addresses the art of negotiation from your perspective.

The Opening Bid

Whether you should go ahead and make your highest bid right away or send up a trial balloon in the form of a lower offer depends on how fair the asking price is, how many buyers you may be competing with, and what other enticements desired by the seller you can offer.

Asking prices often have a good bit of padding built in. You shouldn't offer the asking price, or something close to it, just because that's what the owner wants. Offer what you think the house is worth. If the owner is offended, so be it. You'll find out in a counteroffer or by the lack of any kind of response within the time limit specified in your contract. Occasionally, a house may be priced below market value because of owner ignorance or a desire to sell fast. Should you be the first to spot this, here's the rub: In a hot market, you could offer full price and still find yourself outsmarted by the savvy buyer who offered slightly more than the full price.

Whatever your strategy, don't signal future intentions, either by word or gesture. If, during contract presentation, the seller should ask the agent whether you might go higher or make a bigger down payment, the agent will be obliged to reveal everything he or she knows. Unless your agent signed a buyer representation agreement, he or she will get paid only if you buy this house. "Your" agent wants to get the deal closed, and "your" agent owes primary allegiance to the seller. This person can't fully represent your interests in negotiations with the seller.

The Purchase Contract

A written and signed (ratified) purchase offer can bind both you and the seller. Whether it's called a contract-to-purchase, an offer, binder, or earnest-money agreement, you can be held to your offer once it's signed by the seller. If you leave anything out and the seller accepts and signs the contract, you're out of luck. That's why your purchase offer must cover every minute detail and aspect of the sale.

Do your negotiating in writing. Don't reveal your strategy, and don't make oral offers.

A SCRATCH SHEET FOR NEGOTIATION

Address of property _____

_____

_____

Name of seller _____

Asking price _____

Amount of your offer _____

Payment of mortgage points   ❑ You pay   ❑ Seller pays

Amount of earnest-money deposit _____

Settlement date _____

Items that convey (appliances, lighting fixtures, window treatments, and so on)

_____

Necessary repairs or replacements _____

_____

Other contingencies _____

_____

Property's negative features _____

_____

Notes on comparable properties _____

_____

_____

_____

_____

Your contract should state the date and the amount of the deposit, and name you as buyer and the property owner as seller. It should give the total purchase price and the full legal description and street address of the property you are offering to buy. The contract should name lawyers, brokers, and others involved in the sale, and set out the terms and conditions of their compensation. It should describe the options available to both buyer and seller should either party default. Beyond elements basic to any contract, your offer should contain important protective and escape clauses making the entire agreement subject to, or contingent on, their fulfillment.

Here are some key "subject to" clauses and useful contingencies to be considered for insertion. This list isn't complete; it doesn't take the place of a review by your lawyer and consultation with your buyer's broker prior to signing.

Most sellers tend to measure the seriousness of a buyer's intention by the size of the deposit.

Earnest-Money Deposit

With the exception of court-ordered sales, you are not required by law to make a deposit of a certain size, or any deposit at all. Nevertheless, most sellers tend to measure the seriousness of a buyer's intention by the size of the deposit. A seller could refuse to consider an offer that is not coupled with a reasonable deposit. Conversely, a large earnest-money check just might swing a deal in your favor.

Most real estate agents expect to carry your earnest-money check with them when they go to present a contract to a seller. You'll be asked to make the check out to the real estate agent's firm, his or her managing broker, the escrow or title company, or the lawyer. Whatever name you're given, be sure to add "trustee," "fiduciary agent," or "escrow agent" after the name; this will prevent anyone from being tempted to cash the check and carelessly or maliciously abscond with your money. And never make the check out to the seller.

Find out whether the earnest money will be deposited in a trust account or with a neutral third party, such as a title company, escrow service, or lawyer act-

Keep an eye out for contracts that specify that the seller can keep the earnest money as compensation for his or her time.

ing as an escrow agent. If not, insert that requirement in the contract. Are you putting up a large earnest-money payment? Then stipulate that it be held in an interest-bearing account and that interest earned will be credited to your side of the ledger at settlement.

Set out any conditions for return of your money, including how quickly you'll get it back if the offer expires or you withdraw it, or if for some reason the seller decides not to sell. This will help protect you from having to sue to get your money back from an unregulated individual if the deal goes bad.

Don't allow your deposit to be tied up too long. Keep an eye out for contracts that specify that the seller can keep the earnest money as compensation for his or her time or for any lost opportunities if you pull out or don't meet the terms of your offer. One strategy is for the seller to try to label the earnest money "option money," giving you an option to buy the house for, say, six months (which is longer than the usual time before settlement of 45 to 60 days). If you don't buy the house for whatever reason within that period, the seller keeps the money.

If you don't want your check deposited until the contract has been accepted, write this into the contract. (On the other hand, if a seller balks because he has qualms about your creditworthiness, you could offer to let him have it deposited in escrow to assure him that it will clear.)

Deed and Title Condition

Your offer should state the type of deed and condition of title you'll accept from the seller. If customary in your area, the contract could obligate the seller to pay for the lender's title-insurance policy and possibly to provide you with an owner's policy for the amount of the sale price. (And even if it doesn't, consider the policy cost a negotiating point.) Your contract should also make clear what actions the seller must take to deliver a good title by settlement, and what recourse you have should that not occur. Basically, the interim binder you should request from the title-insurance company and the title-search contingency you insert in your purchase contract give you the chance to decide whether you want the seller to fix any problem or whether the problems merit trying to cancel the purchase. If it comes to that, don't try canceling without getting skilled legal advice. (Chapter 11 discusses how to get a good title.)

Financing

The contract should be subject to your getting satisfactory mortgage financing—satisfactory to you. Make your offer contingent on getting a written loan commitment within a specified time and at terms agreeable to you. State the maximum interest rate and number of discount points you would be willing to pay. Put that way, should you fail to get the desired financing, you will be released from the contract and your deposit will be returned.

Set out how discount points, appraisal fee, and other expenses involved with financing your purchase are to be apportioned between you and the seller. These are typically negotiated through counteroffers and counter-counteroffers.

If you're told it's customary for buyers to pay all points (one point equals 1 percent of the mortgage), don't assume that's so. In many areas and in certain market climates, it's just as customary for sellers to help the buyer by paying a point or so. The point is, what do you want to pay? What can you afford? What could the seller offer that would make it worthwhile for you to back down and pay the point?

Making the contract contingent on financing is important from another perspective, too. Once an offer with this type of clause is accepted, the owner must take the property off the market to give you time to shop for a mortgage.

If you went through a preapproval process, you know what size loan and interest rate you are eligible for. Don't put down unrealistic numbers—a below-market interest rate or a loan bigger than you could get. Such tactics justifiably raise suspicions and make your offer unattractive.

If you're told it's customary for buyers to pay all points (one point equals 1 percent of the mortgage), don't assume that's so.

The contract should state that property taxes will be prorated to the closing date.

Seller Financing

The terms and conditions of any seller financing should be fully and exactly set out in the contract.

Settlement Date and Possession

The sale should be made subject to a settlement date and a possession date—when you will be entitled to take physical possession of your new home.

Settlement usually correlates with the length of time that's required for a title search and mortgage approval—typically 30 days to 60 days. In busy markets lenders and appraisers get backed up, so allow yourself enough time. This is particularly important if you plan to sell your current home and bring cash from that settlement to the closing on your new one. If settlement comes too soon, you could be faced with having to ask for an extension.

Possession usually occurs immediately after settlement. If you need to move in prior to closing, or if the seller needs to remain after closing, the preferred procedure is to arrange for a separate rental agreement between you. Such agreements can have horrendous legal and tax consequences, so all documents should be prepared or reviewed by your lawyer before you accept them.

Settlement Agent

The contract usually specifies the lawyer or title company that will perform the final settlement services.

Prorating

The contract should state that property taxes (among other things) will be prorated to the closing date. Prorating is a method of equitably dividing continuing expenses, such as mortgage interest, property taxes, and insurance, between buyer and seller. Government-backed loans and conventional mortgages may not prorate the same way, but in general it works like this: In January, Mr. Owner pays the annual premium on his homeowners insurance. He then puts his house on the market and sells it; he and the buyer agree to settle at midyear. What happens to the insurance coverage paid for but not used? In many cases, the purchaser "buys" the remaining coverage from the owner by arrangement with the insurer. Payment is made at settlement.

Sale of Current Residence

If your purchase of this house is contingent on the sale of another, this should be carefully stated. It should be clear to all parties exactly what the "sale" of your current home means. Does that mean an acceptable contract in the eyes of the seller? Or one acceptable to you? Sellers are wary of such a contingency and a contract containing it may be far less desirable than others.

Response Time Limit

Your contract should require the seller to accept the offer in writing within a certain time—usually no more than 48 hours—or the offer will be void. How long you give depends on market activity in general and likely buyer interest in that home in particular. Failure to state a time limit invites having your contract "shopped." That means that the seller or agent may use your offer to stimulate slower-moving buyers to get a move on and top your offer.

You are free to withdraw and cancel an offer at any time before the seller has accepted it and you have received notice of that acceptance in accordance with the terms set out in the contract.

Home Inspection

This contingency clause gives you the right to have the property inspected and to withdraw your offer if the inspection report isn't satisfactory to you for any reason. It may also allow for price adjustments to pay for any necessary repairs. Accept no exceptions. You don't want to end up in the same boat some Arkansas buyers did not long ago: Their contracts excluded the foundations, floors, walls, ceilings, roofs, fireplaces, and chimneys! And in at least one state, real estate

Sellers are wary of buyers whose offers are contingent upon the sale of their own homes.

Offset the negative impact of an inspection contingency with a larger deposit or some other bargaining chip.

agents were pushing for a contract that would let buyers cancel only when the inspection report uncovers substantial structural or mechanical problems.

The critical portion of a typical inspection clause reads: "This contract is contingent on a property inspection report which, in the sole judgment of the purchaser, is deemed satisfactory." Such a contingency clause leaves you with an escape hatch as big as the house itself. Consequently, most real estate contracts allow the seller to determine how long you can take to get the job done and by whom. Typically, the seller allows no fewer than three and no more than ten days, and specifies "a recognized professional."

Insert language to the effect that should the home inspector not be able to examine the roof, you retain the right to obtain an inspection satisfactory to you from a qualified roofing professional prior to releasing the inspection contingency but before closing. Many sellers are now providing a Homeowner's Warranty especially for older homes. For about $300 to $400, this policy will cover repairs or replacement (with a deductible of $50 to $60) of the following while the home is under contract and up to a year thereafter:

- **roof**
- **major appliances**
- **plumbing system**
- **electrical system**
- **heating and air-conditioning**

Under normal circumstances, you will pay for the inspection. Since sellers often worry that buyers will raise issues about the condition of the house at settlement, savvy ones demand a copy of the inspection report as part of the deal.

If necessary, offset the negative impact of your inspection contingency with a larger earnest-money deposit or some other bargaining chip that will impress the seller with your interest in the property.

If you haven't lined up an inspector or are uncertain about how to find one, see Chapter 8.

Environmental Tests

You may want to include a clause requiring that the property be tested for radon, lead paint, asbestos, or ureaformaldehyde insulation.

Borrowers buying homes built before 1978 are required to read and sign a lead-based-paint disclosure notice before they sign a sales contract. (HUD lenders are not to process loan requests until they have evidence that buyers have signed this document. Lacking proof, they will return the contract for reexecution—presumably after the buyer signs off on the warning.) Homeowners must also provide a lead-based-paint disclosure form and a federal pamphlet titled *Protect Your Family from Lead in Your Home* to the buyer. (See Chapter 16 for information about what sellers should disclose.)

Termite Inspection

Many contracts require the seller to order and pay for a termite inspection. If yours doesn't, insert language to that effect. Be sure you can void the deal or negotiate with the seller for extermination and repairs if termites, or damage, are found.

What Goes with the House

Specify what furnishings—such as curtains, rugs, chandelier, and so on—are included in the sale. You may assume the seller will leave major appliances, built-in bookcases, sheds, wall-to-wall carpeting, fences, and outside lighting, but such an assumption would be unwise. Customary practices vary; the more specific your contract, the fewer opportunities for later dispute.

Condition of House at Settlement

Specify what must be in demonstrable working order at the time of settlement, as verified during a walk-through of the premises a day or so before settlement. Include electrical, plumbing, and mechanical systems, such as furnaces, air conditioners, and toilets, as well as all appliances. This is no guarantee that these things will continue working after you purchase the house—just that they were functioning properly

Specify what must be in demonstrable working order at settlement, as verified during a walk-through a day or so beforehand.

If you've been preapproved for a mortgage sufficient to swing the deal, let the seller know when you or your agent presents the offer.

when you took title. If you are settling during the winter, it may be impossible to test the air-conditioning at that time, so allow for a test to be done as soon as the temperature permits.

If there are exceptions—such as appliances being conveyed to you "as is," with no guarantee made as to working order—describe them in the contract.

As for cleanliness, note that the house should be left empty of all stored objects and debris (including things in the attic, basement, and garage) and handed over in "broom-clean" condition.

Other Conditions

The list could go on, but every additional condition runs the risk of making your offer more complicated and less appealing.

Presentation and Counteroffer

At this point, your offer—signed and with all clauses initialed—is presented to the seller, either by you, your representative (buyer's agent or lawyer), the seller's agent, or the agent who has been assisting you all along.

If you've been preapproved for a mortgage sufficient to swing the deal, let the seller know that when you or your agent presents the offer. If you haven't been preapproved, then bolster the appeal of your offer by providing a financial statement as evidence of creditworthiness. In the eyes of the seller, your ability to get a loan and get to settlement is as important as the terms of the contract. You will require the seller to take the property off the market while you arrange financing, so his confidence in your financial strength will play a big role in weighing your contract against a rival bid.

Your financial statement doesn't have to have a lot of detail, but it should include information about employment, current home ownership, and other basics.

Once the seller accepts your offer as set out in the contract by signing within the acceptance date specified, the offer becomes binding on both parties, subject to removal of specific contingencies. Rejection of even the smallest provision in your offer is a rejection of the entire thing. If the seller wishes to negotiate, he or she will present you with a counteroffer.

The Counteroffer(s)

The counteroffer typically takes one of three forms: a fresh purchase contract identical to your offer except for the seller's changes; a counteroffer written on the back of the original, or on a separate sheet of paper, accepting your offer subject to certain stated changes; or revisions made by the seller's marking out unacceptable items on your offer and noting substitutions above or below, initialing each change. A time limit is noted, and the counteroffer is dated and signed by the seller.

This is delivered to you. If it's acceptable, you sign and date your acceptance. At that point the contract is considered ratified. If it's not acceptable, you could allow the counteroffer to expire or make a second offer—a counter to the seller's counteroffer. Have a new contract written out. Marking and initialing the document too extensively can only lead to confusion and mistakes.

Sometimes, negotiating goes on for days: offer, counteroffer, offer, counteroffer. More commonly, an agreement is reached on the second or third offer.

If the seller has other contract offers in addition to yours, he may try to play one against the other, often with oral messages. Sometimes a seller or seller's agent won't formally counter a contract but will tell the prospective buyer the offer is "too low," promising acceptance if it is raised. Don't respond; the seller has made no commitment to you, and you have no assurance you'll get the house if you do raise your bid. The seller could change his mind again and keep trying to jack up your bid.

Remind the seller that you have a formal offer on the table and would appreciate a written counterproposal stating the price and terms that would make your offer acceptable. A written response means you're still in the ball game. You can accept the counteroffer and

A seller who has other contract offers in addition to yours may try to play one against the other.

It's not uncommon to put in several bids on one property before getting accepted.

nail down the deal, counter again, or let the response time lapse. Your strategy is to keep the seller involved with only you until your negotiation has run its course. The seller can give a counteroffer to only one buyer at a time; to do otherwise is to run the risk that both parties will accept.

Should you bend? That depends on how much you want the deal to go through. Say you like the house and it meets all major needs. You'd like to settle in time for your children to begin the year in their new schools. Why not give a little? On the other hand, if you're not pressed and you expect similar homes in the neighborhood to go on sale soon, focus on your priorities and hold firm. If this house gets away, you'll probably locate a similar one later. It's not uncommon to put in several bids on one property—or more than one property—before getting accepted. Who knows, you might get a second chance to buy the first house you bid on. You could even end up paying less than you originally offered.

What an Accepted Offer Means

Once your offer is accepted by the seller, or you accept the seller's counteroffer, the agreement becomes a binding contract. If you change your mind after your contract offer has been accepted and signed by the seller, you stand the chance of losing your deposit and you could even be liable for damages for failing to live up to your contract.

Likewise, if the seller simply backs out, you can sue for damages or try to enforce the contract terms.

What if the owner dies before settlement? Your contract should bind the executors of his or her estate to proceed with the sale of the house to you. But you will need a lawyer's help to assert your claim and keep the process on track.

Relocation Loans

Employers sometimes pick up the tab for employees they want to relocate. That can include help in selling your current home or even buying it from you, freeing you to buy a new home where you are being re-located. You may be offered the assistance of a relocation real estate specialist to help you sell your old home. In some cases, you could be offered a guaranteed price for your home if it doesn't sell within a specified period or for a preset price. Your employer might even carry the interest payments on the old home until it is sold.

Guaranteed Sale

In a twist on a once-popular option offered by real estate firms to help eager move-up buyers, some builders promise to buy homes that owners leave behind when they move into one of the builder's new homes. Basically, it works like this: A builder enters into a "guaranteed purchase," or "buy-sell" agreement, with the buyer of one of its new or soon-to-be-built homes. In exchange for the buyer's noncontingent sales contract to buy one of the builder's homes, the builder agrees to buy the old home at a set price after a predetermined time, typically three to six months. If the period elapses with no buyer signed on, the builder must purchase the property. Real estate firms offering such deals today usually bring in outside investors to act as guarantors.

A guaranteed purchase can work to your advantage. But it has a price tag: Builder-purchase commitments are being set low, usually significantly less than market value. You'll be under pressure to sell, something that limits your negotiating hand. Don't sign a noncontingent sales contract before having it reviewed by your lawyer.

Bidding on a
For-Sale-by-Owner House

Theoretically, a house should cost less if bought directly from the owner rather than through an agent. And if the deal is structured right, the seller will do fine, too. What the seller wants is the maximum net proceeds from the sale, so a lower offer

Some builders promise to buy homes that owners leave behind when they move into one of the builder's new homes.

that is not reduced by a sales commission should net as much or more for the seller than a higher offer from which the commission is subtracted.

Many sellers will try for a few weeks to sell the house themselves before listing it with a broker. Even after a seller signs a listing contract, the seller may be permitted to sell the house directly—with no sales commission to the agent—provided the seller finds the buyer, with no help from the agent. In either case, you may save by getting the house for a lower price than it would have sold for through an agent.

How much lower? Well, it could be a full 6 percent lower, which presumes all the savings of the commission end up in your pocket. More typically, the owner will want to share in the savings, perhaps by splitting the 6 percent evenly with you. And if you bring your buyer's broker with you, the seller may be willing to pay the broker an agreed-upon fee or 3 percent.

Have the Home Inspected

Chapter 8

You've made an offer, haggled over the contract, and struck a deal. Now hire an home inspector to give you an objective evaluation of the condition of the home you'd like to buy.

Your purchase contingency should permit you to withdraw your offer if you aren't satisfied with the inspector's findings. If the report reveals that serious structural defects exist, you may want to squash the deal entirely. More typically, the inspection will uncover common flaws and problems.

Your next move depends on your priorities and local sales activity. Don't do anything to void the contract until you've assessed your options. These include trying to bargain down the price or get the owner to pay for repairs. You always have the right to negotiate, and most sellers anticipate making some adjustments after an inspection. If you find yourself dealing with an owner who acknowledges that the house has problems but won't discuss lowering the price or making the repairs you deem necessary, he or she may be having second thoughts about the sale. One possibility: There's a better offer in the making and the owner is quite willing for you to withdraw your offer.

A seller may arrange for an inspection before putting a home up for sale. This helps market the property and shifts some disclosure responsibility from his shoulders to a third party's. Don't remove your inspection contingency until you've read the report and questioned the inspector yourself. Order your own if you have reservations about the report or the integrity or credibility of the inspector.

The inspector you hire should be independent and not beholden to the seller's real estate agent.

Finding a Good Inspector

Start by asking your attorney, friends, real estate agent, and lenders for recommendations. You want someone with a good reputation and recognized professional credentials. Home inspection services may be listed in the *Yellow Pages* under "Building Inspection Services," "Engineers (Inspection or Foundation)," or "Real Estate Inspectors." Look for these qualifications:

Experience. A home inspector's experience in the building field usually comes from a background in contracting, architecture, or engineering. By whatever route, the professional you want is one who knows homes inside and out, who makes a living poking into cellars and attics and crawl spaces looking for design, structural, and equipment flaws, and who then gives you a detailed written report that takes some of the risk out of homebuying.

Impartiality. The inspector you hire should be independent, not beholden to the seller's real estate agent, and not interested in promoting a repair or remodeling business.

Certification and/or professional affiliation. Look for inspectors who are members of the American Society of Home Inspectors (ASHI), which sets the standards for inspections nationwide. Members must pass a set of examinations, provide evidence of having done at least 250 fee-paid inspections that meet standards of practice, and take 60 hours of continuing education every three years. Members are bound by a code of ethics and by prescribed standards of practice.

The National Institute of Building Inspectors, founded by the HouseMaster of America Home Inspection Service (a franchise business), trains its inspectors following the standards set by ASHI, and requires its inspectors to carry liability insurance and meet certain continuing education requirements.

Some inspectors are certified by both organizations (see the box on the next page).

The Cost

Fees for inspecting homes generally vary according to contract price and geographical area, and sometimes according to age, size, and construction of the house. Assuming the home you're interested in is a fairly typical residential property, you should expect to pay, on average, between $300 and $400, depending in part on the home's square footage, sales price, age, and number of rooms. Inspections in large metropolitan areas where homes are more expensive—for example, New York City and San Francisco—may cost more.

Inspectors may do specialized tests—such as those for radon or lead—for an additional fee. Inspections on Sundays, holidays, and after hours, and those that require any long-distance travel, also are likely to command premiums.

The Inspection

A thorough home inspection usually takes two or three hours. Most inspectors encourage buyers to accompany them. You'll have a better understanding of problems uncovered if you do. You can also ask questions of the inspector and get a sense of how serious the problem may be—and how expensive it would be to fix. Come prepared to get dirty. If the house has a crawl space, go down there with the inspector and see whether routine maintenance chores in that space will be within your capacity.

Let the inspector know whether you are handy with a pipe wrench or know something about carpentry so you can get an on-the-spot estimate of the repairs needed and how much they'll cost. Provide information about family size and habits. A water heater usually adequate for four people may be inade-

---

FOR MORE INFORMATION

The American Society of Home Inspectors
(ASHI; 932 Lee St., Suite 101, Des Plaines, IL 60016; 800-743-2744; http://www.ashi.org) can give you the names of its members doing business in your area.

The National Institute of Building Inspectors
(NIBI; 424 Vosseller Ave., Bound Brook, NJ 08805; 888-281-6424; http://www.nibi.com) can give you names of certified HouseMaster inspectors.

quate for your foursome if you all shower in the morning and then again after soccer or evening jogging.

The Report

An inspector may use checklist-type worksheets, adding brief remarks as necessary, or he may present a write-up of the overall condition of the property, along with suggested repairs and improvements.

The report should indicate potential as well as existing problems the inspector can readily observe. For example, the original wiring in a home built before World War II is probably not up to handling today's major electrical appliances. An inspector should note such a shortcoming and give you some idea of what would be involved in bringing the feature up to modern standards.

Special features such as a swimming pool, tennis court, well, or septic system may require a specialist. If you are having a home inspected in winter, some testing

---

WHAT AN INSPECTION REPORT INCLUDES

The report should cover the house from basement to roof and include an assessment of the quality and condition of all the following:

- **Yard:** drainage, fences, grading, landscaping, paved areas, retaining walls
- **Exterior of house:** decks, doors, exterior walls (possibly including insulation), garage, porches, steps, windows
- **Roof and related features:** chimneys, downspouts, gutters, hatches, roofing materials and construction, skylights, vents and fans
- **Attic:** access, insulation, signs of leakage, ventilation

- **Crawl space or basement:** construction, settlement, structural stability, termite or rot damage, water penetration
- **Electrical system:** capacity, fuses or circuit breakers, grounding, obvious hazards, outlets and switches, wires
- **Plumbing system:** drainage faucets, laundry appliances, pipes, sink traps, water heater, water pressure
- **Heating and cooling systems:** type, capacity and condition, controls, and distribution of sources of heat and cooling
- **Kitchen and bathrooms:** fixtures, flooring, plumbing, tile, and ventilation
- **Interior of the house:** doors, walls, ceilings, and floors

may have to be postponed until warmer temperatures arrive; the wording of your contract should set out what obligations the seller must shoulder at that time.

Before removing your inspection contingency, carefully review the written inspection report (see the listing on the previous page).

Back to the Seller?

When a seller finds that a qualified inspector has determined the roof needs repair or the water heater has outlived its expected life span, he may agree to make repairs or replacements or to knock down the price so that you can cover the cost of having the work done yourself.

Suppose something catastrophic is discovered? Perhaps the floors are heaving or the foundation is settling, causing cracks in the interior walls. At this point price is no longer the object; you want out. Assuming the deal was contingent upon an inspection ". . . which in the sole judgment of the purchaser is deemed satisfactory," you're off the hook. Convey your decision to the seller in writing.

Special Situations: New Homes, Condos, and Co-ops

If you're buying a not-yet-built home in a new development, determine whether covenants that dictate the size and style of housing in the development apply only to a particular phase or to all phases of the whole project. Developers sometimes give themselves escape clauses that, for example, permit them to change to a cheaper house if the market changes. Your contract should specify that the house is to be built to the quality standards of the model you saw. If covenants permit the builder to change the model from one phase to another or in response to market condition, and if that's not acceptable, your contract should stipulate what model and standards are to be used in building your home.

If you are having a home inspected in winter, some testing may have to be postponed until warmer temperatures arrive.

Insert a clause in your purchase offer giving you the right to have ongoing inspections done (at your expense) as construction proceeds, plus a final walk-through inspection. Inspection is particularly useful as the foundation is being built and before insulation and drywall go on. At that point, heating, cooling, plumbing, and electrical systems in your house are in place.

Apartment-style condominiums and co-ops also require careful going over by inspectors knowledgeable about and experienced with the special problems and considerations inherent in these types of ownership. For example, an inspector should have the skills needed to assess the condition of large-scale heating plants and plumbing, common roofs, halls, stairs, elevators, and swimming pools.

A typical inspection of a single apartment unit would leave you with little or no information about the condition of the building as a whole. That's a potentially expensive shortcoming: Once you're a co-owner, you will have to ante up your share of the cost of a new roof, electrical system, or furnace.

When an apartment building is converted to condo use, the developer-seller must provide tenants (as prospective owners of units) with an engineering report on the condition of the building. In addition, a tenants association or condo owners association may have, at some point, commissioned its own engineering report. Your contract to buy should be contingent on getting copies of all engineering reports and an inspection that in your judgment is satisfactory (see Chapter 7 for more on home-inspection contingencies).

When going through an engineering report, note recommended or suggested major work. Then find out whether it was done or still lies ahead. If work was done, how was it paid for—out of a reserve fund or by special assessment?

If you remain concerned about the building's condition, consider hiring the engineering or inspection

---

FOR MORE INFORMATION

The Complete Book of Home Inspection, by Norman Becker, P.E. ($17.95, from Home Reporter Systems; 800-328-6775; http://www.hreporters.com).

firm that did the last study for a briefer inspection. (You could hook up with other would-be buyers to share the cost.) Commercial inspectors usually work by the hour, charging from $100 to $200 per hour. A two-hour reinspection should give you the information you need. Weigh the expense against your ability to handle a large and unanticipated bill for major repairs soon after becoming a new homeowner.

New-Home Warranties

Imagine that just two years after you buy a brand-new home, the foundation begins to crack, or the fireplace starts pulling away from its supporting wall. This kind of defect could threaten the soundness of your entire house, and the remedy is sure to be costly. You don't believe you should have to pay—for the work or for legal bills, if it comes to that.

Implied Warranties versus Extended Warranties

If your builder won't fix the problem, you have no alternative but to sue. Many states and local jurisdictions hold builders and developers to an "implied" warranty on the habitability of their homes. (Implied warranties are derived from common law as developed by case law.) In general that means a builder that is authorized to construct homes in a jurisdiction should for a specified time—at least a year or two— replace or repair anything that threatens a home's soundness and the safe functioning of its basic structures and components. While some states have statutes dealing with limitations on when certain actions can be taken in court, implied warranties always must be enforced through litigation.

The desire to avoid costly legal bills and draining court battles if something goes seriously awry helps sell thousands of homes that are constructed by builders who offer the buyers long-term home-protection plans that are backed by insurance. The idea behind long-term warranties is to provide consumers

When going through an engineering report, note recommended or suggested major work. Then find out whether it was done or still lies ahead.

with recourse other than litigation. Warranty plans provide member builders—and buyers of their homes—with ten years of protection against catastrophic losses arising from major design and structural defects. If a member builder refuses or is unable to fix a covered defect, insurance covers repairs that exceed the owner's deductible. (Not all plans charge deductibles—the New Jersey New Home Warranty Program, for example, doesn't.) A built-in dispute-settling process usually is available to mediate between buyer and builder.

What an Extended Warranty Costs, and What It Covers

You don't buy a ten-year warranty policy as you do a homeowners insurance policy. Instead you are automatically covered when you buy a home from a builder currently affiliated with a plan issuer such as Home Buyers Warranty. Each member builder pays a one-time premium to the plan issuer of between 0.2 percent and 0.5 percent of the home's selling price on each home it builds. (The following illustration is based heavily on the 2-10 Home Buyers Warranty plan; other extended-warranty plans will differ.)

During the full ten years of the 2-10 Home Buyers Warranty, the member builder (and your home) remains insured against certain structural defects. Only during the first two years of the plan will you receive additional coverage.

During the first year, member builders warrant their new homes against defects in certain workmanship and materials and certain flaws in the electrical, plumbing, heating, cooling, ventilating, and mechanical systems. The warranty excludes appliances, fixtures, and equipment.

During the second year, builders warrant against certain major electrical, plumbing, heating, cooling, ventilating, and mechanical system breakdowns. The warranty no longer covers defects in materials and workmanship.

During the first two years, you rely on the builder to correct these problems. If, during that period, a

---

MAJOR NATIONAL PLAN ISSUERS

Home Buyers Warranty enrolls about 15,000 builders across the country. For a list of members, write to: Customer Service, Home Buyers Warranty Corp., 1728 Montreal Circle, Tucker, GA 30084; 800-488-8844; http://www.2-10.com.

Professional Warranty Service Corp. (P.O. Box 800, Annandale, VA 22003; 800-850-2799; http://www.pwsc .com) represents builders in all states except Texas, Louisiana, Colorado, and Alaska.

Quality Builders Warranty (325 N. Second St., Wormleysburg, PA 17043; 717-737-2522; http://www.qbwc .com) represents builders nationwide.

Residential Warranty Corp. (5300 Derry St., Harrisburg, PA 17111; 717-561-4480; http://www.rwcwarranty.com) represents builders nationwide.

---

builder defaults on the terms of the warranty or goes out of business, claims are paid through the plan issuer by an insurance company.

Home Buyers Warranty, as the plan administrator, will act as a neutral third party to help you resolve any conflicts covered under the warranty with your builder. Conflicts that otherwise cannot be resolved are generally resolved through arbitration.

Regardless of how often owners change, the builder's ten-year warranty stays with the home for ten years. If you make a claim against your warranty, the plan issuer will in most cases manage and pay for the authorized repairs, less the deductible (around $250), which applies to each claim.

The Limits of Coverage

But buyers who have new-home warranty plans are rarely aware of limits to their coverage. Foundation cracks and basement leaks generally are covered only

BAUIV YOFtrtrst

The sad reality for many owners in new homes that go bad is that they may not get much help from anyone.

during the first year. Certain wiring and plumbing defects are covered for two years. After that, coverage is generally limited to major structural defects that make the home unsafe, unsanitary, or otherwise unlivable.

The sad reality for many owners in new homes that go bad is that they may not get much help from anyone. And they often have to fight to get anything. Builders go broke or refuse to make good. Serious problems appear only after statutory or warranty time limits have expired. Extended warranties that owners believe will protect them fail to do so. And so on.

A builder's ten-year homeowners warranty backed by insurance generally gives you an express warranty (as set out in terms of the contract) rather than an implied warranty. Assurances you get when your builder provides an extended-warranty plan may not be better or more comprehensive—particularly in the early years—than what you would have under an implied warranty. The plan's primary purpose is to offer the possibility of compensation—within terms of the plan's contract—without litigation. (In fact, most warranty claims are settled between builder and homeowner with no involvement by a plan administrator.)

Hashing Out Disputes

When homeowner and builder reach a stalemate over disputed warranted items within the first two years, either may request the plan administrator to arrange for an impartial third party to mediate, at no cost to the buyer. Referees for such disputes are not affiliated with the plan administrator or the builder.

If a mutually acceptable solution cannot be reached, the neutral party decides on the issue, based on the warranty documents. The builder is bound by the decision once it is accepted by a homeowner. He can appeal the decision but faces expulsion from membership if he ultimately refuses to comply. An unmollified owner is free to reject the arbitrated settlement and go to court. (The mandated New Jersey New Home Warranty Program provides that the decision of the neutral third party is final and binding on both parties.)

> ## ONE STATE'S RESPONSE
>
> **New Jersey's New Home Warranty and Builders'
> Registration Act** protects new-home buyers. Under
> the law, all home builders in the state must register with
> the state's New Home Warranty Program. New homes
> are covered by a limited ten-year warranty issued through
> the state's warranty plan or a state-approved private plan.
>
> For more information, contact the Department of
> Community Affairs, New Home Warranty Program,
> P.O. Box 805, Trenton, NJ 08625; or call 609-984-7534
> or 609-984-7563.

Most homeowners accept the mediated decision.
That may not mean they're satisfied, however. The
biggest problems with extended warranties are that
homeowners don't consult their warranty until a
problem surfaces, they fail to give the builder an opportunity to correct the defect, or they wait too long before filing a claim. Owners may feel dissatisfied with
mediated decisions because they did not understand
warranty limitations—either because they spent too
little time reading their policies or didn't understand
what they read.

Another problem is that plan issuers have no authority to get tough on delinquent builders, except by
suing them or expelling them from the program. An
expelled builder can go on constructing homes unless
local or state regulatory bodies decide to take action.
(In New Jersey, if a builder fails to abide by the decision of a plan's dispute settler, its right to build homes
in New Jersey can be revoked or suspended.)

A Long-Term Look at
Homeowners' Experience

One assessment of how homeowners have fared with
ten-year warranties comes from the U.S. Department
of Housing and Urban Development (HUD). Prior to
1980, builders who wanted to sell new homes eligible
for financing insured by the FHA (the Federal Hous-

ing Administration is an agency within HUD that provides mortgage insurance for residential mortgages and sets standards for construction and underwriting) had to get HUD's approval for all plans before starting construction. In addition, the builder needed HUD's okay on the foundation and framing work, and final inspection. In 1980, the department began allowing builders who offered ten-year warranty plans to start construction without submitting plans for approval—as long as they certified that construc-

HOW TO MAKE AN EXTENDED WARRANTY WORK FOR YOU

Find out before you make a purchase offer or sign a contract how state warranty law could affect you.

- **Ask your lawyer for an assessment** and follow that with a purchase contract contingent on receipt of his or her opinion letter.
- **Read all the terms and conditions** of any ten-year warranty policy your builder offers. Have the terms of any warranties entered in the contract.
- **Hire your own inspector to monitor the job** while the house is being built. Critical times: excavation, construction of the foundation, framing-in, and before the installation of drywall.
- **Insist on a final walk-through inspection.** Do not close on the house until all repairs are made.
- **Check drainage and slope.** Grading and drainage are extremely important— and a major source of problems. Make sure the foundation is high enough and the soil is sloped enough—at least six inches for every ten feet—that water will drain away from the house and off the site.

- **Make contractors unambiguously responsible for everything** and for everyone they choose to hire.
- **Keep records and act quickly.** If you have a warranty and problems show up within two years, write directly to the builder. Send copies of all records to the warranty administrator. Hire an independent inspector to support your claims. Keep a diary and copies of correspondence.
- **Dig in your heels.** Give the builder or the warranty administrator a reasonable amount of time to review your claims and make repairs. Be prepared to fight— and put the responsible party on notice that if it doesn't take action, you will.
- **If you bought a new home with a VA or FHA mortgage,** you may be covered under the agency's own four-year structural defect plan (see the accompanying discussion). Complain to the nearest field office and provide copies of all correspondence and documents. If you think you could qualify at some point, keep the agency up-to-date.

tion plans and specifications met local building-code requirements. In addition, structures had to pass local building inspections and the builder must have had previous plans and construction approved by HUD.

HUD anticipated that these warranties would protect homebuyers with three levels of protection. It expected warranty-plan administrators to exert pressure on builders when owners had problems; it thought buyers would benefit by being able to rely on the insurance when a builder became insolvent and couldn't stand by his product; and it was assured that should a builder fail to correct covered defects or deficiencies, or to honor the terms of the plan, the insurance backer would act as a final fallback.

In 1991, HUD testified before a congressional subcommittee that while its overall experience with warranties on single-family homes had been positive, "consumers are too often denied full home protection when warranty companies unreasonably delay claim payments or claims adjusters use high-pressure tactics with homeowners." HUD was disturbed to find cases where on-site claim adjusters used "hardball" tactics with homeowners when settling a claim. For instance, it found, the claims adjuster "may make a cash offer to repair damage but declare that the offer is only good until he reaches his car or office." (Warranty companies must now give homeowners with FHA mortgages ten working days' notice before they must respond to settlement offers.)

In response to its investigation, HUD revised some procedures to ensure that buyers using FHA mortgages to buy new homes are treated fairly and get more support when they go to arbitration over a claim.

In worst-case scenarios, homeowners have ended up in court anyway, suing the plan administrator and the insurance underwriter backing the warranty. Some of them would probably agree that ten-year warranties weren't intended to protect consumers but rather to protect builders from open-ended liability.

If you're faced with a new-home disaster and a recalcitrant builder, state law may permit you to sue or file a claim against the warranty company.

Homeowners who have taken warranty companies to court have also discovered there was little screening of builders and few controls on construction quality.

What You Can Do

If you're faced with a new-home disaster and a recalcitrant builder, state law may permit you to sue or file a claim against the warranty company. Since an express warranty could stand in the place of any implied builder warranty in a court of law, it's helpful to find out what state law might make a builder do to fix a problem—and for how long—in order to judge the value of promises in a ten-year warranty plan. Your decision to buy from a builder whose homes are covered by an extended-warranty plan should take into account your assessment of the financial strength of the builder (the stronger the builder, the better you might fare in court with his own "stand-alone" warranty instead of a ten-year warranty from an insurer), how state courts have treated homeowners who sued builders, and your best guess as to what might go wrong in the house and when it might become apparent (get your inspector to help you with this).

Help from the FHA or VA

The Federal Housing Administration (FHA) and the Department of Veterans Affairs (VA) operate two little-known structural-defect correction programs for buyers who fail to get help from builders or warranty issuers and their insurers. To qualify, you must have bought your new home (resales don't qualify) with either an FHA or VA mortgage, fulfill certain strict requirements, and apply for help within four years. (The FHA's so-called 518(a) program operates under Section 518(a) of the National Housing Act. The VA program comes under Title 38 CFR, Part 36.4364.)

Once your complaint has been reviewed and accepted, it becomes an official "application for financial assistance" and is subjected to further study and, probably, an on-site inspection. The FHA and VA may pay for correcting structural defects that meet their criteria. In certain situations, they may compensate an owner whose home becomes essentially unlivable due to structural defects. If a request is ultimately denied, you will be informed in writing.

To inquire about benefiting from these programs, your first contact point should be either the FHA or the VA field office that processed your loan. It can help you determine whether the house qualifies and the situation meets the agency's criteria, and can advise you on how to go about fulfilling all processing requirements.

How the FHA's Program Works

To qualify for the FHA program, a problem must meet HUD definitions and you must meet all of the following criteria:

The home must be covered by an individual FHA-insured mortgage.

The property, including a condo unit, must have been approved for mortgage insurance before construction started and must have passed a final HUD inspection. (This clause eliminates many owners whose homes were inspected only during construction.)

You must request assistance no later than four years after the date on the first HUD Mortgage Insurance Certificate issued on the property. (HUD/FHA issues this certificate as evidence that a mortgage has been insured and that a lender has met HUD/FHA requirements. The certificate must have been properly endorsed and must be in force on the day your request is received.)

You must have made reasonable, but unsuccessful, efforts to get the builder, seller, or other responsible person to correct the structural defect.

How the VA's Program Works

To be eligible for the VA program:

You must have bought a new home with a VA mortgage, and the Certificate of Reasonable Value (CRV) must have been "predicated upon completion of proposed construction" (see Item 14 on the original CRV). This means the builder sought VA approval before or during construction and the home was checked by a VA compliance inspector during the construction phase. (If the house is enrolled in a ten-year warranty plan and a VA inspector made the final inspection, the home may be eligible, but condo units are not eligible.)

In addition, you must have brought the problem to the attention of the VA no later than four years after the date the VA guaranteed the loan. (Veterans who bring problems to the attention of the VA within the first four years and keep it informed of efforts to get the builder and warranty plan administrator or insurance company to pay for correcting the defect may be eligible for assistance despite the fact that their official request for assistance was made after four years had elapsed.)

Unlike the FHA, the VA does not have special forms for you to complete. Instead, write a detailed letter to the loan guaranty officer of the appropriate regional VA office.

For information and details, contact either the FHA or the VA field office nearest you.

Pick the Right Mortgage

Chapter 9

Time spent shopping for a mortgage is time well spent. A good deal can yield dramatic dividends in the short run and over time if monthly savings are invested elsewhere. Before you rule out one loan or another, read through this chapter and give some thought to your particular needs and aspirations.

Because you obtained preapproval before house hunting, you're ahead of the game. Financial papers are at hand and up-to-date, and you know the general parameters (size and types) of mortgages you qualify for. But don't head back to the lender from whom you received preapproval without shopping further.

The message is simple: Shop for a loan, not a lender. Mortgage lending is mechanical, impersonal, and competitive. Hunt for the best loan—interest rate, points, processing costs, and, on adjustable mortgages, the most favorable adjustment features. Don't pay much attention to who's originating the loan or where the lender is.

And don't place too much value on your current bank or thrift relationship, either. Odds are your loan will be sold once or twice over its term. (The firm servicing your new loan—collecting payments and holding taxes and homeowners insurance in escrow—may change as well.)

The next chapter explains how to shop for a mortgage—who originates them and how to use mortgage reporting or finding services. But before you go into the market, read this chapter to familiarize yourself with the choices and narrow your search to the kinds of loans that best meet your needs.

Compare interest rates by asking for the annual percentage rate (APR) of the loans you're considering.

Learn the pros and cons of fixed-rate and adjustable-rate borrowing. Get acquainted with the jargon of the mortgage business. Then you can ask lenders the right questions and compare confusing offers before putting yourself on the line.

The Basics

There are two basic ways mortgage lenders charge you for using their money: through the interest charges that you pay each month over the life of the loan and through "points," a one-time sum of money (one point equals 1 percent of the loan amount) that you pay up front.

Compare interest rates by asking for the *annual percentage rate (APR)* of the loans you're considering. While there are many ways to state interest rates, the APR includes the cost of points and other fees such as mortgage insurance, making it a useful tool with which to compare loans. Lenders are required by law to give you the APR on a loan if you request it.

A point is prepaid interest that raises the effective yield to the lender without raising the interest rate on a note. From your perspective, points discount the value of a loan. If you pay two points, or $4,000, to borrow $200,000, you've really borrowed only $196,000. But you will pay back the full $200,000 face value of the loan, plus interest.

Paying points to a lender is a standard part of the mortgage business. One point is roughly equivalent to an additional one-eighth of one percentage point on the interest rate of a 30-year fixed-rate mortgage; so the APR of a 6 percent, 30-year fixed-rate mortgage with no points is equivalent to the APR of a 5 percent loan with eight points.

In reality, you won't find lenders charging eight points because the cost of prepaying that amount would preclude all but the most affluent borrowers who would want to be certain that they'd be living in their homes for many years. Since most owners sell or refinance their homes long before their mortgages are repaid, they would be foolish to prepay so much interest. As a result, the differential between a 6 percent loan and a 5 percent one is apt to be around three points.

The cost of points on a buyer's loan is often shared between buyer and seller. (Like everything else in your purchase offer, who pays points should be set out in the contract.) In addition to points, lenders often charge an "origination" fee, usually calculated as 1 percent of the loan amount. Don't confuse the origination fee with the separate loan-application fees you'll pay to cover paperwork and loan approval. Application fees are not tax-deductible, but an origination fee is a charge for the use of borrowed money and, as such, is deductible.

Sometimes an origination fee is labeled a "prepaid point" because it's a prepayment of one of the discount points to be charged at settlement or closing. If, for example, a mortgage calls for a buyer to pay three points (3 percent of the loan amount) at settlement, a credit will be given for the 1 percent origination fee the buyer paid when he applied for the loan, and only the remaining 2 percent will be collected at settlement. (For a discussion of tax implications, see Chapter 3.)

> ### A PERSONAL CHOICE
>
> Your mortgage choice will depend on your answers to questions such as:
> - How long do you expect to live in the house you're buying?
> - Are you stretching to buy?
> - Would you be able to handle a rising loan payment without major stress?
> - Could you count on a higher income should inflation reappear?
> - Could your spouse go to work?
> - Could you swing another income?

Fixed or Adjustable Rate?

After all exotic mortgages are laid aside, the choice for most homebuyers comes to this: Should you get a fixed- or adjustable-rate mortgage?

The standard fixed-rate, fully amortizing home mortgage—with its preset, life-of-the-mortgage, monthly payments covering principal repayment and interest—came into being during the Great Depression and fueled the enormous expansion of home ownership in the decades following World War II. Its beauty was—

> **With an ARM, you, the borrower, assume the risk of rising rates, and you stand to benefit should rates fall.**

and is—the peace of mind homeowners get from predictable monthly payments. Taxes, utilities, and other costs of home ownership may rise, but principal and interest payments remain the same. An obvious drawback, of course, is that if rates fall, the holder of a fixed-rate mortgage cannot capture the benefit of a new, lower rate except by refinancing.

The increasing reluctance of lenders to make fixed-rate mortgage loans in a climate of rising interest rates in the late 1970s led to creation of the adjustable-rate mortgage (ARM). With an ARM, the interest rate you pay rises and falls along with other rates charged throughout the economy. Put another way, you, the borrower, assume the risk of rising rates, and you stand to benefit should rates fall.

What's Best for You?

Let's say that you know which direction interest rates will move. If so, you lock in low interest rates with a fixed-rate loan when it looks like they'll be rising over the next few years. When it looks like rates will go down or stay about the same, an adjustable-rate mortgage should be considered.

But you don't know the direction interest rates will take, and neither do the experts. So leave interest-rate forecasting to those who dare, and concentrate instead on what you can manage. If you're stretching and a sooner-than-expected payment hike could strain your budget, a fixed-rate mortgage is the safe bet. If not, a one- or three-year adjustable-rate mortgage is worth considering. (Five-, seven-, and ten-year ARMs are also available.) ARMs are attractive when the spread between fixed-rate mortgages and the starting rate on the ARM is two percentage points or more, or when you don't intend to stay put more than ten years.

Don't accept an ARM without periodic and lifetime caps on interest rates; typical caps today are no more than a two-percentage-point hike in the interest rate from one year to the next, and no more than a five- or six-point increase over the starting rate during the term of the loan.

Fixed-Rate Loans

A fixed-rate loan locks in your interest rate. With an amortizing, fixed-rate loan, your total monthly payment of principal and interest remains constant, but the portion of each payment allocated to principal grows. By the end of the loan's life, or term, you will have repaid the original loan and all interest you owe.

Long-Term Mortgages

The most common long-term mortgages last 15, 20, or 30 years.

ADVANTAGES. Predictability is the big plus. You know exactly how much interest you will pay over the term of the loan. Total monthly payment of principal and interest is fixed, and in early years it consists primarily of tax-deductible interest. Mortgages without prepayment penalties permit you to shorten the term of the loan at will—and lower ultimate interest cost—by making periodic payments against principal.

DISADVANTAGES. Stability comes at a price. Interest rates on fixed-rate loans are usually higher than starting rates on adjustable-rate loans. Down-payment requirements on conventional, fixed-rate loans are steep—10 percent to 20 percent—unless you obtain mortgage insurance, an added monthly expense that protects the lender from risk of loss. With mortgage insurance you may be able to put down as little as 0 percent to 5 percent. Interest rates on nonconforming or "jumbo" loans may be higher than on conforming loans, and you may pay more points. (The conforming-loan limit is based on the change in average home prices from one October to the next. In 2005, conforming loans nationwide had a ceiling of $359,650 for single-family homes. Anything above that is jumbo.)

While amortization costs remain level over the loan term, monthly payments will increase over the years as property taxes and insurance costs go up.

Predictability is a big plus with long-term mortgages.

WHAT WILL PAYMENTS BE ON A FIXED-RATE LOAN?

This table allows you to calculate your monthly mortgage payment for each $1,000 that you borrow. Only principal and interest are included; insurance and property taxes would be additional expenses. To calculate your monthly payment for a new mortgage, locate the number in the column and row corresponding to the length of the mortgage and the

INTEREST RATE	15 YEARS	20 YEARS	25 YEARS	30 YEARS
4.00%	$ 7.40	$ 6.06	$ 5.28	$ 4.77
4.25	7.52	6.19	5.42	4.92
4.50	7.65	6.33	5.56	5.07
4.75	7.78	6.46	5.70	5.22
5.00	7.91	6.60	5.85	5.37
5.25	8.04	6.74	5.99	5.52
5.50	8.17	6.88	6.14	5.68
5.75	8.30	7.02	6.29	5.84
6.00	8.44	7.17	6.45	6.00
6.25	8.58	7.31	6.60	6.16
6.50	8.72	7.46	6.76	6.33
6.75	8.85	7.61	6.91	6.49
7.00	8.99	7.76	7.07	6.66
7.25	9.13	7.91	7.23	6.83
7.50	9.28	8.06	7.39	7.00
7.75	9.42	8.21	7.56	7.17
8.00	9.56	8.37	7.72	7.34
8.25	9.71	8.53	7.89	7.52
8.50	9.85	8.68	8.06	7.69
8.75	10.00	8.84	8.23	7.87
9.00	10.15	9.00	8.40	8.05

Attractive (that is, low-interest) fixed-rate mortgages usually can't be assumed by subsequent buyers, because lenders want to take every opportunity to replace a low-rate loan with a higher-interest one.

With 20- to 30-year terms, principal balance is reduced relatively slowly compared with shorter-term loans. Twenty-year loans usually don't carry a lower rate than 30-year loans. Though eased by tax deductions, total interest cost is high. A $200,000, 6 per-

interest rate; multiply that figure by the number of thousands of dollars involved. Example: For a 30-year loan of $200,000 at 6%, multiply 200 by $6.00. The monthly payment of principal and interest would equal $1,200.

INTEREST RATE	15 YEARS	20 YEARS	25 YEARS	30 YEARS
9.25%	$10.30	$ 9.16	$ 8.57	$8.23
9.50	10.45	9.33	8.74	8.41
9.75	10.60	9.49	8.92	8.60
10.00	10.75	9.66	9.09	8.78
10.25	10.90	9.82	9.27	8.97
10.50	11.06	9.99	9.45	9.15
10.75	11.21	10.16	9.63	9.34
11.00	11.37	10.33	9.81	9.53
11.25	11.53	10.50	9.99	9.72
11.50	11.69	10.67	10.17	9.91
11.75	11.85	10.84	10.35	10.10
12.00	12.01	11.02	10.54	10.29
12.25	12.17	11.19	10.72	10.48
12.50	12.33	11.37	10.91	10.68
12.75	12.49	11.54	11.10	10.87
13.00	12.66	11.72	11.28	11.07
13.25	12.82	11.90	11.47	11.26
13.50	12.99	12.08	11.66	11.46
13.75	13.15	12.26	11.85	11.66
14.00	13.32	12.44	12.04	11.85

cent, 30-year fixed-rate mortgage costs $231,677 in interest over its term. A 6 percent, 15-year fixed-rate loan, on the other hand, has a total interest cost of $103,789—$127,888 less.

15-Year, Fixed-Rate, Fixed-Payment Mortgage

ADVANTAGES. Principal balance is reduced relatively rapidly compared to longer-term loans. The 15-year fixed-rate loan permits you to own your home debt-free in half the time, and for less than half the total interest cost, of a 30-year fixed-rate loan. It offers some individuals a useful financial planning tool. Interest rates may be lower than those offered on 30-year fixed-rate loans. FHA-insured, low-down-payment, 15-year fixed-rate loans are available; so are VA-guaranteed, no-down-payment, 15-year loans.

DISADVANTAGES. Higher monthly payments make these loans more difficult to qualify for than longer-term mortgages. A 15-year mortgage reduces the number of homes you can afford to buy and locks you into making monthly payments roughly 15 percent to 30 percent higher than you'd make with a comparable 30-year loan. On a $200,000, 6 percent note, monthly payments would be $1,688 for 15 years and $1,199 for 30 years—a monthly difference of $489.

Because the principal balance is paid down faster, total mortgage-interest payments—a key tax-shelter benefit of home ownership—are reduced relative to a traditional 30-year mortgage (see the table below).

THE DIFFERENCE A 15-YEAR LOAN MAKES

This table shows the rapid decline in principal owed over the course of a 15-year mortgage compared with the slower payoff of a 30-year loan. What a difference that makes in the total interest you would pay— $94,150 on the 15-year mortgage, which is less than half the $231,677 you would pay on the 30-year loan. (Note: The total interest you would pay on the 30-year loan by the end of year 15 is $157,936.)

YEAR	PAYMENT NUMBER	15-YEAR FIXED-RATE ($100,000 at 7.5%)		30-YEAR FIXED-RATE ($100,000 at 8%)	
		PAYMENT	PRINCIPAL BALANCE	PAYMENT	PRINCIPAL BALANCE
1	12	$1,634	$191,170	$1,199	$197,544
3	36	1,634	171,986	1,199	192,168
5	60	1,634	150,578	1,199	186,109
7	84	1,634	126,686	1,199	179,279
10	120	1,634	85,553	1,199	167,371
15	180	1,634	0	1,199	142,098

Biweekly Fixed-Rate Mortgage

ADVANTAGES. The biweekly payment schedule of this kind of loan speeds up amortization, reduces total interest costs, and shortens the loan term—usually from 30 years to between 18 and 22 years. You make 26 biweekly payments—which amounts to 13 annual payments—instead of 12 monthly payments. Conversion to a 30-year fixed-rate loan is usually permitted. Payments are deducted automatically from your savings or checking accounts.

DISADVANTAGES. Private companies and lenders usually charge for this service. Registration fees and biweekly debit charges can make this a costly way to shorten the life of a loan and lower interest expense. The same objectives can be accomplished more flexibly with a 30-year mortgage by making an extra payment or two each year or by applying an additional sum to principal repayment when you make a monthly payment. As with other kinds of rapid-payoff mortgages, you trade total interest-cost reductions for reduced tax-shelter benefits.

Community Home Buyer's Program (CHBP)

This low-down-payment, fixed-rate mortgage was designed by Fannie Mae to help creditworthy buyers who can't qualify for standard conventional mortgages. You can choose between a 30-year and a 15-year loan. To qualify you must have income of no more than 100 percent of your area's median household income. Fannie Mae, however, waives income limits in approximately 600 designated cities across the United States.

ADVANTAGES. CHBP loans require less income and less cash. You may be able to pay as much as 33 percent of gross monthly income toward total housing payments (mortgage payments, taxes, insurance, and condo fees, if applicable) and still qualify. (Most mortgage lenders limit you to 28 percent or 29 percent.)

Your down payment can be as low as 5 percent. Many community organizations and state and local

Higher monthly payments make 15-year fixed-rate mortgages more difficult to qualify for than longer-term loans.

> **Each ARM is tied to an index that moves up and down in tandem with the general movement of interest rates.**

agencies provide subsidized loans to low- and moderate-income families to help them buy a home.

You won't have to bring as much cash to closing. In most cases, buyers are required to put two months of mortgage payments in reserve at closing or settlement. This requirement is reduced or waived for CHBP borrowers.

DISADVANTAGES. You will have to pay a monthly mortgage-insurance premium.

Adjustable-Rate Mortgages

ARMs may be called variable-rate loans, adjustable-rate loans, or adjustable-mortgage loans. Whatever the name, they all carry an interest rate that can change periodically during the term of the loan, as well as these four features:

INITIAL INTEREST RATES. Starting rates are generally one to four percentage points below those on conventional 30-year fixed-rate mortgages.

ADJUSTMENT INTERVALS. The adjustment schedule is set out in the mortgage contract. Changes in the rate to be charged on an ARM loan occur at the end of each adjustment period. Some ARMs adjust the interest rate annually, while others have an initial fixed-rate period of three, five, seven, or even ten years, after which the rate adjusts annually.

INDEX. Each ARM is tied to an index that moves up and down in tandem with the general movement of interest rates. The index is used to figure the new loan rate for the next adjustment period. The calculation date—typically one to two months before the anniversary date of the loan—is set out in the contract.

Popular indexes include average rates on one-, three-, and five-year Treasury securities. Another is the Federal Housing Finance Board's National Average

Contract Mortgage Rate (a monthly weighted average of loans closed). This is usually abbreviated as FHFB Series of Closed Loans.

Other common indexes are: the COFI (cost of funds index), which is based on the average monthly rate for marketable Treasury bills and notes; the LIBOR (London Interbank Offer Rate), which averages rates for five major British mortgage lenders; and the Eleventh District COFI, which, although based on borrowing rates in California, Arizona, and Nevada, is used by lenders nationwide.

The cost of funds indexes are considered the least volatile. You can follow the ups and downs of the index your lender uses either in a major newspaper or by calling Fannie Mae's Yield Hotline at 800-752-7020.

Some indexes are more volatile than others. In certain circumstances, the most volatile index will be the least expensive for borrowers over the long haul. While it will go up more quickly than most, it is less likely to "stick" at a high level when interest rates drop. For that reason, a mortgage tied to rates on one-year Treasury securities could give you the best deal when rates fall over a prolonged period.

Find out what index your ARM would be tied to and how often it would adjust. How has the index performed in the past? Where is it published?

ADJUSTMENT MARGIN. The loan rate and the index rate move up and down together, but they aren't the same. "Margin" is the percentage amount the lender adds to the index rate to get the ARM's interest rate. Look for it in the mortgage contract. The margin amount, commonly one to three percentage points, usually remains constant over the life of a loan. Whatever the margin amount, add it to the index rate at the adjustment anniversary to get a new "adjusted" rate.

For promotional purposes, the starting rate of an ARM may be less than the index rate plus margin. Don't be impressed with this kind of discount—it's usually temporary and the rate most likely will rise, although it can rise only so far because it's subject to

> **The loan rate and the index rate move up and down together, but they aren't the same.**

caps. Ask the lender what your interest rate (and monthly payment) would be at the first adjustment date, assuming the index rate didn't change between now and then. The payment will probably be higher (see the discussion of discount ARMs on page 162).

Two Features Many ARMs Carry

CAPS ON INTEREST. There are two types of interest-rate caps:

Lifetime caps, required by law on all new ARMs and on assumptions, limit the interest-rate increase over the life of the loan. With a "5 percent lifetime cap," your rate can't increase more than five percentage points

---

HOW ARM PAYMENTS COULD GO UP OR DOWN

Say you have a $200,000 one-year adjustable-rate mortgage (ARM) with an initial rate of 4%, an annual cap of two percentage points, and a lifetime cap of five percentage points. Here's what the monthly payment would be on a fully amortized loan if payments are adjusted up every year to the maximum and then remain at that level for the life of the loan.

YEAR	RATE	YEARS OF AMORTIZATION	MONTHLY PAYMENT	PRINCIPAL BALANCE AT END OF PERIOD
1	4 %	30	$954.83	$196.477.96
2	6	29	1,192.63	193,884.52
3	8	28	1,447.85	191,951.22
4	9	27	1,580.00	190,195.58
5–30	9	26	1,580.00	—

And this is what the monthly payments would be if interest rates on a $200,000, 7.5% ARM dropped one-half percentage point every year for five years:

YEAR	RATE	YEARS OF AMORTIZATION	MONTHLY PAYMENT	PRINCIPAL BALANCE AT END OF PERIOD
1	7.5 %	30	$1,398.43	$198,156.31
2	7.0	29	1,331.87	195,975.73
3	6.5	28	1,267.99	193,423.13
4	6.0	27	1,206,93	190,464.89
5	5.5	26	1,148.78	187,070.38
6–30	5.0	25	1,093.59	—

over the initial rate no matter how high the index rate climbs. Most adjustable-rate mortgage contracts limit lifetime caps to 5 percent or 6 percent. In some, lifetime caps apply to decreases as well as increases.

Periodic caps limit the interest-rate increase from one adjustment period to the next. For example, your mortgage contract could provide that, should the index rate increase four points in one year, your rate could rise only two points. When rates rise rapidly, periodic caps cushion borrowers from overly steep payment hikes between one adjustment period and the next.

ARM contracts generally allow periodic decreases as well as increases. With ARMs that carry periodic caps, a drop in interest rates doesn't automatically lead to a drop in monthly payments. For example, take a one-year 5 percent ARM with a two-point annual cap. If the index to which it is tied rises three points during the first year, the second-year rate will be capped at 7 percent. At the end of the second adjustment period, if the index stays the same, the third-year rate will rise to 8 percent. This can happen because ARM contracts usually permit loan rates to rise—subject to annual caps—on any adjustment date when the index plus the margin is higher than the current rate you are paying.

The majority of adjustable-rate mortgages sold to major investors in the secondary market—so-called conforming ARMs—have periodic and lifetime limits on interest-rate increases. Most adjustable-rate mortgages today are sold by their originators; most limit interest-rate increases or decreases with periodic and lifetime caps.

CAPS ON PAYMENT. Payment caps limit payment increases to a percentage of the previous payment.

Payment caps can result in "negative amortization" when rising interest rates call for payments higher than the cap would permit. Because the capped payments are not enough to cover monthly interest due

> **With ARMs that carry periodic caps, a drop in interest rates doesn't automatically lead to a drop in monthly payments.**

CHECKLIST FOR COMPARING ARMs

After you've obtained preapproval for the amount of money you may borrow, use this worksheet to assess a lender's adjustable-rate mortgage (ARM) offering.

Lender's name _____

Telephone number_____

Down payment required_____ %

Beginning interest rate (APR)_____ %

Number of points _____

Beginning payment $ _____

Lifetime cap on interest rate?   _____ %

Periodic cap on the interest rate?   yes ❏   no ❏

  What is the cap?   _____ %

How often can payment be adjusted?   _____

Is there a cap on payment?   yes ❏   no ❏

  What is the cap?   _____ %

Does loan permit negative amortization?   yes ❏   no ❏

How much negative amortization is allowed relative to the
    original loan amount? For example, can mortgage balance
    grow to 105% of original loan, 110%, and so on?   _____ %

Loan is tied to which index?

  ❏ 1-year Treasury securities

  ❏ 3-year Treasury securities

  ❏ 5-year Treasury securities

  ❏ Other: _____

  ❏ Federal Housing Board's National Average Contract Rate Series of Closed Loans

Number of adjustments loan calls for   _____

  ❏ First adjustment occurs at   _____months/years

  ❏ Second adjustment occurs at   _____months/years

  ❏ Third adjustment occurs at   _____months/years

Can loan be converted to a fixed rate?   yes ❏   no ❏

  Under what circumstances? _____

  _____

  Cost of conversion option $_____

  Can loan be prepaid in whole or in part at any time without penalty?   yes ❏   no ❏

  If yes, what are the conditions? _____

_____

Is loan assumable by qualified buyer?   yes ❏   no ❏

on the loan, unpaid interest is added to the principal balance. At some point, you will be required to begin making monthly payments large enough to pay off all the principal and interest you now owe over what remains of the loan term. When the day arrives, you could find (assuming rates kept increasing during earlier adjustment periods) that the new monthly payment required to repay a bigger loan over a shortened term is very large indeed.

ARMs with caps on payments are rare today for two main reasons: They are not a good deal for most buyers, and secondary-market purchasers of mortgages are reluctant to buy them after having been burned by higher-than-average foreclosure rates in the past.

Three Other Things to Ask About

There are three other things you should ask about when shopping for an ARM:

ASSUMABILITY. Will you be able to transfer the mortgage to a prospective buyer under the same terms? By assuming the mortgage, the buyer takes on primary liability for the unpaid balance of your existing mortgage or deed of trust against the property. The lender usually must approve the buyer's assumption of liability in order for you to be released from obligation.

CONVERTIBILITY. Can you convert the ARM to a fixed-rate mortgage? A convertible ARM may enable you to lock in a lower rate at some future point. Expect to pay extra for an ARM with a conversion clause—via a higher rate, an up-front fee, a conversion charge imposed on the date you make the change, or some combination of these charges. Some ARM contracts permit you to do this at a predetermined time, commonly after the end of the first adjustment period. When you convert, the new rate generally is the current market rate for fixed-rate mortgages. The ARM program disclosure provided by the lender will provide details about how you could convert your ARM to a fixed-rate loan.

> **A convertible ARM may enable you to lock in a lower rate at some future point.**

PREPAYMENT. Will you have to pay a fee or penalty if you refinance or pay off the ARM early? Prepayment penalties sometimes are negotiable before you sign the loan documents. In many cases, however, you will be permitted to pay off the ARM loan at any time, in full or in part, without penalty.

The 3/I Loan

Because of the appeal of fixed payments to borrowers, lenders offer ARMs that start with a fixed rate and monthly payment for a specified number of years then switch to an adjustable rate and payment for the remaining term. These are known as 3/1, 5/1, 7/1, and 10/1 loans, depending on the fixed period.

The longer-term, fixed-payment periods are particularly attractive, because people often move before the adjustment takes place. But borrowers should be on the lookout for loans that carry any kind of bailout clause that would permit the lender to back out of the mortgage altogether if rates climb above a certain percentage. Be sure that the mortgage you take covers you for the full 30 years in case interest rates rise drastically during the life of the loan.

Discount ARMs Require Caution

As the name implies, "discount" ARMs are offered at initial rates below the sum of index rate plus margin. The discounted rate lasts until the end of the first adjustment period set out in the mortgage contract. Discount ARMs may carry large initial loan fees and possibly extra points, both of which serve to increase overall loan costs.

Discount ARMs are called *buydowns* when the lender is paid a lump sum at settlement in exchange for a lower rate to the buyer. (The payment may be designated as so many "points.") Buydowns can be permanent or temporary and may be paid for by sellers, builders, or buyers. The cost of a permanent builder or seller buydown is usually passed along to the buyer by way of a higher price tag on the property. (Fixed-rate loans can be bought down, too. In such cases, the borrower gets a discounted rate that gradually increases to the agreed-on fixed rate, often over a three-year period.)

Discount ARMs can give unwary borrowers payment shock. If the ARM has a periodic rate cap, you may find it applies only to adjustments made after the discounted rate expires. As a result, there is actually no cap on the first adjustment. Let's see what could happen to your monthly payment with a discount ARM:

- **loan amount:** $200,000
- **index rate:** 3 percent
- **adjustment margin:** 2 percent
- **regular ARM rate:** 5 percent with two-point annual cap; $1,074 monthly payment during first year
- **discount ARM rate:** 3 percent with no cap on first annual adjustment, two-point annual cap thereafter; $843 monthly payment during first year.

> ### THE WHOLE TRUTH
>
> Lenders must provide you with a "Truth in Lending Disclosure Statement" within three days after they receive your application for financing. Use it to double-check important information about your proposed loan. The statement shows you the annual percentage rate (APR), total finance charges, amount financed, total number of payments, amount of scheduled monthly payment, late-payment charges, prepayment penalty (if one applies), and applicable assumption restrictions.

If the index rate sticks at 3 percent, your monthly payment will increase $231, to $1,074, in the second year when the discount ends. If the index rate increases 2 percent during the first year, when the first annual adjustment is made, 2 percent will be added to the 5 percent undiscounted index-plus-margin rate, making your new rate 7 percent. Your second-year payment jumps to $1,329—an increase of $486 a month.

You could end up paying more on a discount ARM than you would on a regular adjustable-rate loan if the full index-plus-margin rate is higher than going ARM rates to begin with. In most cases the discount period is too short to offset the higher base rate you would have to carry during the remaining term of the loan.

Seven-Year Balloon Mortgage with Refinancing Option

When periodic payments aren't enough to pay off principal and interest over the life of a loan, a remaining balance, or balloon payment, will be due. Balloons can be fixed-rate or adjustable-rate loans. Fannie Mae's seven-year balloon is treated as an ARM because it carries a refinance option. In most cases, the balloon lender has no obligation to help a borrower obtain a loan to pay off the expiring balloon mortgage.

ADVANTAGES. Interest rates on seven-year balloons are lower than going rates on 30-year fixed-rate mortgages. Monthly payments are based on 30-year amortization—that is, monthly principal and interest payments would pay off the debt in 30 years. The balloon can be refinanced with a 23-year fixed-rate mortgage in most cases.

Buyers who stay in their homes less than seven years will pay less than they would have with a 30-year fixed-rate loan. If their plans change, they should be able to refinance without requalifying, providing the rate for the new loan is calculated to be no more than five points higher than the balloon-note rate.

Monthly payments can be lowered with a temporary buydown. Lenders may permit borrowers or builders to buy down initial loan-interest rates. A typical charge is 1 percent of the mortgage loan amount

MORE ON MORTGAGES

Applying for Your Mortgage is a brochure available from the Mortgage Bankers Association of America ($ .90 each plus shipping; 1919 Pennsylvania Ave., N.W., Washington, DC 20006; 202-557-2700; http://www.campusmba.org).

Choosing the Mortgage That's Right for You and *Opening the Door to a Home of Your Own* are free publications from the Fannie Mae Foundation (800-611-9566; http://www.homebuyingguide.org). Both are available in booklet form or may be read online.

Consumer Handbook on Adjustable Rate Mortgages is free and available in hard copy or online from lenders or Publication Fulfillment, Board of Governors of the Federal Reserve Systems (MS-127 Washington, DC 20551; 202-452-3245).

How to Save Thousands of Dollars on Your Home Mortgage, 2nd Ed., by Randy Johnson (Wiley, $17.95).

for each one-quarter-point reduction in the interest rate. (The less time you stay in the home, the less you benefit from buying down the rate.)

DISADVANTAGES. You could lose the right to refinance by falling behind on payments or by putting a lien on the property. In addition, if interest rates rise significantly by refinancing time, you could be turned down. If the new rate is more than 5 percent above the balloon-note rate, you could be required to requalify for the new rate and have your home reappraised.

You will be charged fees and costs to refinance.

In most cases, the balloon lender has no obligation to help a borrower obtain a loan to pay off the expiring balloon mortgage.

No-Down, No Kidding

Lenders are also offering to finance 100 percent of the cost of a new home. This opens the market to many first-time buyers who otherwise would have insufficient savings to cover a down payment.

The no-down mortgage usually consists of a first mortgage, either fixed or adjustable, of up to 80 percent of the home price (maximums of $500,000 or more), and a second mortgage—usually a variable-rate line of credit—for the remaining 20 percent. To further entice homebuyers, the no-downs are offered with no private mortgage insurance fees. You might even find a no-down for 107 percent of the value of the home for amounts of $325,000 or more.

So what's the catch? These mortgages are generally offered at rates 3 percent to 4 percent higher than conventional mortgages. But if you're having a hard time saving up for a down payment, this may be the solution to your problem. You can buy the home, pay off the down payment within a few years, then refinance the mortgage when more attractive rates are available.

Making a Mortgage Choice

Deciding which mortgage is best requires a close look at your present circumstances, future earnings, and financial goals. Clear forecasting of

AN ARM AND FIXED-RATE EXAMPLE

Say you're expecting a job-related move within three to six years. You could consider a 30-year, three-year adjustable-rate mortgage (ARM) with a 2% periodic-adjustment cap and a 6% lifetime cap on a $200,000 loan. Assume that you could get this ARM with an initial interest rate 1.75% points lower than what you could get with a 30-year fixed-rate loan (points paid at settlement are equal). The following figures show how you would fare with an upward adjustment of two percentage points at the end of year three.

4.25%, 30-YEAR, THREE-YEAR ARM ($200,000)

YEAR	INTEREST RATE	PAYMENT	BALANCE
1	4.25%	$ 984	$196,628
2	4.25	984	193,110
3	4.25	984	189,440
4	6.25	1,212	186,660
5	6.25	1,212	183,700
6	6.25	1,212	180,551

economic conditions a few years down the road would help, too—but don't hold your decision hostage to your predictions about interest rates and economic cycles. That's something even experts fail to do with precision. Instead keep your needs in the forefront. Do you intend to stay put for many years? Then getting the best interest rate is important. Paying 6 percent rather than 6.5 percent on a $200,000, 30-year fixed-rate mortgage will save you $65 each month. Tuck that amount each month in a mutual fund and you've saved $780 a year, not counting long-term appreciation and compounding.

On the other hand, say you plan to put the home up for sale three to five years hence. Then points and closing costs (and the ability to pay off the mortgage without penalty) are more important than getting the absolute lowest available rate. For most homebuyers, the choices are these:

- **Will your down payment be small or large?**
- **Do you want a long-term or short-term loan?**
- **A fixed-rate or adjustable-rate mortgage?**

Over a six-year period, monthly payments on the three-year ARM would cost you nearly $7,300 less than those on the fixed-rate loan, and you would have reduced your mortgage balance by $2,245 more than you would have with the fixed-rate loan. If rates on the ARM increased less than two percentage points in the third year—or fell—savings would be greater.

8%, 30-YEAR, FIXED-RATE $100,000 MORTGAGE

YEAR	INTEREST RATE	PAYMENT	BALANCE
1	6%	$1,199	$197,545
2	6	1,199	194,936
3	6	1,199	192,168
4	6	1,199	189,229
5	6	1,199	186,109
6	6	1,199	182,796

■ **Will you pay points for the lowest-rate mortgage** or will you shop for a loan with few or no points and therefore a higher rate?

Go for Equity?

Another way to look at the problem is to ask yourself what you want from your home in addition to its shelter value. Choose a mortgage that helps move you closer to those objectives.

Suppose that ten years from now you will need a home-equity loan to finance college educations for your children. From your perspective, tax benefits from mortgage-interest payments are less of a priority than equity buildup. You could accomplish this by making a large down payment, of course, and borrowing it back as necessary. If that's not possible, you could choose a 15- or 20-year loan—using the mortgage as a form of forced savings, as it were. Or you could opt for a 30-year fixed-rate mortgage and make additional voluntary payments against the principal. (Before you

> **If you plan to stay in the house, it may be wiser to pay a point or two to get the lower interest rate.**

choose the latter, determine whether your loan contract would permit the lender to charge you a prepayment penalty. If so, and you can't get that provision removed, chances are you'd do better not prepaying but investing that extra sum elsewhere.)

Before embarking on a major campaign of prepaying principal, however, give thought to alternative uses of the money. What kind of return on your money could you anticipate from stocks, bonds, mutual funds, and other types of investments? How does that compare with the amount of equity you could "accrue" in your home over the same time period? Keep in mind that once you put money into repaying your mortgage, you will earn no current income, and you can get it out only by borrowing it back via a home-equity loan or some sort of refinancing.

The Vanishing Point

From time to time, the points (prepaid interest charges on mortgages) you will be asked to pay to get a mortgage loan shrink or even vanish. This can be a boon because you can borrow for less and drive a harder bargain on price.

In the early 1990s, for instance, lenders were sometimes waiving points on conventional loans. (Points on FHA-insured and deeply discounted adjustable-rate mortgages remained customary.) Lenders could afford to forgo points because the yield curve was skewed in their favor: Lenders were paying 3 percent or 4 percent for money they could lend out to would-be homeowners at 8 percent or better. That was profit enough without points. Lenders were also finding that borrowers were shopping hard to minimize closing costs.

Should you take a zero-point loan? The irony is that if you plan to stay in the house, it may be wiser to pay a point or two to get the lower interest rate. Pay one point ($2,000) on a $200,000 mortgage with a rate of 5.75 percent instead of 6 percent and you break even in under four years, assuming a 25 percent tax bracket.

When the spread between short-term and 30-year rates is around three percentage points, mortgage points are common.

Whatever your decision, keep in mind that as circumstances change and interest rates rise and fall, your initial loan choice in most cases isn't set in stone. You can refinance or take out a home-equity loan, even sell and move on. You don't have to bet right on the cheapest loan to come out ahead in the long run. Buy the home you like in a good neighborhood, and odds are it will appreciate modestly in line with inflation over the coming years.

Find a Lender, Get a Loan

After you've picked the type of mortgage best suited to your needs, you're ready to find a lender. A decade or two ago, finding one didn't require much comparison shopping. Loans were fixed-rate and rates didn't vary much, so most people dealt with a local institution they already had a relationship with. Today things are more complex.

Although your real estate agent can help you find a lender, usually without charging a fee, this is something you can do yourself. As noted in the previous chapter, lender name recognition and location are less important than the quality of the deal. Check with several mortgage companies, use a reporting service (see pages 174–75), and check the online services (see page 20). Rely on your own efforts, including lots of time spent on the computer and lots of telephone calls.

If there isn't a mortgage reporting service covering your area, begin the search at your own bank or savings and loan. If you were preapproved by a lender or mortgage company, by all means determine whether the firm can offer you a competitive deal. You'll save time dealing with the same company, but you aren't obliged to do so. If you decide to switch to another lender, you must be approved all over again.

The Secondary Market's Role

Most home mortgages are sold once they have been closed. The buyers—organizations with such names as Fannie Mae, Ginnie Mae, and

Most home mortgages are sold once they've been closed. The buyers make up what's known as the secondary market.

Freddie Mac, as well as a number of private firms—make up what is known as the secondary market. It acts as a conduit, linking the world of the homebuyer to Wall Street by purchasing mortgages from lenders and reselling them, or securities backed by them, to investors. Because it is so big, the secondary market affects what loans are available and what buyers have to do to get them.

By selling the loans they originate, savings institutions, mortgage companies, and commercial banks get their cash back to reinvest, and they also earn fees for continuing to service the loans. Those who buy the loans, usually government or government-backed agencies or large mortgage bankers, get the right to receive the principal and interest paid by borrowers. They, in turn, package their mortgages and sell securities backed by the pooled loans. Pension funds and other institutional investors are the biggest market for mortgage-backed securities.

The secondary market helps redistribute available mortgage funds by buying mortgages in regions where the demand from homeowners outstrips lenders' deposits and selling them in other markets where available credit exceeds loan demand.

Sources of Mortgage Money

The lender you choose will take your loan application, follow through on credit checks, property appraisal, and other details leading to settlement and transfer of title. A "lender" is likely to be a loan originator who immediately sells your loan and others to secondary-market mortgage buyers and repackagers such as Freddie Mac or Fannie Mae, as described above, rather than an institution that lends you money and holds your loan in its own portfolio of investments. An originator will have the promissory note prepared—establishing the amount of debt, terms of repayment, and interest rate you have contracted to pay—and have the mortgage or deed of trust drawn to secure the property for the lender should you default on the note.

Independent Mortgage Companies

Independent mortgage companies—such as Countrywide Funding, to name the largest—make just more than 70 percent of all home mortgages, including most VA-guaranteed and FHA-insured loans. Mortgage bankers work closely with the secondary market by selling their loans to agencies buying standardized, or conforming, home mortgages. You will be expected to meet secondary-market standards covering creditworthiness, down-payment size, and appraisals. Once your application is approved, you will get a loan commitment binding the lender for a specified length of time to the rate and terms set out in the contract. Although the terms of your loan will not change, do not be surprised if the company servicing your loan changes. You will be notified where your mortgage payments should be sent.

Savings Institutions

Savings and loan associations and savings banks originate less than a quarter of home mortgages. Most are conventional loans—those not guaranteed by the VA or Rural Development, or insured by the FHA—and most conform to standards set by secondary-market agencies because these institutions, like mortgage bankers, sell the mortgages they originate.

Commercial Banks

Commercial banks are active in residential lending. Many have affiliations with mortgage bankers or operate their own mortgage-banking subsidiaries. Banks also are a major supplier of loans for mobile-home buyers.

Government-Backed Loans

USDA GUARANTEED RURAL HOUSING LOAN PROGRAM.

Through the Rural Housing Service (RHS), a part of the U.S. Department of Agriculture's Rural Development (USDA/RD) office, qualified low- and moderate-income families can receive loan guarantees for purchasing rural property. To qualify for the program,

You will be expected to meet secondary-market standards covering creditworthiness, down-payment size, and appraisals.

you must have adequate income, a stable employ-ment profile, and good credit history. You must also plan to live in the home you purchase.

Other RHS rules require that the property be located within an area that's designated as "rural" by the USDA, and that your adjusted family income not exceed 115 percent of the median income for the area. You can find out about area designations and income calculations from a local lender or a Rural De-velopment office.

Loans guaranteed under this program are 30-year fixed-rate mortgages. Closing costs and required repairs may be included in the loan if the total amount doesn't

FOR MORE INFORMATION

A First Stop

Check in at http://www.kiplinger.com/ personal finance/rewards/home, where you'll find current average national mort-gage rates and links to a variety of online calculators (including how big a mortgage you can afford and how big your monthly payment will be) and to the Web sites of mortgage-shopping services and mortgage brokerages.

After that, you may wish to try some of the following sources, depending on your indi-vidual situation:

Leads to Local Mortgage Brokers

State and local boards of Realtors may give you names of mortgage brokers active in your area. Or contact the National Association of Mortgage Brokers for the location of your state's association, which will in turn refer you to some local brokers (NAMB, 8201 Greensboro Dr., Suite 300, McLean, VA 22102; 703-610-9009; http://www.namb.org).

Mortgage-Reporting Services

HSH Associates (1200 Route 23, Butler, NJ 07405; 800-873-2837 or 973-617-8700; http://www.hsh.com) surveys more than 2,000 lenders weekly in more than 30 states and over 2,500 lenders monthly in all 50 states. Its Homebuyer's Mortgage Kit ($20 plus $3 for shipping and handling) provides a list of lenders and information on at least three loans from each, including discount points, down payments, interest rates, an-nual percentage rate, terms, and maximum mortgage amounts. The kit contains a 56-page booklet, *How to Shop for Your Mortgage.*

Help for Low- and Moderate-Income First-Time Buyers

If you aren't able to locate the correct agency providing help to qualified low- and moderate-income first-time buyers in your state, you can access a list of state housing finance agencies (HFAs) that provide first-time buyer loans by checking http://www .ncsha.org, the official Web site of the Na-tional Council of State Housing Agencies.

exceed the market value of the property. For further information on the program, see the contact information in the RHS listing in the box shown below.

FHA-INSURED HOME LOANS. The Federal Housing Administration (a part of the Department of Housing and Urban Development—HUD) insures a wide variety of mortgages, including fixed-rates and ARMs. Down payments are low—as low as 3 percent. You can be charged an origination fee for services of up to 1 percent of the loan amount, and you are not restricted from paying points. The FHA doesn't set the interest

Help for Rural Buyers

If you are unable to get credit from private providers of mortgage funds but you meet certain income and rural-residency requirements, you may be able to buy a home through the U.S. Department of Agriculture's Rural Housing Service (RHS). Contact the RHS office in the county where you would like to buy or build. Addresses of offices can be obtained by writing to the Rural Housing Service National Office (U.S. Department of Agriculture, Room 5037, South Building, 14th St. and Independence Ave., S.W., Washington DC 20250) or by checking the agency's Web site (http://www.rurdev.usda.gov/rhs).

Help for Union Members

For information about the AFL-CIO's home-loan program for affiliated unions, contact your union or write to Union Privilege (1125 15th St., N.W., Suite 300, Washington, DC 20005). You may also log onto http://www.unionprivilege.org. or call 202-848-6466.

Help from the VA

In addition to eligible veterans of military service, members of the National Guard and military reservists with six or more years of service are also eligible for VA-guaranteed loans. Also, a direct loan program for Native American veterans buying on trust lands (reservations) is currently available.

Regional VA offices can provide you with information on eligibility requirements and other details. Look in the blue pages of the phone book under "U.S. Government" for the VA office that's nearest you. You can also call 800-827-1000 for more information, or visit the VA Web site at http://www.homeloans.va.gov. From the home page you can click on "Information on the Home Loan Program" and then on "Pamphlets on the VA Home Loan Program" to download VA pamphlet 26-4.

> **FHA lenders will qualify you using a set of debt-to-income ratios that are a bit more generous than those applied by mortgage lenders making conventional loans.**

rate on loans it insures, so you'll need to shop around for the best rate.

The FHA limits the amount it will insure to whichever is less: 95 percent of the local median home price or 87 percent of the loan limit set by Freddie Mac. An FHA-approved lender can determine the cap in your area.

FHA-mortgage insurance premiums usually will be collected in one lump sum at settlement. For single-family homes (what the agency calls Section 203(b) property) the premium is 1.75 percent of the loan amount for first-time homebuyers. You are allowed to increase the size of your mortgage to cover the cost. (Loans repaid at an early date may entitle you to a refund.)

FHA lenders will qualify you using a set of debt-to-income ratios that are a bit more generous than those applied by mortgage lenders making conventional loans. Family housing expenses should not exceed 29 percent of gross income, and total indebtedness should not go over 41 percent of income. Rules permit lenders to make exceptions where there are "significant compensating factors," such as a history of paying rent in excess of the mortgage amount and availability of cash reserves after closing. These factors are not set in black and white, so don't rule out a low-down-payment FHA loan without checking with more than one major lender in your area.

Other FHA-loan features include:

- **You're allowed to include most closing costs in the mortgage amount.** See Chapter 3 for information on how points and other loan-origination fees are handled for tax purposes.
- **FHA loans are assumable.** In most cases the FHA will require a credit check on the assuming homebuyer.
- **Loans carry no prepayment penalty.** You can make additional payments or pay off the loan at any time.
- **FHA loans are available from** FHA-approved lenders, including savings institutions, mortgage bankers, and commercial banks. Mortgage bankers, however, do the bulk of the business.

So-called direct-endorsement lenders can process your loan, which should reduce the time to loan approval. (You'll have to ask whether a lender is direct-endorsement—lenders won't tell you.) And, because appraisals are the bottleneck in loan approvals, you'll want to find out whether a direct-endorsement lender has an appraiser on staff.

VA-GUARANTEED LOANS. The Department of Veterans Affairs (VA) protects lenders against losses on mortgage loans made to eligible veterans by guaranteeing a portion of the loan in the event of foreclosure. VA-guaranteed loans are either fixed-rate or adjustable-rate loans with repayment periods of as long as 30 years and one month.

In most cases, no down payment is required by the VA. You'll have to fork over cash if you can't qualify for the monthly payments or if the cost of the property is more than the VA establishes as its "reasonable value."

The VA sets no limit on the size of mortgage it will guarantee, but Freddie Mac, Fannie Mae, and other investors in the secondary market do. As a rule, your entitlement (the guarantee amount) must be at least 25 percent of the loan amount. If you are also making a cash down payment, that amount plus the entitlement must equal 25 percent. The VA does have a maximum guarantee, however. In most states, it will guarantee no more than $89,912 on loans over $144,000. Using your full VA entitlement for a no-down-payment loan, the maximum you could borrow would be $359,650. In Hawaii and Alaska, the maximum guarantee is 25 percent of the loan amount up to $134,868, making the maximum VA home loan in those states $539,475.

You'll be responsible for the following closing costs: discount points, appraisal, credit report, survey, title search, recording fees, and VA funding fee. You should not be charged brokerage fees for your loan. On no-down-payment loans, the VA collects a funding fee equal to 2.15 percent of the loan at settlement. (This is reduced to 1.5 percent of the loan amount with a

> **The VA protects lenders against losses on mortgage loans made to eligible veterans by guaranteeing a portion of the loan in the event of foreclosure.**

If you are having trouble getting a loan, consider using a mortgage broker.

down payment of up to 10 percent and 1.25 percent with a down payment of 10 percent or more.) You will pay a higher funding fee if you are a reservist, if you borrow to refinance (interest-rate-reduction refinancing loans, or IRRRLs) or if you buy a manufactured home. A 3.3 percent fee is charged for subsequent use of the program. Certain disabled veterans may be exempt from paying.

You'll have to negotiate paying loan points with the seller (see Chapter 3 for a discussion of points).

VA loans can be paid off in full at any time without penalty. You can prepay the principal when you make your regular monthly payments as long as additional payments are $100 or more. (If you have an old mortgage and your monthly installment is less than $100, the prepayment must be at least as much as the payment.)

If you buy a new home that was appraised by the VA prior to construction and inspected along the way to ensure compliance, the property may be covered by the VA's structural-defect program. Builders of such homes must warrant that they were built according to the approved plans and specifications. A similar builder warranty may be provided on new manufactured (mobile or modular) homes (see Chapter 8 for information on builders' extended warranties and the VA/FHA structural-defect program).

See also the contact information in the VA listing in the box on page 175.

Mortgage Brokers

Mortgage brokers act as intermediaries. A broker keeps tabs on the mortgage market through ties to local, regional, and national lenders and can refer a prospective borrower to a mortgage banker, savings institution, commercial bank, or even an individual investor interested in buying mortgage paper. Brokers don't lend and can't approve loans or make loan commitments to borrowers.

If you are having trouble getting a loan, consider using a mortgage broker. You may pay a flat fee, or you may pay an additional point or so to the lender, who then pays the broker at settlement.

Credit Unions

Credit unions are a good source for loans. You must be a member, however, and membership is often based on some criterion of affinity, such as residency in a given city or state, employment, or membership in an association or club. Loans are generally available from the largest credit unions. If you are a credit union member or are eligible to become one, you may find the mortgage rates and terms it offers quite competitive.

Public Agencies

State and local housing-finance agencies make below-market-rate financing available to eligible low- and moderate-income first-time buyers through the sale of tax-exempt bonds.

Employers and Unions

Don't overlook your employer as a source of assistance. An employer may pay points, subsidize the interest rate, or even act as lender. Such programs are most commonly available to employees who have been asked to relocate from areas where home prices are modest to areas where they are sky-high.

Unions are another possibility. The AFL-CIO offers its affiliated unions "Union Privilege" benefits (see page 175). Among the benefits is a mortgage and real estate program that makes first-time home loans available to eligible members for as little as 3 percent down. Interest rates are at or below national averages. What's more, buyers who sign up for the program, use a participating real estate agent, and obtain a program mortgage may be eligible for a credit toward closing costs.

Certain parts of the program are open to parents and children of union members.

An employer may pay points, subsidize the interest rate, or even act as lender.

Other Types of Financing

Those borrowers who don't fit the mold designed by secondary-market mortgage buyers such as Fannie Mae, Freddie Mac, and Ginnie Mae can have a hard time buying a home. If you are self-

If you're self-employed, involved in a divorce, or otherwise unable to qualify for a mortgage, seller financing is one alternative.

employed, involved in a divorce, or otherwise unable to qualify for a mortgage originated by a bank, thrift, or mortgage company that will turn around and sell your loan to the secondary market, one alternative is to look for property being sold with seller financing. Another is to seek out a mortgage broker who will try to locate an investor to buy your note.

Obviously, the more a buyer has to pay in interest each month, the less house he can afford to buy. So when interest rates are high, many would-be purchasers can't qualify for long-term mortgages big enough to buy many homes listed for sale. As a result, sellers must step in to fill the gap between down payment and first mortgage. Sellers who take back below-market-rate notes in effect discount the prices of their homes.

When rates are low, sellers who own homes free and clear of debt are often willing (and in some instances, even eager) to finance purchases. In such cases, a seller is doing essentially the same thing as a commercial lender—carrying the entire note and securing it with a first mortgage or deed of trust. What's in it for sellers? When yields on certificates of deposits, money-market funds, and short-term bonds are so low, a seller may earn much more on a note secured by property—in this case, a former home. He may be able to get an above-market rate (more than the going long-term mortgage rates), enough to compensate for the added risk and complications of having documents drawn and executed. Where homes aren't selling promptly, one being offered with seller financing may pull more prospects—particularly those who can afford to buy but who are nevertheless outside institutional lending parameters for one reason or another.

First-Mortgage Financing

As a buyer, the appeal of this kind of financing lies in its flexibility. Assuming documents are properly and carefully drawn, you'll be in the same basic situation you would have been had you obtained a mortgage or deed of trust from an institutional lender.

MORE ON SELLER FINANCING

Owner Will Carry: How to Take Back a Note or Mortgage Without Being Taken, by Bill Broadbent and George Rosenberg (Creative Solutions Inc., 1380 Broad St., San Luis Obispo, CA 93401; 800-366-6037; http://www .arnettbroadbent.com/ownerwillcarry.html). Available for $39.95 (plus $4.40 shipping). A $7 discount is available if you mention *Buying and Selling a Home*. The book includes a CD-ROM program that will amortize a note with stepped payments and so reduces or eliminates a dangerous balloon payment. This book addresses take-back mortgages in detail from a seller's viewpoint. But it should reward anyone who intends to buy a home with seller financing and is willing to study and act on what the authors propose.

Because you are likely to be trading a higher price for favorable terms, be prepared for more lengthy negotiations. What rate you pay, how often and how much, prepayment and late-payment penalties, and whether the note carries a due-on-sale clause are all subject to bargaining. To protect your interests, you'll need your own representatives—a buyer's broker and lawyer—to assist you in negotiating and reviewing documents.

In their book, *Owner Will Carry* (see the box above), Bill Broadbent and George Rosenberg point to four areas, in addition to the interest rate and payment frequency, likely to require negotiation and compromise between buyer and seller:

DUE-ON-SALE PROVISION. This clause enables a lender to demand full payment of the remaining loan balance should you sell or transfer all or part of the property without her consent. You want a loan without a due-on-sale clause because your loan would be assumable. The seller (soon-to-be lender) will want to include this clause to protect her stake in the property.

Possible compromise: A due-on-sale provision that gives the seller/lender the right to approve a new

You want the seller to pay all closing costs. The seller wants you to pay them. Possible compromise: Split them equally.

buyer after checking character references, credit, and loan-paying ability.

BALLOON PAYMENT. Though payments on seller carryback loans are commonly structured to amortize principal and interest over 30 years, most are due in full—hence the name "balloon"—three to seven years after the sale. Because the seller/lender doesn't want her sale proceeds tied up too long, you should expect a balloon payment as part of the deal. Your concern should focus on your ability to refinance the loan when it comes due. Suppose rates are much higher at that time or your spouse is unemployed. Then what?

Possible compromise: Postpone the balloon payment as long as possible. The more time you have, the better your chances of refinancing at favorable terms and before the deadline. The loan balance will be lower, too. Try for ten years and negotiate a protective clause into the note giving you the right to extend the term for a specified period of time. You could suggest a two-year extension, for example, coupled with a higher rate, a bigger monthly payment, a one-time partial payment on the balloon, or even a combination of those.

LATE-PAYMENT CHARGE. The seller will want a penalty big enough and soon enough—say 6 percent of the payment amount if payment is not received within five to ten days—to discourage delinquency. You certainly don't consider yourself a deadbeat and you do not want the clause.

Possible compromise: Keep the seller's penalty at 6 percent but extend the time to a more reasonable 15 days.

CLOSING COSTS. You want the seller to pay all closing costs. The seller wants you to pay them.

Possible compromise: Split them equally. Even if that's not acceptable, suggest the 50/50 split as a starting point for further negotiations.

Seller financing isn't restricted to situations in which the owner has no mortgage debt. Seller carryback second mortgages and wraparound loans are options when there is an assumable mortgage on the property.

Carryback Second Mortgage

Here a note, secured by a second mortgage or trust deed, closes the gap between the price of the property and the combined amounts of the down payment and the balance due on an assumable first mortgage. The interest rate is negotiated between seller and buyer and may be more or less than the going rate on commercially originated second mortgages.

As Broadbent and Rosenberg make clear in their book, carryback financing can be a "win-win transaction for both buyer and seller." That's because a seller/lender may be able to earn a higher rate on a carryback note than he could earn elsewhere, and the buyer/borrower's overall cost of funds may be no more than if he got a loan from an institutional lender.

You will want to be sure the first mortgage you intend to assume is, indeed, assumable and what, if any, conditions or fees the first-mortgage lender or servicer may impose on you or the seller. You could be required to get approval by passing certain income and credit tests, for example. Failure to fulfill the requirements could cause the lender or servicer to call the loan using a due-on-sale provision in the mortgage.

Payments on seller carrybacks typically are figured as though the loan would be paid back over 25 or 30 years, but loans are due in full, in the form of a balloon payment, 3 to 10 years after the sale. This means you will have to refinance by that time.

Should a buyer default and foreclosure result, the seller/lender gets reimbursed after the first-mortgage holder's claim is satisfied. If a property ultimately sells for less than (or close to) the sales price it commanded when the carryback second note was placed on it, the seller/lender could lose money.

Carryback financing can be a "win-win transaction for both buyer and seller."

Protect your interests by requiring the seller to select a neutral collection agency where you can send your wrap payment.

Wraparound Mortgage

When there is an existing, legally assumable first mortgage on a property you want to buy using a down payment plus a seller carryback second mortgage (see above for discussion of carryback notes secured by second mortgages or trust deeds), you can expect a savvy seller or agent to start throwing around terms like "wrap" or "wraparound." The reason: Such financing may provide a better return to the seller. Wraps—like other forms of creative financing—typically carry balloon payments.

Instead of financing the second-trust or second-mortgage note, the seller may suggest carrying back what is called an "All-Inclusive Trust Deed" note for an amount equal to the assumable first mortgage plus equity. The rate you will be offered on the wrap will be less than what you would have paid for a carryback second and more than the rate on the assumable first. You'll be making one payment to the seller/lender covering the assumable first and the amount you'd otherwise be paying for the carryback second—at a blended rate. This puts more money in the seller's pocket and also earns her the benefit of principal reduction that is occurring as payments are made on the first. The blended rate plus the value of principal reduction on the assumable first boosts the seller's overall yield or return on the all-inclusive trust deed.

Wraps remove the seller/lender's concern that the buyer won't make payments on the assumable first loan because the buyer will now make just one payment—to the seller. The seller then makes the payment on the first loan. Broadbent and Rosenberg suggest that you, as buyer/borrower, protect your interests by requiring the seller to select a neutral collection agency where you can send your wrap payment. The agent then becomes responsible for making payments on the assumable first loan and disbursing remaining funds to the seller.

Land Contract

Also known as a conditional sales contract, contract for sale, or contract for deed, this type of financing is actually an installment sale whereby the buyer gets only the right to obtain absolute ownership to the property. The buyer doesn't get title to the property but must wait until some point agreed on in the contract—usually after a certain amount has been paid toward the principal or when the contract is fully paid. Often that's years down the road. In the interim, the seller retains what is known as "bare legal title."

Much can go wrong with land contracts. As part of the deal, the buyer may agree to take over payments on the seller's existing mortgage—an arrangement that a mortgage lender may contend violates the due-on-sale provision of its mortgage contract. Lenders may be able to foreclose on such mortgages, leaving the buyer/borrower with nothing to show for his payments except a worthless contract. Never sign a land contract before getting expert legal advice.

Equity Sharing

In a shared-equity arrangement, the homebuyer and an investor—frequently a parent, relative, or friend— buy a house or condo apartment together. It's one way for first-time buyers who otherwise couldn't afford to buy, or who wouldn't qualify for a mortgage, to do so. For example, rather than making a loan or gift to help a child into home ownership, parents become part owners and rent their share of the place to the child. As investors, the parents share in the appreciation of the house. As landlords, they also get rental income and the tax deductions that go along with rental real estate.

Both parties enter into a contract that specifies who pays what portion of the down payment, mortgage interest, property taxes, and monthly costs; how much rent the child will pay; and how equity will be split when the house is sold. Parents could make the down payment and pay most of the mortgage interest and taxes. Or equity could be split 50/50, with each party putting up half the down payment and agreeing to pay half of the ongoing expenses. The possibilities are limited only by the needs and desires of the contracting parties.

Equity could be split 50/50, with each party putting up half the down payment and agreeing to pay half of the ongoing expenses.

Homebuyers who can't manage the monthly payments with a traditional mortgage may be able to choose a 40-year loan with lower payments.

40-Year Mortgage

Homebuyers who can't manage the monthly payments with a traditional mortgage may be able to choose a 40-year loan with lower payments. Fannie Mae has been test-marketing the extralong loans through several credit unions nationwide. For buyers on the margin, adding an extra decade to a conventional 30-year mortgage can mean the difference between affordable and out of reach. But the savings are minimal.

Buyers pay a higher rate to stretch payments. A $200,000, 40-year loan at 6 percent will save just $64 per month compared with a 30-year fixed-rate loan at 5.73 percent. And the longer loan will cost an additional $109,000 in interest over the life of the loan.

In addition to the higher interest rate, another significant disadvantage is that home equity increases at a very slow rate. A homeowner may have little or no equity if he or she moves soon after buying the house.

Another option for homebuyers who want to hold down monthly payments is to obtain a loan that's paid off at a 40-year rate until a balloon payment comes due, say in five years. With a lower rate of 4.5 percent, the payment would be $899 a month on a $200,000 loan, about $200 less than the full-term 40-year mortgage. Unfortunately, buyers can't predict what rates will be when they have to refinance. And they still have the problem of having little or no equity if they move soon after buying the house.

Interest-Only Loans

Interest-only mortgages allow the homebuyer to pay only interest on the mortgage in monthly payments for a defined period of time. At the end of the interest-only term, usually five to seven years, the payments rise substantially. At that point, most homeowners must choose from three options—start paying off the principal by making those bigger payments; refinance; or pay the balance in a lump sum.

Interest-only mortgages were originally marketed to affluent buyers, and might be appropriate for sophisticated investors who will invest the mortgage savings and earn returns that exceed the rate of home appreciation. They might also be appropriate for buyers who expect their incomes to be much higher in a few years. And they might make sense for people who work on commission or receive large annual bonuses who will make the interest-only payments but can pay above and beyond the amount due when they get their commission or bonus checks since there is typically no prepayment penalty on interest-only loans.

But financial advisers frown on these loans for the typical consumer, even though they are now available in amounts under $200,000. A buyer runs the risks that the house will lose value, that their incomes will not increase enough to cover the increased mortgage payments once they have to start paying principal, or that they will run into financial difficulty if their earnings decrease due to unforeseen circumstances, such as a period of unemployment. They then risk foreclosure or being forced to sell the home.

Using a Reporting Service

Reporting services provide details on a variety of mortgages, including conventional, FHA, and VA loans. Some may include rates on second mortgages and other types of loans as well. You should be able to get a handle on the types of loans being offered (adjustable-rate and fixed-rate, for example), loan life spans, interest rates, points, and length of time the lender will guarantee the rate you're offered at application time. For adjustable-rate mortgages, look for information on the index base, adjustment margin, and periodic and lifetime caps.

Reports are updated on a regular basis, often weekly, and you should be able to buy just one or two. Many metropolitan newspapers publish abbreviated lists in weekly business or real estate sections.

Mortgage information is now readily available online. You can access daily and weekly rate quotes for mortgages and home equity loans, the qualifications for special Fannie Mae programs, estimates of closing

Mortgage information is now readily available online.

Rate quotes are usually guaranteed for a set period; some aren't guaranteed at all.

costs, an analysis of different mortgages, programs available for veterans and active-duty military personnel, as well as many other helpful bits of information.

See the listing on page 174 for more information.

Fine-Tuning Your Choice

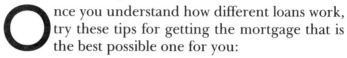nce you understand how different loans work, try these tips for getting the mortgage that is the best possible one for you:

Use reports and other loan sources to identify the best loan prospects. Discuss details with promising lenders over the phone or in person before making a final selection. Make sure advertised loans and rates are available.

Use the annual percentage rate (APR) to compare loans. The APR is the cost of your mortgage loan expressed as a yearly rate. It reflects the effect of origination fees, points, and (if applicable) mortgage insurance by adding them to the loan rate as though they were spread out over the term of the loan. Lenders often promote a particular mortgage loan by advertising the interest rate or the monthly payment. By law, they also must divulge the APR.

Find out how long an advertised or stated loan rate will stick. In other words, if you applied for a loan today at an advertised rate, could the lender raise it tomorrow? At the end of 30 days? Would it be available at settlement 45 days or 60 days hence? Rate quotes are usually guaranteed for a particular period; some are not guaranteed at all, giving the lender the right to charge you the current market rate on settlement day. If the rate at closing is much higher, you conceivably could be shocked with "disqualification" at the 11th hour.

When rates could be upwardly mobile, lock in the rate you want by paying a loan-commitment fee. A lock-in guarantees you the rate quoted at the time of application for the lock-in period. The charge for this service varies, depending on market conditions. In times of moderate interest rates, the range can be from no charge for 60-day lock-ins to 0.5 percent of the loan amount for 90 days and 1 percent for 120 days. If rates are expected to go up significantly, banks would probably reinstate a charge for the 60-day lock-in.

> ### MORE ABOUT "LOCK-INS"
>
> A useful brochure, *A Consumer's Guide to Mortgage Lock-Ins,* prepared by the Federal Reserve Board and the Office of Thrift Supervision, is available free from your lender. You can also read it online at http://www .hsh.com/pamphlets/lockins.html.

The Loan-Application Process

You've found the mortgage you want and you're ready for the next step: loan application. The process costs money. Lenders levy the fee to cover the costs of running credit reports, filling out mortgage-insurance applications, having appraisals conducted, and the like. Some lenders will charge you a flat fee, anywhere from $100 to $400, while others will charge separately for the different services required. These fees are usually nonrefundable. For budgetary reasons alone, you'll want to avoid multiple applications. But if you feel shaky about the prospects of approval, or want to play one lender against the other for the best rate, you may be tempted to apply to more than one. Don't do it. A lender will almost certainly discover that you've applied elsewhere. After all, you just gave the company the right to examine your credit history—including the names and dates of all recent credit-check inquiries. If you applied elsewhere or have been turned down, it will show up on the computer screen. You may be able to rescind a contract you signed, but using that right to obtain the lowest rate isn't kosher, and you won't get back nonrefundable fees. Worse, you could get turned down everywhere else as a result.

Here's what you can expect:

You will need raw material, and lots of it, for the application: income and balance-sheet figures and evi-

Be prepared to give contact information for someone who can verify financial information about you— most likely, your employer's human resources office.

dence, copies of past income-tax returns, and the title to your car (to prove it is either free of liens or not encumbered by a loan). Take with you the paperwork you pulled together during the preapproval process. Much of the information should be applicable.

Be prepared to give contact information for someone who can verify financial information about you—most likely, your employer's human resources office. If you have substantial nonsalary income from investments, you'll be asked to substantiate this through an accountant, stockbroker, trust officer, or similar source. If you are self-employed (a definition that could be triggered by as little as a 5 percent to 10 percent ownership stake in a closely held company you work for), you may be asked to submit financial information about the company.

Application forms are usually filled out during the interview or over the phone, with the help of a loan officer, but you could also fill them out at home and return them, or fill them out online at the lender's Web site.

For conventional loans carrying private mortgage insurance (PMI), check with your lender regarding the necessary documentation.

In addition to the application fee, you may be asked to pay a "loan origination fee" or "prepaid point"—typically 1 percent of the loan amount—when you apply, before approval is made. This is just another way of charging you prepaid interest—the points you may have to pay at settlement. Remember that the more points you pay up front, the lower the rate should be on the loan.

Find out what will happen to your origination fee if the lender decides not to approve your loan. Will the 1 percent origination fee be refunded? Get the answer in writing before you pay.

Check whether the quoted interest rate is guaranteed, and for how long. If you think that interest rates may risc while your application is being processed, consider paying for a "lock-in" (see the box on page 189).

The federal Real Estate Settlement Procedures Act (RESPA) requires a lender to provide you with a "good-faith" estimate of closing costs once you complete a loan application or within three business days. The RESPA statement reflects the lender's experience in the area where your property is located. The estimate must include costs for such items as points, an appraisal, title search, title insurance, survey, recording of deeds and mortgages, and attorney's fees. You can ask for a hypothetical calculation of such items as property taxes and hazard insurance, based on your anticipated closing date (see discussion of settlement costs in Chapter 12).

Private Mortgage Insurance

Lenders usually require buyers getting conventional loans with down payments of less than 20 percent to carry insurance provided by a separate private mortgage insurance company. The insurance is designed to protect lenders from losses in the event borrowers stop paying on their loans; premiums typically are paid by homebuyers.

Insured, low-down-payment mortgages are more attractive—and less risky—investments than uninsured ones, and lenders who wish to sell low-down-payment loans must have them insured. VA-guaranteed and FHA-insured loans also protect lenders against borrower default.

Private mortgage insurance generally covers 25 percent to 30 percent of a first-mortgage loan. This permits lenders to make loans up to 95 percent or 97 percent of the appraised value of a home while taking about as much risk as they would assume making a loan of 63 percent to 72 percent of value. A loan-to-value ratio (LTV or LV) expresses the relationship between the amount of a loan and the value of property being pledged as security. For example, on a $200,000, 90 percent LTV-ratio loan for 30 years at a fixed rate,

Buyers getting conventional loans with down payments of less than 20 percent usually carry private mortgage insurance.

By law, lenders must cancel PMI automatically when your equity reaches 22 percent (based on regularly scheduled monthly payments).

the borrower making a 10 percent down payment assumes the first $20,000 risk of any loss in property value. The insurer takes 25 percent on the remaining $180,000, or $45,000. The lender then is left holding the bag only for losses beyond $65,000. In other words, the down payment plus insurance together reduces the lender's loan-to-value ratio on the property from 90 percent to 67.5 percent.

Insurance premiums vary from company to company and according to the type of loan being insured. Coverage is available for both conventional adjustable-rate and fixed-rate mortgages. First-year premiums may range from 0.38 percent to 1.04 percent of the mortgage amount, depending on, among other things, the loan amount and type and the size of the down payment. After that, premiums will either stay the same or gradually decline in proportion to your mortgage balance.

You'll be expected to pay one or more monthly premiums, or the entire premium, in advance on the day of settlement. Some lenders are now including the cost of private insurance directly in the interest rate you're charged. If your lender offers this service, make sure you know the cost of the insurance and requirements for cancellation.

What does this mean for you? Before you take out a mortgage, find out what private mortgage insurance requirements there are and what circumstances in the future would warrant cancellation of the policy. By law, lenders must cancel PMI automatically when your equity reaches 22 percent (based on regularly scheduled monthly payments). However, the lender may still demand that you pay for an appraisal, roughly $250 to $300, to verify that the home's value hasn't declined since you took out the loan. In addition, the lender may also reject your request if you've had a payment past due during the 12 months before you became eligible to drop PMI, or 60 days late during the preceding 24 months. Lenders must also send their current customers annual notices of their cancellation rights.

MORE ON MORTGAGE INSURANCE

For more information on FHA mortgage insurance, you can obtain a free brochure, *Guide to Single Family Home Mortgage Insurance,* by writing to the Federal Consumer Information Center, P.O. Box 100, Pueblo, CO 81002. You can also view or order this and other housing publications online at http://www.pueblo.gsa.gov.

Some lenders require private mortgage insurance coverage of second mortgages. If it is required, your lender will make the arrangements.

If Fannie Mae or Freddie Mac purchased your mortgage, you have a good chance of dropping PMI. Both say that lenders must agree to drop the insurance if a new appraisal shows that you now have 20 percent equity and have paid your mortgage on time for 12 months. Freddie Mac will also usually require that you've had the loan from two to five years. If your case is based on increased market value, be prepared to pay $250 to $300 to an appraiser selected by the mortgage servicer.

If you took out an FHA mortgage and put less than 5 percent down, you must ask the lender to drop the mortgage insurance. With 5 percent down, the insurance automatically expires after 12 years; with 10 percent down, it will cease after seven years.

If your lender has a "no-cancellation" policy, request that they consider your case as an exception. If you get no satisfaction, you have the option to refinance and find a lender with a more acceptable policy.

Credit Life Insurance— Something You Can Do Without

Your lender may try to talk you into buying credit life insurance that would pay off the mortgage in the event of your death. Even if your lender doesn't offer it, you may be deluged with

There are better and cheaper ways to provide protection for your family than mortgage life insurance.

mortgage life insurance solicitations after you buy your home.

Mortgage life insurance is usually decreasing-term insurance, in which the premium stays the same but the amount of coverage declines each year, in step with the declining balance owed on your mortgage. It is often promoted as valuable protection for your family, to keep them from losing the house if you die.

Mortgage life insurance does this, but there are better and cheaper ways to provide the same protection. One problem with mortgage life insurance is that the beneficiary is the mortgage lender, not someone you designate. Perhaps your spouse, for example, needn't and shouldn't pay off the balance on the mortgage, because the interest rate on it is much lower than the then-prevailing rate and there is sufficient income to keep making the payments. Since mortgage life insurance automatically pays off the lender, your spouse won't have a choice about how to use the insurance money. He or she would own the house free and clear but may have to refinance, possibly at a higher interest rate, to tap the equity for some worthwhile purpose, like college expenses.

Undeniably, any new homeowner with a family to protect should boost his or her life insurance coverage, so that the insurance proceeds—if invested conservatively—would yield enough income to continue paying the mortgage and other basic expenses of living. For a young person, annually renewable term life insurance offers the most coverage for the lowest current cost, even though the premiums will rise each year. Before buying mortgage life insurance, shop for the best deal in term coverage.

The Wait and the Tension

From the time you submit your completed loan application—and appraisal and credit reports are received—you might have to wait from seven to ten days for approval. In some cases, you can obtain approval within 24 hours. If you are turned down, you must be told why.

When homes are selling briskly, the time between a loan application and loan approval may gradually increase. Appraisers and credit bureaus get swamped.

Make sure you haven't been forgotten or put on a back burner. During the process, remind the loan officer of your settlement date and check on how everything is going.

Buyers with impeccable credit records who are able to make hefty down payments may be able to locate a "no-doc" loan through a mortgage broker. Because you do not have to provide the extensive income verification and credit documentation usually required to obtain a mortgage loan, the time to closing may be shorter. However, you can expect to pay extra points and fees and possibly a higher interest rate for the convenience.

You should have assessed how long the application process would take and proposed a suitably distant date back when you submitted your purchase contract. If it now appears you miscalculated, ask the seller for a new, later settlement date and explain that processing delays beyond your control have made it necessary. Most sellers will agree to a good-faith postponement of settlement, and this kind of delay is generally not grounds for voiding a contract.

During the wait between application and approval, the settlement clock is ticking and you are at the lender's mercy. When interest rates are falling, though, you may have some leverage. If rates have come down since you applied, remind the loan officer that he or she could lose your business by delaying settlement. If delays force you to reschedule the settlement, you might be inclined to reshop the mortgage and shift to another lender who can offer a new, lower rate or assure you of faster approval. If this is a real possibility (or a persuasive bluff), make sure your loan officer knows you're considering it; it could speed things up.

You might have to wait from seven to ten days for approval. In some cases, you can obtain approval within 24 hours. If you are turned down, you must be told why.

Get a Good Title

f you build a new house and it burns to the ground, you'll still own the land, even if you failed to cover the house with insurance. But if you buy a home with a faulty title—perhaps due to fraud, forgery, conflict between long-ago heirs, unpaid liens from contractors, or just a title-search error—you could lose everything. Is it likely? According to industry experts, despite the best efforts of observant escrow-closing officers and title searchers-examiners, title scams are a continuing problem, accounting for about 20 percent of annual losses at one title insurance company.

When your lender requires title insurance on the home you intend to buy, it is not for your benefit. Lender coverage assures the institution that it has a valid first lien and that it will be protected against title hazards that aren't listed as exceptions in the policy. Lender's title insurance is issued in the amount of the mortgage and decreases as the mortgage is paid off. It leaves your equity unprotected.

When you take title to your home, you want assurance of secure ownership and marketable title now and in the future, if you wish to sell or pass the property along to someone else. Unfortunately, the title being conveyed to you—essentially the seller's right to own, possess, use, control, and dispose of the property—may not be all it seems. Rights conveyed to you in a properly executed and recorded deed may be seriously compromised. That's why you'll want the protection of owner's title insurance, regardless of the customary closing practices in the state where you're buying. If providing you with an owner's title isn't customary and automatic through the seller, make your purchase offer

If a title problem threatens to delay settlement, let your lender know how much time may be necessary to clear the title.

contingent on being able to obtain such insurance, even if you have to buy it yourself.

How the Process Works

You should also request a title insurance interim binder to be issued before closing. An interim binder is a preliminary commitment to insure and is based on a search and examination of the public records. It gives a description of the property and shows such things as the owner, title defects, liens, or encumbrances of record.

Following examination of the title evidence, the company will normally insure the title. If problems are discovered, the company may still agree to insure the title if certain conditions have been met by the closing date. Alternatively, it could make the insurance coverage subject to specified exceptions.

Basically, an interim binder gives you the chance to decide whether you want the seller to take remedial action or whether problems disclosed in the search and examination merit canceling the purchase. If problems show up after the binder is issued, the title company may be liable, depending on the policy's provisions.

Title examination takes place before your purchase is completed, usually while your mortgage loan application is being processed. Lawyers or other title specialists—who may be selected by you—handle the work.

If title problems turn up, they should be cleared up before you complete your purchase. Otherwise you may be burdened with claims and loss of equity. Clearing a title can require the release of a debt lien or use of a quitclaim deed (see page 205). If the snag is the result of record-keeping neglect, such as the failure to show a paid-up second mortgage as satisfied in the record, the task may be simple. But problems such as contested wills can be nightmares. You could even be faced with trying to void your contract. If it comes to that, don't try canceling without skilled legal advice.

Insist on being kept informed and on understanding each step in the title-protection process.

If a title problem threatens to delay settlement, let your lender know how much time may be necessary to clear the title. Loan commitments often expire after 30 or 45 days, sometimes earlier. If you don't get a commitment extension in writing, you could lose your loan, or at least the interest rate you were promised.

Hazards of a Clouded Title

There are circumstances, such as assuming an old loan or using seller financing, that may tempt you to save money by foregoing a title search and new owner's title insurance. The savings aren't worth the risk. Regardless of how great a deal you've found or the customs of the region, you should obtain an owner's title insurance policy.

The wisdom of buying title insurance boils down to this: You need the protection. Title problems are numerous and varied, and they're on the increase. Some possibilities:

You are buying a house from a supposedly single man or woman. The title search reveals two names on the ownership record and describes them as married: "John and Jane Clark, husband and wife."

You are buying from a middle-aged brother and sister from out of town. They are selling you a home their parents bought for their retirement. The father died several years ago and the widowed mother passed away just recently. A title search reveals that the property is in her name, but there is no will on file to direct what she wanted done with it.

You are buying from a couple who borrowed $20,000 seven years ago to add a room to their house. They have long since paid back the loan but have forgotten that her parents recorded it as a second mortgage when they made the loan. A title search shows the second mortgage but no evidence of its having been paid.

> **The wisdom of buying title insurance boils down to this: You need the protection.**

You are buying a house to which the owner added central air-conditioning two years ago. He had a fight with the air-conditioning contractor over some damage to a ceiling that occurred during installation. When the contractor refused to correct the damage, the seller refused to pay the final installment on his contract. The contractor filed a mechanic's lien on the property, and it has never been removed.

You are buying a property that is beautifully landscaped. A title search shows that the landscaper has a lien on the property. The seller explains that several of the trees died and when the landscaper refused to replace them, the seller refused to make final payment.

You are buying a house at a great bargain from a man who is in trouble with the Internal Revenue Service, which has placed a lien on the property.

You are buying a house from an aged widow. She and her husband bought the property many years ago, and

---

AVOIDING SURPRISES

Never take title to a property—not even as a gift—without full knowledge of its legal and financial condition. Common problem areas include:

Unpaid taxes. Make sure there are no unpaid property taxes from prior years. The title policy or interim binder should note any pro rata portion of taxes unpaid in the current year.

Restrictions. Restrictive covenants or easements tell you where and what you can and can't build. The title company may be responsible for damages caused by restrictions it failed to list in the interim binder.

If a listed easement, such as a utility right-of-way, concerns you, get legal advice before closing.

Community standards. Within the private restrictive covenants section, the title policy should certify that structures comply with existing community standards. Then you'll be protected if, for instance, the previous owner built the deck two feet too close to the road and your neighborhood association demands you dismantle it.

Encroachments. Be sure the policy affirms that nothing on your property encroaches on your neighbor's property, and vice versa.

when he died last year, she thought she was the sole owner. Now a title search reveals that the deed by which she and her husband acquired title was defective. The deed says only "Horace and Henrietta Jenkins." It should have shown their relationship and the manner in which they intended to take title.

You are buying a house that has a newly paved driveway. Your seller is proud of having improved the value of his property by converting his joint driveway into a private driveway. He bought his neighbor's half in a friendly deal last year when the neighbor built a new driveway on the opposite side of his house. There is just one problem: The expanded driveway doesn't appear in the public records.

The paving, sidewalks, and gutters in front of the house you have under contract are all new. A title search shows that your seller has not paid the city's special assessment for the improvements.

You plan to build a garage on the west end of your lot as soon as you move in. A title search reveals an easement of eight feet over the length of your future yard, extending across the garage site. The gas company owns the easement, which was granted by the development company that built your house.

You are planning to get away from it all by building a house on a piece of land 50 miles from town. A title search reveals that your property was carved out of a large farm that was never legally subdivided. The land description was one of those down-home "from the apple tree to the stone marker" jobs. That sort of inadequate land description and the resulting defective deed occurs in the city, too, when neighbors get together and swap bits of land. Sometimes an owner with an oversize yard sells a rear 20 feet to a neighbor with a short yard. Or neighbors buy a vacant lot between them and split it. They erect a fence along the newly created lot line and consider the job finished,

Inadequate land description and the resulting defective deed occurs in the city, too, when neighbors get together and swap bits of land.

Title insurance companies are regulated by state law, but in most states, rates vary enough to make shopping around worthwhile.

never thinking to get a survey and a proper deed for their new half lot and have it recorded.

Sometimes it is the owner's financial manipulations in a business that cloud the title. In the case of a bankruptcy or an unincorporated business or partnership, the owner's personal residence may be attached to satisfy part of his business debt. Another business owner may not be in trouble, just expanding, and has pledged his personal residence—the one you're about to buy—as part of the security required to obtain a business loan. Until that lien is paid or he arranges with his creditor to substitute other property as security, he can't deliver a clear title to you.

Less Than Best

By the time you close you should feel sure that the title you're getting is what you expected and what it's represented to be. You could encounter the following methods, other than title insurance, for assuring that a title is good. Neither, however, carries the full protection of title insurance.

Abstract Plus a Lawyer's Opinion

Title is usually in the form of an abstract, which is a historical summary of everything found in a search of public records that affects ownership of the property. It includes not only the chain of ownership, but any recorded easements, mortgages, wills, tax liens, judgments, pending lawsuits, marriages, and anything else that affects the title. When a property is sold, a lawyer examines the abstract, and gives a written opinion as to the title—including who the owner of record is and her judgment on whether anyone else has any right to or interest in the property. The opinion is often known as the certificate of title.

Lawyer's Record Search and Opinion

The lawyer searches through the public records and issues her certificate of title.

Buying Title Insurance

Regardless of customary title assurance practices in your state, you can buy title insurance for a one-time fee. (Iowa has a state title guaranty fund, but private title insurance is available to residents through insurance companies located outside the state.)

You pay for title insurance at settlement. Title insurance companies are regulated by state law, but in most states, rates vary enough to make shopping around worthwhile. An owner's policy could cost about $3.50 per $1,000 of home value; lender protection about $2.50 per $1,000 of the loan amount.

When you're checking the fees charged by different firms, find out exactly what is covered in each case. In some areas of the country, companies routinely quote a single fee that includes the costs of handling the closing as well as the search, title report, and insurance-risk premium. In others, the quote may include only the report and risk premium, and in a few states, only the premium.

The easiest way to get coverage is to piggyback on your lender's coverage. As mentioned, the lender will generally require mortgagee (lender's) title insurance to protect its interest in the property and improve the mortgage's marketability.

The face amount on the lender's policy is the amount of the loan and will decline gradually as the debt is paid off. The lender's policy does not protect you. To protect yourself, you must request and pay for an owner's policy. (In some localities, the seller customarily provides owner's title insurance for the buyer.) While you may be able to buy owner coverage at some later time, it's easier and cheaper to buy both the lender's and the owner's title insurance at once.

Your owner's policy is for the purchase price and will continue to protect you and your heirs after you sell. Your policy is the title insurance company's contract with you to make good any covered loss caused by a defect in the title or by any lien or encumbrance that was recorded in the public records and was not revealed to you when the policy was issued. It doesn't

The lender's title insurance policy does not protect you. You must request and pay for an owner's policy.

Be sure you understand what kind of deed you will receive from the seller and what rights will be conveyed to you.

cover title defects you cause while you own the property. The title company also will identify title problems and pay for a legal defense against an attack on the title, in whatever manner is provided for in its policy. The company has a number of options for handling valid claims: It can pay, negotiate an acceptable settlement, or appeal the claim in court.

Ordinarily, you can expect an owner's policy to cover you against such things as loss or damage from forgery, failure to comply with the law, impersonation, acts of minors, marital status, and competency questions. Policies are sometimes amended by adding special endorsements or by removing exclusions. For example, the insurer may include a rider that will increase the face amount on the contract as your home appreciates.

Nearly all title policies follow the same standard format, regardless of the issuing company. Take time to read yours, and if possible have someone knowledgeable go over the details with you before closing. Pay close attention to what it covers and to the exceptions and exclusions.

Title Documents You May See at Closing

You'll be wading through a dizzying number of legal papers at closing, and you'll find yourself signing your name over and over again, sometimes on several copies of the same document. Obviously, that's not the most auspicious time to be asking dozens of questions about deeds, titles, and insurance protection—or for getting good answers. The time for that is before making a purchase offer. Get information and answers as you proceed. Here's a brief rundown on some of the common documents relating to title transfer.

Warranty Deed
This document officially transfers title to the buyer. The seller, not the buyer, signs it and thereby agrees to pro-

> ## ONE WAY TO SAVE
>
> One way to save money and still get full title protection is to get a reissue rate. If the seller has owner's title insurance, find out whether the company offers a reissue rate. You may get a break even when a company reissues insurance on a title policy made as long as ten years ago. In some cases a reissue rate may be obtained from a company other than the original issuer.

tect the buyer against losing the property because of claims against it. When the deed is recorded at the local courthouse, the buyer usually keeps the original deed.

In some states a different type of deed, such as a bargain and sale deed, security deed, grant deed, or special warranty deed, is used in lieu of a general warranty deed to transfer title. Be sure you understand what kind of deed you will receive from the seller and what rights will be conveyed to you.

Quitclaim Deed

This is a device often used to deal with title problems. Anyone with a potential claim against the property can sign it, thereby releasing rights he or she might have had, although this alone isn't enough to ensure a clear title for the new owner.

Mortgage Deed or Deed of Trust

The basic purpose of either document is to secure the loan. When a debt is secured by a mortgage, the borrower signs a document that gives the lender a lien on the property.

Owner's Affidavit

The seller swears in this document that there are no unpaid liens, assessments, or other encumbrances against the property. The affidavit protects the purchaser, lender, and title company. If the seller is lying, he or she can be sued for damages by the buyer, the lender, or the title company.

Purchaser's Affidavit

Sometimes the buyer is required by the lender to swear that there are no existing or pending suits, judgments, or liens against him or her. If the buyer is lying, that is sufficient grounds for foreclosure.

Get Ready for Settlement

There is no way to guarantee a smooth path from a ratified contract to the settlement table, but doing your part is at least half the job. Major steps at this stage are finding the right loan and getting the application under way.

Expect minor problems and delays along the way. On the seller's side, title problems are a common cause of postponed settlements. On your side, bureaucratic snags such as extensive credit checks and slow appraisals can bog things down. In many cases, there isn't much you or the seller can do but wait.

Should you run into problems—say, a delay in mortgage approval that prevents you from being ready to go to settlement—contact the seller immediately and work out an extension. You shouldn't be penalized if the problem is one you couldn't have anticipated. At this point, neither party is likely to be looking for a way out.

While you're waiting for completion of all the processes now in motion, you should:

- **Review the lender's commitment letter.** Note any conditions of the loan offer that are stated in the lender's commitment letter. Make sure all conditions are met before closing.
- **Decide how you want to take title to the house.**
- **Apply for homeowners insurance on your new home.**
- **Get an exact accounting of settlement costs,** and make sure the money and necessary documents will be there at closing.
- **Select a date for the walk-through of the house.** You may wish to have a walk-through two weeks or so

Before you can take title to your new home, you'll have to decide what form of ownership you want.

before you intend to close if you expect work will need to be done by the owner. Then a final inspection can be made just prior to settlement.

■ **Contact the utility companies** about establishing service in your name. Arrange for electricity, gas, oil, and water to be turned on in your name on the day of settlement so that there will be no interruption in service. Make these arrangements a few weeks in advance, because utility companies may require deposits, credit checks, and advance notice.

■ **Review the adequacy of your disability and life insurance policies.**

How to Take Title

Before you can take title to your new home, you will have to decide what form of ownership is desirable.

If you're single, you'll probably buy the house in your name alone.

Husbands and wives generally own their property through joint ownership, in one of two forms, either joint tenancy with the right of survivorship or tenancy by the entirety.

Under either form of joint tenancy, when one spouse dies, the other becomes sole owner of the property. This happens automatically, bypassing probate, avoiding delays, and usually trimming the costs of settling the estate. For federal-tax purposes, half the value of all property owned by a married couple as joint tenants is included in the estate of the first spouse to die.

The two kinds of joint ownership differ in some respects, and many states don't recognize tenancies by the entirety. Get advice from your lawyer. If you are living in a community-property state (Arizona, California, Idaho, Louisiana, Nevada, New Mexico, Texas, Washington, or Wisconsin), state regulations may affect the availability and treatment of certain joint ownership arrangements.

The advice of a good trusts-and-estates lawyer is particularly important if you are a member of a step-family or are wealthy. For example, a couple whose total wealth exceeded $3 million in 2005 and who died more or less simultaneously would have spared their heirs federal estate taxes if their property had been divided equally between them so that each spouse's estate got the benefit of the $1.5 million starting point for taxation. (Note that the estate tax exemption will increase gradually until 2010, when the estate tax will be repealed. The tax may be reinstated in some form in 2011.)

To save on estate taxes someday, you may want to put the new home in the name of one or the other spouse alone. But your lender may not want the house owned by one spouse exclusively if all or most of the earnings to pay the mortgage will be derived from the other spouse.

And consider this: Titling the house in only one spouse's name could affect the division of property in case of a divorce.

If you are buying with a partner who is not your legal spouse, you can choose among the forms of ownership discussed below. Consult your lawyer on which is most suited to your needs.

Tenancy in Common

Each owner has separate legal title to an undivided interest in the whole property, and each one is allowed to independently sell, mortgage, or give away his or her interest.

It's wise for two single owners to have a written agreement setting out each individual's rights to deal with his or her legal interest in the property. The agreement also should specify the percentage of ownership interest each person has in the property, particularly if they have not contributed equal amounts. When one of the owners dies, the other does not automatically get the deceased's share unless that person specifically made such an arrangement in his or her will. If the will doesn't cover this, or if an owner dies without a will, state law determines who gets the deceased owner's share.

An agreement between two single owners should specify the percentage of ownership each person has in the property.

Joint Tenancy

Under this arrangement, each person has an equal interest in the property regardless of the amount contributed at purchase. If one owner dies, that person's share passes automatically to the other without going through probate.

Form a Legal Partnership

The best strategy for unrelated individuals to buy a home may be in a limited partnership, in which the partnership, not the individuals, takes the title. If a partner dies, the heirs would acquire the interest in the partnership; other partners could be among the heirs if the deceased willed it so. A partnership also avoids problems if one person goes into bankruptcy or has other legal difficulties that could cloud the title, because the partnership is separate from any legal entanglements of individual partners.

If you choose to set up a limited partnership, consult a lawyer experienced in partnerships who can help you draw up the agreements. The points to address include:

■ **How ownership will be divided,** which in turn determines who pays how much of the down payment, monthly payment, maintenance, and repairs. The contract should also describe how any profits or losses from rent or sale of the place will be divided and how tax benefits will be distributed.

■ **How use of the house's space is to be divided.**

■ **Which constitutes a deciding vote** and under what circumstances such a vote is considered necessary.

■ **Which owner will act as managing partner** and thus be responsible for signing checks and paying expenses.

■ **How much advance notice a withdrawing partner must give** and how the buyout price will be set.

Insurance on Your New Home

You'll be required to take out a homeowners insurance policy, something you should do anyway. The lender wants to cover the amount of its mortgage loan so it could recover the money in the event of a total loss; you want full-value coverage, perhaps enhanced by an inflation-adjustment mechanism that keeps the coverage rising with home values. You may also want other special protections.

HO What?

The term *homeowners insurance* is to some extent a misnomer: Standard policies cover much of what you own, give you personal liability protection, and protect you from credit card losses and even medical bills.

There are several types of homeowners policies that differ in the number of perils they cover and the degree of protection they offer. The most popular type is HO-3, often called "special form." But the best policies are usually called "deluxe" or "executive" policies. In insurance lingo, they're HO-5, embellished HO-3, or HO-3 with HO-15. These policies typically have higher coverage limits for contents and include sewer- and drain-backup coverage. They cost about 15 percent more than HO-3 policies, and they're not available everywhere, but go for the extra protection if you can get it.

If you are buying a condominium, you will use an HO-6 form; and unique older houses may be insured with a special HO-8 policy, available in some states.

All of these policies exclude floods, earthquakes, war, and nuclear contamination. Policies may differ by company and according to state requirements.

Property and Liability

A typical homeowners HO-3 policy combines two basic types of insurance with some additional coverage:

PROPERTY PROTECTION. This part of the policy reimburses you for losses or damages to the house and its contents. The amount of insurance coverage is based on the anticipated cost of replacing the entire structure, with coverage on personal property usually figured as the cash value at the time of loss. There are set monetary limits for specific classes of objects. They range from $200 for currency, to $1,000 for jewelry,

Standard policies cover much of what you own, give you personal liability protection, and protect you from credit card losses and medical bills.

> ### FAIR ACCESS
>
> If you discover that the home you want can't be insured through the regular insurance market (say, if your home is in an area that is especially vulnerable to losses due to fire, windstorm, vandalism, or civil unrest), you may be able to buy basic coverage under the **Fair Access to Insurance Requirements (FAIR)** plan. FAIR is in effect in 35 states and the District of Columbia. For information, contact your state insurance department, the Insurance Information Institute (110 William St., New York, NY 10038; 212-346-5500; http://www.iii.org), or the National Insurance Consumer Helpline (800-942-4242).

furs, and manuscripts, to $2,500 for silverware. Recently, however, major insurance companies have started to withdraw the option of reimbursing clients for the amount it would take to replace possessions and are instead reimbursing them for lesser dollar amounts.

LIABILITY INSURANCE. This protects you against personal liability, medical payments for injuries to others, and damage to other people's property. It typically applies to you and any other family members living in the house.

Insurance experts recommend at least $300,000 of liability coverage (although most people buy $100,000 coverage), which is paid to others for injury or damage that you or a family member might have caused, or for an accident that occurs around your home. You'd be covered, for example, if the mailman trips on the porch steps. If someone is injured at your home, medical-payments coverage typically pays at least $500 of the injured person's bills. Injuries caused by a family member who is away from the home may also be covered. And the injury needn't have been your fault for the coverage to apply. You'd also be covered for legal defense if needed.

Extended personal liability or umbrella insurance may be worth considering. It dramatically increases your personal-liability coverage at comparatively little cost and extends your coverage beyond damages assessed for physical injury to such things as libel, slander, character defamation, shock, mental anguish, sickness or disease, false arrest, wrongful entry or eviction, and malicious prosecution. You may purchase umbrella policies at a cost of between $175 and $250 for $1 million of additional liability coverage.

REMODELING UPGRADE. If you do any remodeling in the future, make sure you boost your coverage. If you don't notify the company promptly, you could void your replacement-cost guarantee.

HOME-OFFICE COVERAGE. More insurers are now including limited coverage for home offices in the basic policy—primarily covering computer equipment. Check with your agent for coverage under your policy.

ADDITIONAL COVERAGE. You can select a policy that will help cover costs, including provisions for housing and restaurant bills, should your home become uninhabitable. Many policies routinely pay up to $500 if a credit card is stolen or forged in your name.

How Much Coverage Do You Need?

Once you've pinned down the type of policy that suits your needs, the next step is to figure out how much coverage you want on the house and its contents. The basic building block of any policy is the amount of coverage on the house. This should be based on the replacement value—that is, what it would cost to rebuild the structure.

Because you are unlikely to experience a total loss on your home, you may be tempted not to insure for the full value. But insuring for less than full value is false economy. You won't be fully protected for a partial loss unless your coverage at the time of the loss is at least 80 percent of the replacement cost. That provision could become a problem as construction costs rise or as you improve the house. You can protect

(continued on page 216)

You won't be fully protected for a partial loss unless your coverage at the time of the loss is at least 80 percent of the replacement cost.

HOW HOME INSURANCE POLICIES COMPARE

These are the principal features of standard homeowners policies. The policies of some companies differ in a few respects. Policy conditions may also vary according to state requirements. You can usually increase coverage for some items by paying an additional premium.

	HO-2 (Broad Form)	HO-3 (Special Form)
Perils Covered (see key below)	items 1–16	all perils, except those specifically excluded, on buildings
Covered item or loss	**Amount and limits of coverage**	
House and attached structures	based on structure's replacement value	based on structure's replacement value
Detached structures	10% of insurance on house	10% of insurance on house
Trees, shrubs, plants	5% of insurance on house; $500 maximum per item	5% of insurance on house $500 maximum per item
Personal property	50% of insurance on house; 10% for property normally kept at another residence or $1,000, whichever is greater	50% of insurance on house; 10% for property normally kept at another residence or $1,000, whichever is greater
Loss of use, additional living expense; loss of rental unit, uninhabitable	20% of insurance on house	20% of insurance on house
Special limits on liability	money, bank notes, bullion, gold other than goldware, silver other valuable papers, deeds, manuscripts, passports, tickets and stamps, and outboard motors—$1,000; trailer not used with boats— stones—$1,000; theft of silverware, goldware, and pewterware—	
Credit card loss, forgery, counterfeit money, electronic fund transfer	$500	$500
Comprehensive personal liability	$100,000	$100,000
Damage to property of others	$500	$500
Medical payments	$1,000 per person	$1,000 per person

Key to Perils Covered: 1. fire, lightning 2. windstorm, hail 3. explosion 4. riots or civil commotion 5. damage by aircraft 9. theft 10. volcanic eruption 11. falling objects 12. weight of ice, snow, sleet 13. leakage or overflow of water or steam from a of an appliance for heating water 15. freezing of plumbing, heating, and air-conditioning systems and domestic appliances 16. dam-

The special limits of liability refer to the maximum amounts the policy pays for the types of property listed. Usually jewelry, furs, boats, and other items subject to special limits must be insured separately if you want more coverage.

HO-4 (Contents Only)	HO-6 (Co-op or Condo)	HO-8 (Limited Coverage)
1–16	1–16	1–10

Amount and limits of coverage

no coverage	$1,000 on owner's additions and alterations to unit	based on structure's market value
no coverage	no coverage	10% of insurance on house
10% of amount of personal-property insurance, $500 maximum per item	10% of amount of personal-property insurance, $500 maximum per item	5% of insurance on house, $25 maximum per item
based on value of property; 10% of that amount for property normally kept at another residence or $1,000, whichever is greater	based on value of property; 10% of that amount for property normally kept at another residence or $1,000, whichever is greater	50% of insurance on house; 5% for property normally kept at another residence or $1,000, whichever is greater
20% of personal-property insurance	40% of personal-property insurance	10% of insurance on house
than silverware, platinum, coins, and medals—$200; securities, etc.—$1,000; boats including their trailers, furnishings, equipment, $1,000; theft of jewelry, watches, furs, precious and semiprecious $2,500; theft of firearms—$2,000		theft on premises limited to $1,000; no coverage for theft of items (named at left) off premises
$500	$500	$500
$100,000	$100,000	$100,000
$500	$500	$500
$1,000 per person	$1,000 per person	$1,000 per person

age 6. damage by vehicles not owned or operated by people covered by policy 7. damage from smoke 8. vandalism, malicious mischief plumbing, heating, or air-conditioning system 14. bursting, cracking, burning, or bulging of a steam- or hot-water heating system or to electrical appliances, devices, fixtures, and wiring from short circuits or other generated currents

yourself by getting an inflation guard, which automatically raises your coverage in step with rising prices. But check on the value of the house and contents at least every two years to see that you are adequately covered.

A better solution is to shift the responsibility for keeping replacement-cost coverage up to 80 percent from your shoulders to the insurance company, through what is called an inflation-guard clause (or a replacement-cost endorsement). Your coverage will automatically increase by a specified percentage at regular intervals. Your premium will also increase as coverage increases. This option can cost as little as 10 percent of a year's base premium or as much as three times the standard coverage. You can also buy replacement-cost coverage for personal property.

Most policies can be customized to meet your needs. You should be able to buy add-on coverage to insure silverware or art, for example, not covered in standard policies. (See also the discussion of package plans in the box on the preceding pages.)

Cutting Costs

Prices for equivalent homeowners policies can vary by hundreds of dollars from company to company. As you shop, take the following steps to ensure that you are getting the most for your money:

- **Get price quotations** from at least three companies.
- **Ask about plans that bundle options** together at reduced prices.
- **Find out whether you'd get a price break** if the insurer provided both your home and auto coverage.

For each policy, compare these items:

- **The amount you wish to insure the house for** and the cost of a replacement-cost endorsement on the policy.
- **The cost of content coverage.** Half the amount of coverage on the structure (minus depreciation) is standard; decide if more coverage seems necessary.
- **The cost of replacement coverage** versus actual cash coverage on the contents. If possible, opt for replacement coverage.

- **The deductible.** As a general rule, don't ask for a deductible lower than $250; it's too expensive. Consider a deductible of $500 or even $1,000 to save more money.
- **The cost of floaters** you may need for antiques, jewelry, computer software, and the like.
- **The liability limits.** The standard amount is $100,000, but $300,000 is desirable and not that much more expensive. If you have a high net worth, obtain an umbrella liability for $1 million or more.

Flood Insurance

The most important risk excluded from most homeowners policies is damage caused by flooding from rivers, dams, and other natural sources. If you buy a home in an area the government has designated "flood prone," you may be able to purchase flood coverage through the federal government's National Flood Insurance Program (NFIP). Under the 1994 National Flood Insurance Reform Act, homeowners who receive federal disaster assistance must purchase flood insurance and maintain it for as long as they own their home. If you cancel the policy and your home is flooded again, you'll be ineligible to receive federal assistance.

You can purchase flood insurance from a licensed property/casualty insurance agent or broker, or from a private insurance company.

More than 20,000 communities participate in the NFIP, administered by the Federal Insurance Administration, part of the Federal Emergency Management Agency (FEMA). Most owners living in such a community will be eligible for some coverage once required flood-management programs have been initiated. Protection isn't cheap; the average homeowner's annual premium is $352, although individuals living in higher-risk areas will have a higher annual premium.

You'll have to wait 30 days from the time you purchase the policy until it goes into effect. Deductibles are applied separately to the building structure and contents even if they are damaged in the same flood. Minimum deductibles are set at $500 for buildings and $500 for contents.

For more information, contact your insurance company, or call the NFIP at 888-379-9531. More information is also available at http://www.floodsmart.gov.

Earthquake Insurance

Although standard homeowners policies don't include coverage for earthquake damage, you should be able to buy a special earthquake endorsement with your policy or get a separate policy.

Unfortunately, cost deters most owners from even taking out earthquake insurance. And that in turn makes coverage more expensive because the risk is being carried by a smaller pool of individuals. In California, for example, where less than 15 percent of homeowners have earthquake insurance, an earthquake endorsement usually averages about $2.80 per $1,000 of coverage, depending on the home's construction and location. Residents in higher-seismic-risk areas pay higher rates than those in lower-seismic-risk areas. Wood-frame houses cost significantly less to insure than brick homes. Most policies carry a high deductible—usually anywhere from 10 percent to 15 percent of your coverage limit.

California isn't the only part of the country where homeowners are at risk for earthquakes. Homes situated in parts of Arkansas, Colorado, Idaho, Illinois, Indiana, Kentucky, Massachusetts, Mississippi, Missouri, Nevada, New York, South Carolina, Tennessee, Utah, Washington, and Wyoming are also at higher-than-average risk. If you have difficulty obtaining earthquake coverage, call your state insurance department for assistance.

Earthquake insurance pays off only on devastating claims and it will not shield you from having to absorb a major financial loss. In addition, the deductible usually applies separately to the structure and its contents.

Despite the cost, it's important to consider buying earthquake insurance if:

■ **Your home was constructed before World War II,** when codes covering a structure's ability to withstand shifts in the earth were weaker; this is particularly important for homes not framed with wood.

■ **Your home is located within ten miles of a fault.**

■ **Your home is on unstable soil,** such as a hillside, landfill, or flood-control plain.

Insurance on Your Life

If your new home represents a higher financial burden than you've ever carried before, and you have a spouse or children to protect in the event of your death or disability, this is a good time to review your insurance needs. Have an accountant, trusts-and-estates lawyer, financial planner, or trusted insurance professional review your situation on disability and life insurance.

Depending on your age, your best bet may be conventional term life insurance whose proceeds, if invested wisely, would produce enough annual income to pay the new mortgage and other basic living expenses (see the discussion of credit life insurance and its drawbacks in Chapter 10).

On to Settlement

You are only days away from becoming an owner. The search has been expensive in terms of both time and money. Now it's time for you to pay for the property and for the seller to deliver the deed.

There is no standard name for this next step. Depending on where you live, it is known as title closing, settlement, or closing of escrow. The closing officer in your area may be a title company, an abstract lawyer, or a regular real estate lawyer. Occasionally, it is a broker or lender.

When closing involves an actual meeting, the process commonly is called settlement. If no meeting occurs, it's often known as escrow and is handled by an escrow agent. In escrow cases, the buyer and seller

(continued on page 222)

When you buy a new home, it's a good time to review your life-insurance needs.

SETTLEMENT COSTS WORKSHEET

You'll receive a copy of this form—or one with similar language, sequence, and numbering of the line items—from your real estate agent, prospective lenders, and whoever conducts your settlement. Required by the Department of Housing and Urban Development, this

	AGENT'S ESTIMATE	LENDER'S ESTIMATE	ACTUAL COST
800. Items Payable in Connection with Loan			
801. Loan origination fee % (of loan)			
802. Loan discount (points) % (of loan)			
803. Appraisal fee to			
804. Credit report to			
805. Lender's inspection fee			
806. Mortgage insurance application fee to			
807. Assumption fee			
808.			
809.			
810.			
811.			
900. Items Required by Lender to Be Paid in Advance			
901. Interest from (date) to (date) @$ /day			
902. Mortgage insurance premium for months to (end date)			
903. Hazard insurance premium for years to (end date)			
904. years to			
905.			
1000. Reserves Deposited with Lender			
1001. Hazard insurance (number of) months @$ per month			
1002. Mortgage insurance months @$ per month			
1003. City property taxes months @$ per month			
1004. County property taxes months @$ per month			
1005. Annual assessments months @$ per month			
1006. months @$ per month			
1007. months @$ per month			
1008. months @$ per month			

format makes it easier for you to compare estimated settlement charges and to identify and question any unexplained items. (Unless otherwise stated, the word "to" refers to who will receive the payments.)

	AGENT'S ESTIMATE	LENDER'S ESTIMATE	ACTUAL COST
1100. Title Charges			
1101. Settlement or closing fee　to			
1102. Abstract or title search　to			
1103. Title examination　to			
1104. Title insurance binder　to			
1105. Document preparation　to			
1106. Notary fees　to			
1107. Attorney's fees　to			
includes above item numbers:			
1108. Title insurance　to			
includes above item numbers:			
1109. Lender's coverage　$			
1110. Owner's coverage　$			
1111.			
1112.			
1113.			
1200. Government Recording and Transfer Taxes			
1201. Recording fees: Deed $　; Mortgage $　; Release $			
1202. City/county tax/stamps:　Deed $　; Mortgage $			
1203. State tax/stamps:　Deed $　; Mortgage $			
1204.			
1205.			
1300. Additional Settlement Charges			
1301. Survey　to			
1302. Pest inspection　to			
1303.			
1304.			
1305.			
1400. Total Settlement Charges			

The key to reducing money shock at settlement is to know ahead of time what you'll have to pay.

typically sign an agreement requiring each party to deposit certain funds and documents with the agent. When all the papers and money are in, the escrow is "closed." The agent records the documents and makes the appropriate disbursements.

Settling on a home can be as serene as a treaty signing or as stressful as divorce proceedings. All in all, the more planning and monitoring you have done, the more likely you are to have a peaceful closing.

As the buyer, you probably selected the person or firm to perform the settlement, so you can rely on their competence and integrity. If the seller specified the agent, take along your own lawyer or have a lawyer of your choice review the documents before you sign them.

The Costs You Face

The key to reducing money shock at settlement is to know in advance what you'll have to pay. You should have gotten ballpark figures when you started looking, and once your purchase offer was accepted, you received detailed estimates from your lender.

Settlement costs are influenced by such things as the state in which you live, your closing date, how you financed your purchase, and what the lender required as an inducement to lend you money.

The government's Real Estate Settlement Procedures Act (RESPA) applies to most home loans, including VA, FHA, and other government-backed or government-assisted loans; loans eligible to be purchased by Fannie Mae, Ginnie Mae, or in other federally related secondary-mortgage markets; and loans made by lenders who invest or make more than $1 million in residential loans each year. Assumptions and seller financing are excluded.

When you apply for a new loan from a lender covered by RESPA, you must be given a "good-faith" estimate of fees or be sent one within three business days. You must also be given a Department of Housing and Urban Development pamphlet entitled *Settlement Costs and You,* which describes how the closing process works and explains terms you will encounter.

The day before settlement, you are entitled to see the Uniform Settlement Statement. This is a duplicate of what you will get at settlement. Where there is no meeting, the escrow agent is required to give you a copy when escrow is closed.

Use the worksheet on pages 220–21 to check the lender's and agent's estimates against actual amounts as you get them. This may give you some warning if there are substantial changes before settlement. The worksheet, like HUD's Uniform Settlement Statement, breaks total settlement charges into broad categories, including:

COSTS ASSOCIATED WITH GETTING A LOAN. These include the lender's charge for processing the loan, loan discount points and/or origination fees, appraisal fee, borrower's credit report, mortgage insurance, and, if relevant, loan-assumption fee.

ITEMS TO BE PAID IN ADVANCE AT CLOSING. Among them are mortgage interest, property taxes, and mortgage- and hazard-insurance premiums.

Once you become an owner, you pay interest on your monthly mortgage loan in arrears; that is, you pay for the use of the loan at the end of each month. Payments made on the first of each month cover interest owed from the previous month. To make this work, the lender collects interest in advance at settlement for the period between closing and the end of the month. For example, if settlement is August 15 and you make your first mortgage payment October 1, the lender will collect interest through the end of August.

Lenders also often require advance payment of as much as the first year's premiums for mortgage and hazard insurance at closing. In some cases a buyer can arrange for the seller to transfer the remaining hazard insurance, paying the seller on a prorated basis for the remainder of the policy term.

RESERVES FOR INSURANCE, TAXES, AND ASSESSMENTS. The borrower may be required to pay an initial amount

In general, items paid for in advance by the seller would be prorated in favor of the seller at closing.

at closing to set up a reserve fund, or escrow account. Each month a portion of the regular payment will be added to the reserve to assure sufficient sums to pay future taxes and insurance premiums.

TITLE COSTS. These pay for various transactions, notably the title search required by the lender. An examination is made of the public records to determine whether the title you receive has any ownership or financial claims against it or restrictions on the use of the property. Other related charges include title insurance, document preparation, notary fees, and the lender's attorney fees.

RECORDING AND TRANSFER CHARGES. Such charges cover recording of the loan and property documents at the county courthouse, as well as related transfer taxes.

ADDITIONAL FEES. These fees might cover lawyers' and buyer-broker services, property survey, and pest inspection. In general, items paid for in advance by the seller, such as property taxes, would be prorated in favor of the seller at closing. Items paid in arrears—interest on an assumed loan, for example—would be prorated in favor of the purchaser.

Run through the worksheet and note which items are to be paid in full or in part by you. Local custom influences whether the buyer or the seller pays a particular charge. You can do things differently, but only if your purchase contract stated clearly how each item was to be handled. Otherwise, it's not unreasonable for the seller to expect you to abide by the prevailing custom.

In some areas, for example, buyers pay for a title-insurance policy because their lenders demand it. In others, the seller absorbs the charge as a selling cost. Likewise, you may discover that buyers always pay the local tax for recording the deed, or that sellers always pay it. (To find out what closing costs might be involved in the purchase of a $200,000 home, see an example of the worksheet on the opposite page.)

HYPOTHETICAL SETTLEMENT COSTS

In this example:

(1) The buyer is paying a 1 percent loan origination fee, and the seller has agreed to pay one point on the buyer's $200,000 home mortgage.

(2) Because interest is paid in arrears—for the previous month—and because the buyer's first regular monthly payment won't be due until March 1, the lender collects interest for the period from January 2 through February 1 at closing.

(3) Each month lenders frequently collect $1/12$ of the annual property taxes—along with the principal and interest payment—to be held in escrow until payment is due. How much is paid at settlement depends on the closing date and when taxes are collected in a given locale.

(4) The lender is collecting and will be paying a full year's premium on hazard insurance covering at least the value of the mortgage; the lender is also starting a reserve fund for future premiums.

In some locales and in other circumstances, the buyer's closing costs may include an assumption fee (if the buyer is taking over the seller's mortgage), mortgage insurance, and various other charges.

Total settlement charges are generally less if the buyer is assuming an existing loan or paying all cash, rather than getting a new mortgage. (These settlement calculations are based on average costs for a $200,000 loan.)

The Purchase

Location Montgomery County, Md.	
Date of Closing	February 1
Sale Price	$ 240,000
Down Payment	40,000

Buyer's Costs

Credit report	$ 50.00
Loan origination fee (1%) (1)	2,000.00
Interest to February 1 (2)	917.00
Six months' property tax (3)	1,000.00
Hazard-insurance premium (4)	700.00
Two months' insurance reserve (4)	200.00
Lawyers' fees (includes title-exam fee and binder)	600.00
Recording fee	100.00
Survey	200.00
State recordation tax	660.00
Transfer taxes	800.00
County transfer tax	1,500.00
Title insurance (lender's coverage)	400.00
Title insurance (borrower's coverage)	600.00
Total	**$ 9,727.00**

Seller's Costs

Sales commission (6%)	$ 14,400.00
Loan discount point (1%) (1)	2,000.00
Appraisal fee	400.00
Closing fees	150.00
Termite inspection	60.00
Total	**$17,010.00**

Schedule a walk-through of the house shortly before settlement, but allow time for the seller to correct any last-minute problems.

What to Bring to Closing

In order for things to go smoothly, each person is responsible for bringing certain documents and for being prepared to write the necessary checks. Many closing costs can be paid by personal check, but ask the lawyer who is handling the closing. A certified or cashier's check is usually required; find out to whom checks should be made payable.

The seller and his attorney, or the settlement lawyer you've both agreed on, are responsible for preparing and bringing the deed and the most recent property-tax bill. They also will bring other documents required by the contract. This can include the property insurance policy, termite inspection, documents showing the removal of liens, a bill of sale for personal property, loan documents, and so on.

Your responsibilities include bringing the cashier's check or having adequate funds in your checking account for the down payment and other settlement costs, arranging for your attorney to represent your interests at the meeting, bringing the loan commitment, bringing photo identification, and informing the lender of the meeting's time and place.

If your lender requires payment of the first year's premiums for mortgage and hazard insurance at the closing, be prepared to pay or to bring proof that the premiums have already been paid. Finally, it's a good idea to bring a copy of the purchase contract. You may need to refresh your memory.

The Final Inspection

The house you're buying must be handed over to you in the condition specified in the contract (see the discussion of condition in Chapters 7 and 8).

To verify this, schedule a walk-through of the house shortly before settlement, but allow time for the seller to correct any last-minute problems.

If the house is vacant, it should be empty of debris and in the "broom-clean" condition you specified in the contract. Take along a simple device for testing all the electrical outlets—a plug-in nightlight, for example. Turn on the furnace and air conditioner. Flush toilets and turn on faucets. Put the washing machine and dryer through a cycle. In short, put the house through its paces.

If anything needs fixing or further cleaning (aside from things that were conveyed only in "as is" condition), tell the seller immediately. Neither you nor the seller wants to postpone the settlement, but make it clear that you won't go to closing until a second walk-through proves satisfactory.

Prepare a File for Your Taxes

Congratulations! You're now a homeowner. Tax benefits weren't your primary motivation for buying, but now they take on more importance.

If you haven't read Chapter 3 carefully, do so after closing. Now is the time to begin keeping records of costs you incur on your new home—from settlement expenses to improvements that add to the home's value. Some expenses can be deducted from taxable income in the year you buy the home; others will merely increase the tax basis.

When Your Mortgage Is Sold

It may not be long after you assume ownership of your home—possibly after only one or two mortgage payments—that your mortgage lender will sell your mortgage. Servicing mortgage loans—collecting monthly payments, and reserving taxes and insurance premiums in escrow—is big business and quite separate from mortgage lending. Some lenders sell the servicing immediately after originating the loan; others sell blocks of loans as a way to raise cash. At least half of all mortgage debt in America is being serviced by companies other than the loan originators or the lenders. Problems with loan service are common, particularly once a loan is transferred from lender to service company.

Problems with loan service are common, particularly once a loan is transferred from lender to service company.

Here's how to respond to four of the most common servicing problems:

Notification

It seems little enough to ask that somebody promptly let you know if your mortgage is transferred. Several states have laws requiring timely notification. On loans in which they have an interest, Fannie Mae and Freddie Mac require both the old and the new servicers to advise you of the transfer. The Mortgage Bankers Association recommends that its members notify you as well.

If your loan is transferred, you should get a "good-bye" letter from your old servicer before receiving a "hello" letter from the new one. Don't redirect payments unless you've been told to do so by your current servicer. If your first notice comes from the new servicer, contact your current lender to make sure the transfer is legitimate.

Homeowners Insurance

If your mortgage servicer fails to pay an insurance premium, you should get a warning from your insurer before the policy is canceled. Some companies send just

---

CALLING FANNIE OR FREDDIE

If you have an intractable problem with your mortgage servicer, it's time to contact the owner of your loan. In any correspondence, be sure to include the mortgage company's name, your loan number, name, address, and home and work phone numbers.

If Fannie Mae bought the loan, call 800-732-6643 to discuss the problem. Depending on the complexity of your situation, it may step in to facilitate.

For Freddie Mac loans, call or write to the Regional Director of Loan Servicing at the regional office closest to your mortgage company (ask your original lender for the address). For more information, visit the Freddie Mac Web site at http://www.freddiemac.com.

Regional offices are in:
- New York City (212-418-8900)
- McLean, Va. (703-902-7700)
- Atlanta (770-857-8800)
- Dallas (972-395-4000)
- Chicago (312-407-7400)
- Woodland Hills, Calif. (818-710-3000)

one notice to the homeowner and mortgage servicer. Should you get such a notice, don't ignore it. Contact both your servicer and the insurer to see that coverage is maintained. In theory, if a mortgage servicer is responsible for paying an insurance premium and fails to do so, resulting in a loss of coverage, the servicer would be liable for losses suffered by the homeowner. But such a situation would compound an already upsetting and stressful event and could force you to sue in order to recoup.

Property Taxes

Many borrowers have complained that their servicer failed to pay property taxes on time. Some found that when the company got around to paying the bill, the late payment was deducted from their escrow account. If you get tangled in that kind of mess, write to both the lender and the taxing authority. You may have to wrestle with the lender to get it to pay what it's already taken your money for, and persuade the taxing authorities to stop harassing you over a problem you didn't create.

Escrow Problems

Mortgage transfers are often accompanied by an increase in your monthly payments. And although terms of the loan don't change, there's a good chance that the amount required for deposit into your escrow account will.

It's difficult to know whether you're being asked to pay too much into your escrow account. Because insurance and tax bills come due at different times of the year, lenders are allowed to keep a cushion in the account. That means the amount you pay into escrow each month will be more than the total of your tax and insurance bills divided by 12. Many contracts permit lenders to keep a cushion covering up to two months, the maximum allowed under the Real Estate Settle-

---

INTEREST DUE

Lenders must pay interest on funds held in escrow accounts in California, Connecticut, Iowa, Maine, Maryland, Massachusetts, Minnesota, New Hampshire, New York, Oregon, Rhode Island, Utah, Vermont, and Wisconsin.

---

ment Procedures Act (RESPA). Lenders may use a combined total to calculate the cushion or view taxes and insurance as separate accounts.

Keep track of what is in your account. You should get periodic statements of exactly how much is in there and when payments are made from it. If it appears that the amount is too much, ask for an escrow reanalysis.

If you have a problem that you haven't been able to get fixed, find out from the original lender the name of the secondary-market firm—like Fannie Mae or Freddie Mac—that bought your loan. These giants have a strong interest in the proper servicing of the loans they buy and resell; they want to know about problems with servicing firms that do business with them (for contact information, see the box on page 228).

Your servicer must respond within 20 business days and must abide by certain other procedures. When the National Affordable Housing Act was passed in 1990, certain provisions were added to RESPA dealing with complaint resolution. Among them are: a stipulation that under certain conditions an aggrieved consumer may recover actual damages up to $1,000.

Buying a Vacation Home

Chapter 13

A simple log cabin in the Ozarks. A weathered cottage on Cape Cod. A ski condo in Aspen. A secluded home tucked into a cove on the Caribbean island of St. Lucia. A resort time-share in Pennsylvania's Pocono Mountains. The words *vacation property* may be used by the owners of each, although the financial, legal, and tax consequences of ownership can be as different as the environments.

There are many reasons to buy a second home—some personal, some financial. You could enjoy a vacation spot so much you believe you'll want to keep returning over and over. Rather than renting a different house or hotel room each time, you want to feel at home and be recognized as part of a community—and that means having your own place where you can put down roots, entertain friends and family, and stash vacation gear.

If your goal is merely to lock in predictable vacation costs where you like to go each year, a fractional interest or time-share might make sense. Some kinds of time-shares are not real estate per se but are in effect a prepaid right to use a given unit for a certain length of time each year. If so, keep expectations for financial gain low or nonexistent; it's usually difficult to sell a time-share for what you paid for it.

You may dream of buying a vacation home where you believe you'll retire one day and convert that second home to your primary residence.

Or you may have financial motivations uppermost in your mind. If this describes you, make sure you check out all the angles before succumbing to the fast talk of a resort salesperson. Buying a vacation home to avoid rising rents might make sense in some areas, but not in others; it often costs the vacationer less to rent the nicest house in a given community for a month than it costs the owner to pay the mortgage, taxes, and maintenance on that same house for a month, particularly in the early years of ownership.

Price appreciation is another matter. Some people buy in a given vacation community because they've witnessed firsthand a rapid rise in home prices (and probably rents, too) over the previous several years; they want to get in on the action. Carefully selected homes in the most sought-after communities can, in fact, appreciate nicely, making them good investments as well as nice places to spend a vacation. But appreciation is highly variable from region to region and resort to resort. Some who hastily bought time-shares or resort houses from persuasive salesmen have found they can't even recover their original investment in the slender resale market.

DEFINING YOUR NEEDS

Carefully consider the following points:
- **How large** a residence do you need?
- **What style** is practical and desirable?
- **How far** from your home is acceptable— a few hours drive? a long plane trip?
- **How frequently** will you want to visit your vacation home? Only on weekends? Just two weeks annually?
- **Will the home be exclusively** for your own use, or will you want to rent it out for part or all of the year?
  If it's the latter,
- **Are you willing to curb** your taste for the unusual and buy what renters want and like?

Study Before You Buy

It takes study, cool analysis, and good luck to make a smart decision. In many ways, though, buying a vacation property is like buying a principal residence, so the preceding chapters of this book should be useful to you. There are also special considerations, such as those addressed in the accompanying box.

Then, as you head out with your dreams, your maps and the classified ads, keep these points in mind:

A DEPRESSED PRICE ISN'T THE SAME THING AS A BARGAIN. The property may have been grossly overpriced to begin with or severely inflated by a speculative orgy. If there's an abundance of listings, try to find out why from independent sources, such as the local tax assessor or a real estate agent. If a lot of people were burned, it could happen again. Perhaps the area has become less desirable.

LOCATION, LOCATION, LOCATION. That trilogy is just as important for a vacation home as it is for your principal residence. Overbuilding tends to run in cycles, and it generally happens in bigger, better-known, heavily promoted areas with large numbers of builders and hard-charging chambers of commerce. You may find better prospects in older, quieter, and less-exotic communities with fewer absentee owners. The more time you can spend looking and comparing, the better you're likely to do.

CHECK THE FINANCIAL VIABILITY OF RESORT OPERATORS. When you buy a home near ski slopes or golf greens, your property's value is directly tied to the quality of the resort's management. Investigate its financial health before you risk your own. You should be able to obtain quarterly statements and annual reports on a publicly held development. A privately held resort is not required to disclose financial information, but some sleuthing can uncover clues. Try to find out whether the company pays creditors and employees on time. The county clerk's office can tell you if liens have been placed against the property, and the local Better Business Bureau can tell you about any complaints or if the resort is reorganizing under bankruptcy protection. Also ask homeowners about the company's reputation. Search libraries and electronic data bases about the resort and its owners for articles, and then follow up.

At some resorts—such as Wintergreen, in Virginia's Blue Ridge Mountains—ski, golf, and racquet amenities are owned by a partnership of homeowners. That means you can probably get copies of federally mandated property reports and other financial documents.

Location is as important for a vacation home as it is for your principal residence.

You can probably fully deduct mortgage interest and property taxes you pay on a second home.

DON'T SPECULATE. Don't assume today's prices make appreciation a sure bet. Remember that many investors' hopes were dashed even when all the tax benefits were in place and prices were steadily moving up. Most of today's buyers are families who plan to use the property for vacations and weekend getaways. If a rental market does start to hum, overbuilding could soon spoil things.

CHECK YOUR ACCESS RIGHTS. Find out whether homeowners are guaranteed preferred access to golf courses or ski slopes. Does the guarantee transfer with the property? Get it in writing.

UNDERSTAND TAX BENEFITS. Albeit to a lesser extent than in the past, Uncle Sam still subsidizes your home away from home. You can probably fully deduct mortgage interest and property taxes you pay on a second home.

BUY FOR ENJOYMENT. Buying a place where you can escape for fun, relaxation, tranquility, and companionship could do wonders for your health and spirits, and could be one of the best investments you'll ever make. In terms of real value, a well-established, desirable, family-oriented community with good recreation facilities could be a far better choice than a neon-splashed strip of highrise condominiums and cocktail lounges.

Don't buy where you haven't visited many times as a vacationer. Most of all, never buy a home on a first visit to a new resort community or time-share resort that uses intensive sales pressure to convince people to commit themselves on the spot.

While on a vacation in the community you're considering, devote a few days to a thorough investigation of the market. Look at the houses or time-shares for sale. Find out how much homes have sold for in that area, and ignore advertised asking prices. Talk to leading real estate brokers in the community. If you're planning to rent the house out, contact several management firms who specialize in finding tenants, collecting rent, maintaining, and making repairs when you're not around. Talk to all the year-round residents you can find, and drop by the local newspaper, chamber of commerce, or library to learn what you can about zoning, future developments, and commercial growth in the area.

IF YOU'RE BUYING OVERSEAS. Thousands of Americans have been enticed by foreign communities or lower land costs (or both) and have purchased homes abroad. In most cases, mortgage-interest payments on foreign properties are deductible on U.S. tax returns.

The first area of concern when buying a foreign residence is to find a reputable real estate agent in the country that interests you. Familiar American companies such as Century 21 and Coldwell Banker hang shingles abroad, and many smaller firms are linked through international referral networks. Domestic firms can also counsel you on the details of an international move, such as quarantine rules for pets.

Another source of information is foreign banks, which have branch offices in most major American cities. Not only can they provide referrals, but they can often offer financing as well.

In most cases, mortgage-interest payments on foreign properties are deductible on U.S. tax returns.

Vacation-Home Strategies

Most would-be buyers soon have their choices limited by the lofty price tags attached to the most attractive vacation properties. The scenarios below show the kinds of properties that make the most sense depending on your plans for its use.

Personal Use Only

Affluent buyers are often looking for a unique or unusual property. They want it to reflect their status in life and aren't interested in rental income. They intend to use the property for their own and their family's enjoyment, but long-term appreciation and estate building are primary *investment* objectives. The home may qualify as a second residence; if so, mortgage interest

Less-affluent vacation-home buyers need rental income to help carry their investment.

will be fully deductible as long as the combined debt secured by the vacation home and principal residence doesn't exceed $1 million.

Good bets include the most sought-after (and expensive) categories of vacation property: rural acreage near growing metropolitan areas; waterfront property; and apartments or town houses in cities that are hubs of international travel and cultural and recreational attractions.

Some Rental and Business Use

Other affluent buyers look at vacation property with a sharper focus on its potential medium-term investment return. Appreciation and some tax shelter are important financial objectives. They may own more than one property—because it is financially rewarding and because it gives them more than one getaway place. They actively seek rental income and use professional management. Such owners may restrict personal use of a property to maintain deductions and tax shelter (a strategy that demands careful analysis). And they may use it for business purposes, such as entertaining clients or customers.

Choices of vacation property purchased for financial reasons could include condos or town houses in popular resort areas, or perhaps a condo hotel suite in a sought-after area where the climate permits either one long vacation season or two peak seasons.

Limited Personal Use, Heavy Renting

Less-affluent vacation-home buyers need rental income to help carry their investment. They also need appreciation and tax shelter to make ownership sustainable. They may manage the property on their own or seek renters to supplement those lined up by their manager. They may not use the property themselves in the early years of ownership, or may do so only out of season (see the discussion on the trade-offs between personal and rental use, beginning on page 242). Owning vacation property in an area that becomes overbuilt—driving down rental rates and slowing appreciation—is a serious financial risk.

Best purchase prospects include resort property in areas with perennial popularity and with, as in the above category, either one long rental season or two rental seasons (for example, a part of New England with winter skiing and summer camping).

Less-Than-Full-Time Ownership

Finally, there are those who dream of owning a beach cottage or a mountain hideaway but cannot afford the down payment or the cash outlay that an unrented property would drain from their budget. "You can't spend all your time on vacation, so why own a vacation place all the time?" they reason.

And, because so many people are in this group, developers and salespeople have spent hours upon hours figuring out how to help them "own"—ways that people wouldn't consider for a primary residence but that may make sense for a vacation home.

If you belong in this category, consider vacation ownership—fractional interests and time-shares—in quality developments.

FRACTIONAL INTEREST. Fractional interests may be sold as quarter-shares (13 weeks), fifth-shares (ten weeks), or tenth-shares (five weeks). Essentially, you buy title to a number of weeks spread throughout the year. If you buy a quarter-share, for example, you get to use the property every fourth week. Each year, the sequence shifts forward a week, giving you the opportunity to use all the weeks of the year within a four-year period. Some fractional-interest contracts use a mix of floating and fixed time periods.

Fractional interests offer better prospects for appreciation than time-shares (see the discussion on the next page). Pay attention to marketing costs, which range from zero to 25 percent. Buyers paying a 25 percent premium in sales expenses such as commissions will have to wait a long time before counting paper profits.

The resort developer is the most likely source of funds to finance a fractional interest, and terms vary widely. Prices for "fractionals" range from $50,000 to

With a fractional interest, you essentially buy title to a number of weeks spread throughout the year.

$1.5 million, depending on the location, size, and number of weeks. Owners also pay annual fees from $450 to $14,000. Check with a knowledgeable accountant regarding tax consequences and interest deductions.

TIME-SHARES. This is a popular means of dividing ownership of vacation property, and it's often the cheapest way to buy into a resort. You become one of the owners of a property, typically a condo apartment. Usually, ownership is divided into 52 parts— one for each week of the year—and the parts are sold one or more at a time.

FOR MORE INFORMATION

PERIODICALS AND NEWSLETTERS
Hideaways International (767 Islington St., Portsmouth, NH 03801; 800-843-4433; http://www.hideaways.com). Guide to vacation homes for rent and for sale worldwide; magazine published six times a year; membership also includes a quarterly newsletter and a biweekly electronic newsletter. Photographs and information describing some of their properties are available on the Web site.

John T. Reed's Real Estate Investor's Monthly (John T. Reed Publishing, 342 Bryan Dr., Alamo, CA 94507; 925-820-7262; http://www.johntreed.com). Practical advice for investors from an expert in the field.

ADVISERS AND BROKERS
The Counselors of Real Estate (430 N. Michigan Ave., Chicago, IL 60611; 312-329-8427; http://www.cre.org). Members of this organization, which is affiliated with the National Association of Realtors,

offer advice and analysis on property matters on a fee basis.

Condolink (7811 L St., Omaha, NE 68127; 800-877-9600; http://www.condolink.com). Company conducts sales and rentals of condos worldwide, as well as sales and resales of time-shares.

The following two companies are involved in sales and resales of time-shares, and are licensed to handle time-share exchanges:

Second Market Timeshare Resale (East Coast) (P.O Box 4050, Harrisonburg, VA 22801; 800-368-3541) offers an Internet vacation resort guide with approximately 4,000 listings on its Web site, http://www.2ndmarkettimeshares.com.

TRI West (West Coast) (13353 Washington Blvd., Los Angeles, CA 90066; 800-423-6377; http://www.triwest-timeshare.com) offers the Bluebook, listing historical prices of sales and resales by rental weeks at about 3,000 time-share resorts, on its Web site.

Time-share resorts also offer "lock-out" units, which are essentially duplexes comprised of two apartments. You can use the whole unit for large families, use one section and rent out the other, or rent out both sections during your week.

Some well-recognized names such as Disney and Marriott have also entered the vacation-ownership market. With their presence in the field and the advent of larger lock-out units, an average one-week time-share can now run anywhere between $5,000 and $50,000. Annual fees generally range from about $5 to $750.

Time-share ownership can be in the legal form of tenancy in common (sometimes called time-span ownership) or interval ownership. Tenancy in common gives you an undivided interest in a property, prorated according to the amount of time you purchase. Interval ownership lasts only for a specified number of years. When those years are up, you and the other interval owners become tenants in common. Under either type of ownership, you don't always get a specified unit for a fixed time period. Instead, you may choose from interchangeable units and floating weeks.

One form of time-sharing—known as a vacation license, vacation lease, or club membership—carries no ownership rights at all, only the right to use the property each year for a number of years. Ownership stays in the hands of the developer.

Whatever the form of purchase, you normally cannot get a mortgage to buy a time-share. Financing typically is covered by a personal loan over a five- to ten-year period with a 10 percent down payment, and the lender usually is the developer. Check with your accountant and lawyer about the tax implications. Don't rely on assurances from a salesperson.

If guaranteeing yourself a slot at your favorite resort once a year is your goal, a time-share may suit the bill. It locks in the cost of staying at a particular place, yet it provides the flexibility to vacation elsewhere, too. For an annual fee, usually between $80 and $90, you can become a member of a time-share exchange group

> **Whatever the form of purchase, you generally cannot get a mortgage to buy a time-share.**

If you're buying with partners, head off problems with a written partnership agreement.

that works out vacation-place swaps with other time-share owners around the world. Exchanges cost from $120 to $190.

But a time-share doesn't make sense if you'd like to sell at a profit eventually. This caveat is particularly pertinent if the unit is new and the developer still is selling others. Heavy marketing costs, which may include free airfare and lodging to lure potential buyers to the resort, push up the cost of the units. Developers don't devote time to reselling units until a resort is completed and sold out. Most time-shares are resold for half—or less—of what their owners originally paid and take months to sell, if they can be sold at all.

One way to buy a time-share is through a time-share auction. These events can be attended in person or handled through the mail. Sponsored by either Century 21 TRI Timeshares or TRI West (see box on page 238), the auctions are held several times each year and advertised in most major newspapers.

At auction, you should expect to pay significantly less than the original price. If you're thinking of bidding higher than about 35 percent, you might as well go to the ordinary resale market, where you will find a wider selection.

Buying with Partners

Friends often get together to buy a vacation home, either as tenants in common or in a legally constituted partnership.

Owning as tenants in common, friendly as it sounds, can cause headaches. Head off problems by anticipating and addressing them in a written partnership agreement. Use your real estate lawyer to draw up the agreement, but ask a lawyer in the vacation locale to check relevant regulations.

Make sure the contract addresses the following:

■ **How ownership will be divided,** which in turn determines who pays how much of the down payment, monthly payment, maintenance, and repairs. The contract should also describe how any profits or losses from rent or sale of the place will be divided and how tax benefits will be distributed.

- **Who gets to use** the property when.
- **What constitutes a deciding vote** and under what circumstances a vote is considered necessary.
- **Which owner will act** as managing partner and thus be responsible for signing checks and paying the routine expenses.
- **How much advance notice** a withdrawing partner must give and how the buyout price will be set.

A limited partnership should protect the existing mortgage when a new owner enters the picture if the documents make clear that it is an interest in the partnership—not an interest in the property—that is being transferred. (See the discussion of limited partnerships in Chapter 1.)

Taxes Take No Holiday

O ne thing you can't get away from at your get-away-from-it-all vacation home is taxes and some exasperatingly convoluted tax rules.

When It's Just for You and Yours

First, look at the bright side. If your home away from home is only that—a second residence that you never rent out—the tax benefits come with few complications. You can deduct the mortgage interest on a second home just as you can on your principal place of residence. (See Chapter 3, page 29, for information about possible changes to the tax law regarding mortgage interest deductions.)

Only two homes to a customer, though. Congress apparently figures that anyone who can afford more than two homes can handle the mortgage interest without the help of a tax deduction. Interest on any additional homes—and on any debt on the first and second homes that exceeds the $1 million cap—falls in the category of nondeductible personal interest.

If you own a second residence that you never rent out, the tax benefits come with few complications.

The IRS does not care about rental income you receive if you rent the place for 14 or fewer days a year.

A motor home or boat can qualify as a second residence for the purpose of deducting mortgage interest. To meet the IRS definition of a home, the boat or recreational vehicle must have basic living accommodations, including cooking facilities, a place to sleep, and a toilet. (However, if you are subject to the alternative minimum tax, interest on a loan for a boat you use as a second home can't be deducted as mortgage interest.)

Property taxes are deductible, regardless of how many homes you own.

Points paid to get a mortgage on a vacation home are not deductible in the year paid. Instead, they're deducted proportionally over the life of the loan.

When You Also Rent

It's when you start renting out the vacation home—as many owners do to help pay the freight—that things get tricky. The IRS does not care about rental income you receive if you rent the place for 14 or fewer days a year. You can charge as much as you want, and as long as your tenants stay no longer than two weeks the rent you receive is tax-free. Rent for more than 14 days, though, and you become a landlord in the eyes of the IRS. You must report rental income, and you qualify to deduct rental expenses.

How much time tenants use the property compared with how much time you enjoy it yourself determines whether the house is treated as a personal residence or a business property. This distinction is the key to the tax ramifications.

If your personal use accounts for more than 14 days during the year or more than 10 percent of the number of days the place is rented (26 or more personal days compared with 250 rental days, for example), the house is considered a personal residence. Hold personal use below the 14-day/10 percent threshold, however, and the house is considered a rental property.

Because the tax consequences turn on personal use, it's important to know that the IRS takes a broad view of what counts. Personal use includes:

- **Any day the property is used** by you or any part-owner (unless it is rented as a principal residence to a part-owner under a shared-equity arrangement).
- **Any day it is used by a member of your family,** whether or not rent is paid. For this test, a member of your family includes your spouse, brothers and sisters, parents and grandparents, and children and grandchildren.
- **Any day it is rented** for less than fair market rent.
- **Any day the property is used by someone** in connection with an arrangement that gives you the right to use another dwelling, such as if you trade a week at your beach home for a week at a mountain resort.
- **Any day it is used as a result of your donating** its use. If you donate use of your vacation home to a charitable organization—to be auctioned off at a fundraising event, for example—the period the property is used under the arrangement counts as personal use.

Note that time you spend at the place doing repairs or general maintenance does not count as personal use. As long as that is the primary purpose of staying at the vacation home, the day isn't counted. You must keep detailed records showing the dates of personal use, rental use, and repair and maintenance days.

The breakdown between personal and rental days is crucial because it determines whether the property can produce tax losses. Such losses—available only if personal use is limited so that the property qualifies as a rental rather than a residence—can often be used to trim your tax bill by sheltering other income, such as your salary.

Prior to 1994, the IRS classified all losses on rental property as "passive" losses and limited the amount of loss that could be deducted. Now, however, if you meet the requirements of material participation (one being that you devote more than 750 hours in real property services annually) then the loss becomes an active loss. Needless to say, most vacation homeowners will not fall into this category.

> **The breakdown between personal and rental days is crucial because it determines whether the property can produce tax losses.**

Any passive losses unused when you sell the property can be deducted against the profit on the sale or any other income.

The passive-loss rule does have an important exception. You are allowed to deduct up to $25,000 of rental losses in which you "actively participated" if your income is $100,000 or less. For incomes over $100,000, the $25,000-loss figure is reduced gradually and phased out completely at an income level of $150,000 or more. "Active participation" requires that you own at least 10 percent of the rental property and you make decisions such as approving tenants, rental terms, and repairs.

Expenses you can't deduct because of the passive-loss rules aren't lost forever. Unused losses are held over to future years when they can be used to offset income from the vacation home or other passive investments. Also, any passive losses unused when you sell the property can be deducted against the profit on the sale or any other income.

Even if the $25,000 exception will protect your rental write-offs, you have to watch out for another potential trap. Limiting personal use of your vacation home may mean giving up the right to take some mortgage-interest deductions.

Remember, the law only permits mortgage-interest deductions for loans secured by your first and second residence. If your vacation place is a business property, then the mortgage isn't covered. Part of the interest could still be deductible—the portion attributable to the business use of the property—but the rest would be considered personal interest, and therefore is not deductible.

That rule has led some tax advisers to recommend that taxpayers intentionally flunk the 14-day/10 percent test by increasing personal use of vacation property. That way, you preserve the full interest write-off. Part of the interest would be deducted as a rental expense and the rest as personal mortgage interest. What you give up, of course, is the opportunity to claim a tax loss.

Allocation of Expenses

To figure your vacation-home deductions, you have to allocate expenses to personal or rental use. There are two ways to do this—the IRS method and another approach that has been approved in court cases—and the one that's best for you depends on your circumstances.

According to the IRS, you begin by adding up the total number of days the house was used for personal and rental purposes. Then figure the percentage of time it was used for rental. That's the percentage of total expenses you can deduct against rental income.

Let's say you have a cabin in the mountains that you use for 30 days during the year and rent out for 100 days. The 100 days of rental use equals 77 percent of the total 130 days the cabin was used during the year. Using the IRS formula, 77 percent of your expenses—including interest, taxes, insurance, utilities, repairs, and depreciation—would be rental expenses.

The IRS is also particular about the order in which you deduct those expenses against your rental income. You deduct interest and taxes first, then expenses other than depreciation, and then depreciation. The sequence is important, and detrimental, because of the rule that limits rental deductions to the amount of rental income when personal use exceeds 14 days or 10 percent of total use. Remember that mortgage interest and property taxes not assigned to rental use could be claimed as regular itemized deductions instead. But by requiring you to deduct those expenses against rental income—that might otherwise be offset by depreciation you won't get to claim—the law squelches the write-off for taxes and interest as an itemized deduction.

By using a different allocation formula, though, you can limit the interest and tax expenses used to offset rental income and thereby boost the write-off of other rental costs. Courts have allowed taxpayers to allocate taxes and interest over the entire year rather than over just the total number of days a property is used. In the example above, assuming 100 days of rental use, that method would allocate just 27 percent (100 divided by 365) of the taxes and interest to rental income. That would leave more rental income against which other expenses can be deducted. The extra taxes and interest can be deducted as regular itemized deductions.

Although the court-approved formula can pay off when the 14-day/10 percent test makes the property a personal residence, the IRS version can be more appealing if the place qualifies as a business property. You need to look at the specifics of your situation to determine the best method for you and seek the advice of your accountant.

Squeezing Tax-Free Profit from a Vacation Home

Although the sweet, new rules that grant tax-free status to most home-sale profit apply only to your principal residence, there's a way to stretch the tax shelter around a vacation home. Simply move into the place after you sell your main home and live in it for at least two years before you sell. If you acquired it in a tax-free exchange, you must have owned it for at least five years before you sell, but you still have to have lived in it only two out of the previous five years. After living in the house for two years, the house becomes your home in the eyes of the IRS and you get a second bite at the tax-free apple. Any profit attributable to depreciation will be taxed at 25 percent.

Part II

For Sellers

Alternatives to Selling

Chapter 14

There are as many reasons for selling a home as there are for buying one. Some people sell because they are relocating and believe they must sell their current house to get the cash they need for a new home. Others sell because they need more space for a growing family—or less space because the children have grown and left. Still others, due to retirement, ill health, or a reduction in income, sell because they need the money that's tied up in their home for living expenses.

Whatever the reason, give some thought to whether you might meet your objectives without selling. Don't expect to hear about these alternatives from real estate agents. In a business fueled by sales commissions, it's a rare agent who will advise you not to sell. Nor should an agent advise you on something that is really a financial-planning decision. If you're unsure about selling, check with your lawyer or accountant—or seek advice from a financial planner.

If your present home is too small, what about remodeling or adding on? Moving to another home is usually the most expensive solution to the tight-space problem. Sales commissions, closing costs, moving and decorating costs—not to mention picking up and moving—take a big toll financially and emotionally.

Would remodeling make sense? Do you like the neighborhood well enough to justify the cost and hassle of a building project? Is your lot big enough for an addition? Would your improved house be too big or fancy for the neighborhood, making it hard to recover the cost of your improvements if you had to move?

Money for remodeling or for a down payment on a place in the new hometown could be right under your nose.

Must you seek permission to remodel from a community review board?

Moving to a new job? Study housing markets in your current and future hometowns. If houses are appreciating in value rapidly where you live now, but less so where you're headed, consider converting your home to a rental property.

But where will the money for remodeling or for a down payment on a place in the new hometown come from? It could be right under your nose. You could tap the equity in your current home via a full refinancing, traditional second mortgage, or home-equity line of credit. These possibilities are discussed below. Beginning on page 265 is a discussion of special options for older homeowners who want to stay put but need the money they could get from selling the house.

Tapping Your Home Equity

Your home equity is the difference between what the place is worth and what you owe on loans secured by the property. If you could sell for $200,000 and the balance on your mortgage is $120,000, for example, your equity is $80,000.

Your equity should increase each year as your home appreciates and monthly payments reduce what's owed on the mortgage. Home equity could be the major building block of your net worth.

More and more homeowners have been dipping into that equity by borrowing against it. The appeal of this kind of debt is that interest paid on the loan is generally fully deductible on your tax return, while interest paid on other consumer loans is not. (But be cautious: Casual use will drain your home equity; worse, it could cause you to lose your home.) If the money will be used to improve your home, the sky's the limit. You can deduct up to $1 million of mortgage debt used to buy a home or make major improvements. For other home-equity debt, the cap is $100,000 (beyond the loan you took to buy the house). It's deductible for any use except buying tax-exempt bonds or single-premium life insurance.

In other words, the government subsidizes the cost of borrowing if the loan is secured by your home. Consider what that means on a $10,000, ten-year loan at 7.5 percent. In the first 12 monthly payments, interest totals $750. If the loan is secured by your home and the $750 is deducted in the 25 percent bracket, the federal government effectively pays $188 of the interest. (Your state government might help, too, assuming you also get the benefit of the deduction on your state return.)

Home-Equity Options

Home-equity loans and lines of credit have become the preferred choice of most borrowers. Banks are offering a wide array of enticing options to make it easier for homeowners to get at their equity to pay for such things as reducing nondeductible credit card debt, college tuition, a new car, or home improvements. There are deals that allow you to set up mini fixed-rate loans under a line of credit or fixed-rate loans that can be adjusted when rates drop, and lines of credit that can protect you from an overdraft in your checking account or let you tap 100 percent of your home's value, instead of capping it at the usual 75 percent to 80 percent.

LOAN VERSUS LINE OF CREDIT. The first thing you need to decide is whether to apply for a fixed-rate loan that offers fixed payments over a set period of time or a line of credit that you can tap at will. Your choice will depend on your plans for the money and how disciplined you are at handling available cash and repaying debt.

A fixed-rate loan is akin to a second mortgage— you borrow a set amount and repay it in fixed monthly installments over 10 to 30 years. It is usually the best option if you need a given amount all at once—for a home improvement, say, or to start a business. With the fixed-rate loan, you are also unable to tap the equity at will.

A line of credit, on the other hand, replaces certainty with flexibility. You might arrange for a $50,000 line, for example, then borrow $1,000, $4,000,

Home-equity loans and lines of credit have become the preferred choice of most borrowers.

A line of credit is the way to go for people who will be borrowing irregular amounts to pay college tuition or to buy a new car.

or $5,000 simply by writing a check. Payback is as flexible as withdrawal, often with interest-only payments allowed during, say, a ten-year borrowing period. You will pay interest only on what you borrow, so if you don't borrow you won't owe anything. A line of credit is the way to go for people who will be borrowing irregular amounts to pay college tuition or to buy a new car.

HOW IT WORKS. Banks set a maximum credit limit at anywhere from 75 percent to 100 percent of the loan-to-value (LTV) ratio of your home. Determining your limit is not quite as easy as you might think. If a lender uses an 80 percent LTV ratio, for example, you could borrow up to 80 percent of the appraised value of your home, but the 80 percent figure includes all home debt. Let's say that your home is appraised at $300,000 and you owe $150,000 on a first mortgage. You would be eligible for a credit limit of $90,000. (The $300,000 multiplied by 80 percent equals $240,000, less your outstanding mortgage of $150,000, leaves you with available equity of $90,000.)

Home-equity debt usually carries a variable interest rate that's somewhere between one and three points above the prime rate. Say that the prime rate was 6.5 percent. That would produce a home-equity debt rate between 7.5 percent and 9.5 percent—considerably lower than the 14 percent to 17 percent or more you could pay on credit card debt or unsecured loans. Many banks also offer a lower teaser rate of 4 percent to 7 percent for the first six months to attract new customers. (A few go as low as 0 percent, per bankrate .com.) When you add in the tax savings, you just can't beat those rates. Let's say that you have a 7.5 percent home-equity loan and that you're in the 25 percent tax bracket. Your after-tax loan rate will be 5.63 percent (7.5 percent − [7.5 × 0.25] = 5.63).

Deals that allow up to 100 percent of equity borrowing are more costly. Expect to pay up to five points over prime—still a good deal compared to credit card rates. These deals may also come with dollar caps—say, a top loan of $10,000—regardless of how much equity you have in your home.

Home-equity lines are usually structured to expire far sooner than 30-year mortgages, although a few come due only when you sell. Generally, the loan period is divided into two segments—a "draw" period and a "payback" period. During the draw period, typically five years or so, you can borrow at will simply by writing a check. As you pay back the loan, your credit limit is restored accordingly. The length of the draw period is set out in your contract, along with minimum withdrawal amounts and any restrictions on how often you can tap the credit line.

The contract also spells out what happens when your draw period ends. You may be able to renew the credit line, for example, or be required to pay the outstanding balance at once. Alternatively, you could be required to repay the outstanding balance over a fixed period—say, ten years.

WHAT TO LOOK FOR WHEN YOU SHOP. Bankers are competing hard for new home-equity debt, so there are plenty of excellent deals to be found. That's great news for the consumer, but it also means you need to shop around to find the best deal for you.

You should be able to find a bank that's offering zero closing costs. This means that the bank will pick up the cost of the appraisal and document handling, which includes a credit check, title search, and similar charges. (Low introductory fees and waivers of closing costs may not be offered if you opt for a 100 percent deal.) Even though there may be no closing costs, look at the fine print to see if there are annual fees associated with the deal or if you're obligated to repay closing costs if you shut down the credit line within a year without selling your home.

You might pay an extra one-half percentage point or so on your interest rate for the privilege of avoiding closing costs. If you plan to borrow a large amount, you may want to ask your lender to lower the interest rate if you pay the closing costs up front (usually $200 to $300).

For those not comfortable with variable rates, banks offer loans with convertible features. That means if the prime rate goes down, your rate does too. If the

> **Even though there may be no closing costs, look at the fine print to see if there are annual fees associated with the deal.**

HOME-EQUITY LOAN WORKSHEET

Knowing the answers to these questions, adapted from a Federal Trade Commission checklist, will help you compare home-equity loans from different lenders. Before you compare, have in mind how much you want to borrow.

	LENDER		
	A	B	C
What size credit line is available?	_____	_____	_____
What is the length of time for repayment?	_____	_____	_____
Is there access to loans by check or credit card?	_____	_____	_____
Is the interest rate fixed? What is it?	_____	_____	_____
Is the interest rate variable?	_____	_____	_____
What is the initial rate?	_____	_____	_____
What is the maximum rate?	_____	_____	_____
How often can the rate be adjusted?	_____	_____	_____
What index is used?	_____	_____	_____
What margin, if any, is added to the index?	_____	_____	_____
Can the loan be converted to a fixed rate?	_____	_____	_____
What closing costs does the borrower pay:			
Points (percent of line of credit)	_____	_____	_____
Application fee	_____	_____	_____
Title-search fee	_____	_____	_____
Appraisal fee	_____	_____	_____
Lawyer's fee	_____	_____	_____
Other fees	_____	_____	_____
Is there an annual fee? What is it?	_____	_____	_____
Are there fees per transaction? What are they?	_____	_____	_____
What are the repayment terms:			
Is the monthly payment fixed?	_____	_____	_____
How much is it?	_____	_____	_____
Is the monthly payment variable?	_____	_____	_____
How much is it to begin with?	_____	_____	_____
How much is the maximum?	_____	_____	_____
Do payments cover both principal and interest?	_____	_____	_____
Are payments interest-only?	_____	_____	_____
Is there a final balloon payment?	_____	_____	_____
Can a balloon be refinanced or extended?	_____	_____	_____
What's the penalty for late payments?	_____	_____	_____
Is there a penalty for early repayment?	_____	_____	_____
What are the default provisions?	_____	_____	_____

prime goes up, you have the option of converting the balance of the loan or line of credit to a fixed-rate loan at the going rate. There should be no additional charge for the conversion. If your home-equity loan carries a fixed rate already, there are some banks that offer to reset the rate once during the life of the loan at no extra charge.

Most lines of credit offer you easy access to your credit by giving you a checkbook that you can use to tap your money whenever you need it. Some lenders also offer lines of credit linked to credit cards, debit cards, even ATM machines. You may even find a bank that's willing to hook your line of credit to your checking account so that you never again need to worry about bouncing a check.

With so many options available, you need to shop around and find the deal that offers the options that most suit your needs and lifestyle. If, for example, you know that you'll be tempted to spend more money if the credit is readily available, then you may not want a line of credit hooked to your checking account. When funds are less accessible, you'll be less likely to draw on them for a spontaneous purchase. A separate checking account may be more in tune with your needs. And remember that whatever terms you choose, you're putting your home up as collateral; if you can't repay, you could lose your home. Compare each loan you consider, according to these points:

Payment terms. These should be spelled out clearly. For example, you might be told that your line of credit is good for ten years, with a minimum monthly payment of $100 or 1/360 of the loan balance plus finance charges, whichever is greater. At the end of this ten-year draw period, you would have another five years to pay any remaining balance. Minimum terms during the repayment period would be 1/60 of the outstanding balance plus finance charges.

Watch out for negative amortization, which means that interest payments are too low to let you pay back the loan during its term. The balloon payment at the

Watch out for negative amortization, which means that interest payments are too low to let you pay back the loan during its term.

If something on your credit report turns sour, your borrowing rights could be frozen or reduced.

end could catch you off guard. If you can't pay or refinance, you may have to sell or face foreclosure.

Payment example. You must be given an example of what the minimum monthly payments would be if you borrowed a certain amount—say, $10,000—and the interest rate reached its maximum level.

Lenders' fees. These could include loan-application fees (typically around $125), one or more "points" (each at 1 percent of your credit limit), and a maintenance fee (often $50 to $75 or so).

Third-party fees. These fees usually include amounts for home appraisals, credit reports, and legal fees, and might total between $800 and $1,000.

Rate features. Most home-equity loans are pegged to the prime rate. Lenders currently add from zero to three points to the prime to come up with their index rate. Should you encounter an equity line pegged to some other index—the 90-day Treasury bill or the LIBOR (the London Interbank Offered Rate), for example—ask the lender to provide you with a historical example showing how changes in the index rate in the past would have affected minimum payments due on the home-equity line compared with what you would have experienced with a loan tied to the prime. (An index that responds quickly to rising rates will also reflect a drop in rates much more quickly than a sluggish one such as the index of 52-week Treasury bills.)

You must also be told about any annual or lifetime rate caps that apply. The index must be one that is out of the lender's control. Banks aren't allowed to use their own cost of funds as an index or change the index at their discretion.

As a rule, lenders can't accelerate payments or change the contract terms once the line has been opened. But a rainy-day fund could dry up just when you need it. Most home-equity lenders check borrowers' credit every year or so. If something on your credit report turns sour, your borrowing rights could be frozen or reduced. A sudden drawdown when you haven't used any credit for an extended period or a request to switch to easier payback terms could also trigger a check. Lenders have the right to reappraise your home periodically to make sure there's still enough equity cushion for their safety.

Once you've found a good home-equity loan, compare the deal with a traditional second mortgage (see the following discussion) before you commit. You can't simply compare the APRs on the two loans, however. The APR on second mortgages takes into account the interest rate charged, plus points and other finance charges, while the APR on a home-equity loan is based solely on the periodic interest rate and excludes any points, annual fees, or other charges.

After you commit yourself, you have three business days to back out of the loan if your principal residence serves as collateral.

PAYING OFF THE LOAN WHEN YOU SELL. You may be required to advise the lender when you put your house on the market. In any case, at settlement you must repay the home-equity loan along with your original mortgage. You'll face minor additional fees because clearing title involves an extra step. Your settlement lawyer must prepare a release, which can cost from $50 to $100, and file it, usually at a cost of another $25 to $50.

Second Mortgages

Lenders typically offer second mortgages—also called second trusts—of usually 15 years. Unlike an open-ended equity line, second mortgages involve borrowing a fixed amount of money up front and then making payments of principal and interest over a fixed period to amortize the loan. You generally can borrow up to 75 percent or 80 percent of your home's appraised value; if you can find a lender willing to count the value remodeling will add to the property, you may be able to borrow more.

> Once you have found a good home-equity loan, compare the deal with a traditional second mortgage before you commit.

You can borrow $25,000 or less for specific improvements to your home with an FHA Title I loan.

Interest rates are higher than those on conventional ARMs and fixed-rate first mortgages and adjustable-rate home-equity loans. Adjustable-rate second mortgages may be more competitive, but their spread over the index rate is commonly two to four percentage points. Rates are most often adjusted monthly.

The application process for a second mortgage is similar to that for a first. You won't get approval until your home is appraised, your credit checked, and title insurance written. Turnaround time for approval can be fairly short; you could close within two or three weeks of applying.

You'll also have to pay closing costs, which typically amount to 2 percent or 3 percent of the loan amount. For second mortgages of less than $15,000, lenders are often satisfied with a drive-by appraisal, verification of existing title insurance, and a credit report. As with home-equity loans, lenders may allow you to finance the closing costs as part of the loan.

Even with a higher interest rate, adding a second trust on top of a first mortgage usually costs far less, over the whole term of your home ownership, than refinancing with a new first.

FHA Loans

You can borrow $25,000 or less for specific improvements to your home (sorry, no swimming pool) with an FHA Title I loan. FHA-insured Title I loans are fixed-rate and can be obtained through contractors or from banks or other lenders. (Lenders inspect finished projects when you borrow more than $7,500. On all loans, you'll be asked to certify that the completed work qualifies as a home improvement.) Loan terms run from six months to as long as 20 years.

If you borrow less than $7,500, the loan won't be secured by a lien on your home. But interest payments on such unsecured personal loans are not deductible as mortgage interest for federal tax purposes. Larger loans are secured by your home and interest is deductible up to the value of the home.

To learn more about FHA Title I loans for home improvement, call HUD at 800-767-7468 and leave your name and address on the recording. HUD staff will send you a brochure describing the program and a list of lenders operating in your area. Or check on-line at http://www.hud.gov/fha/sfh/title/sfixhs.html.

Full Refinancing

First, here's the good news. An owner who trades a $200,000 fixed-rate, 30-year mortgage at 8 percent for the same loan at 6 percent is happily saving $269 a month before taxes. Refinancing means paying off your old loan and getting a new first mortgage. Now the bad news. It generally means paying fees for origination, appraisal, and credit check, and points, too.

What if your rate is 7.5 percent, or you paid to refinance a couple of years ago, or you have an adjustable-rate mortgage (ARM) with an adjustment due soon? Is refinancing worth it?

A home-equity loan or second mortgage may be the fastest way to tap your equity, but refinancing could be the better route in any of the following situations:

- **Interest rates** have fallen 2 percent or more below what you are now paying;
- **Rates** aren't quite 2 percent less, but you plan to stay put; or
- **You figure** you could pay off a new loan in less time with roughly the same payment you are making on your current mortgage.

Do you have remodeling in mind? Say your home is worth $400,000 and the mortgage balance is $150,000. You could refinance for $250,000 at a new lower rate, use $150,000 to pay off the old loan, and free $100,000 of home equity for remodeling. Lower interest rates mean you could get a bigger loan without a big increase in monthly payments. For example, the principal and interest payment on a $200,000, 8 percent, 30-year, fixed-rate mortgage is $1,468. With rates at 6 percent, if you refinanced for $260,000 and used

YOUR REFINANCING WORKSHEET

This worksheet lets you figure out how long it will take to pay yourself back if you refinance. Figures for the example, based on a $200,000 loan, are typical. To compute your new monthly payments for the second step of the Payback section, refer to the table on pages 152 and 153.

	EXAMPLE	YOUR LOAN
The Cost of Refinancing		
Points	$ 2,000	$_____
Application fee	125	$_____
Title search and insurance	600	$_____
Inspections	400	$_____
Survey	200	$_____
Lender's underwriting fee	400	$_____
Credit report	50	$_____
Appraisal	400	$_____
Lawyer's fees	400	$_____
Recording fees	100	$_____
Transfer taxes	1,000	$_____
Other (prepayment penalty, etc.)	+ 0	+_____
Equals Total Cost of Refinancing	**$ 5,675**	$_____
The Payback		
Current monthly mortgage payment (principal and interest; based on 30-year fixed-rate at 10%)	$ 1,468	$_____
Subtract new mortgage payment (P&I; 30-year fixed-rate at 8%)	- 1,199	-_____
Equals pretax savings per month	$ 269	$_____
Multiply your tax rate (eg., 27%) by pretax savings and subtract result	- 67	-_____
Equals your after-tax savings per month	$ 202	$_____
Divide total cost of refinancing by monthly savings	$ 5,675 ÷ 202	$_____ ÷_____
Equals Number of Months to Break Even	**28**	

the money left after paying off the old loan for home improvements, monthly principal and interest payments on the new loan would be $1,559—just $91 more than on the old loan.

Refinancing can make sense even if you don't need to tap the equity in your home. Consider refinancing anytime there's a difference of two percentage points or more between your fixed-loan rate and current rates. The two-point rule works in your favor when you stay in the house long enough for lower monthly payments to offset the costs of refinancing—usually several years. Refinancing with less than a two-point differential can be advantageous if you plan to live in your home for a long time. Even a 1.5-point spread can do the trick when you stick around more than seven years. (Since ARM rates can change, refinancing from a fixed-rate loan to an ARM is more problematic.)

Figuring the Cost

In the worksheet (opposite page), first add up the cost of points and other fees, which can average 2 percent to 5 percent of the mortgage amount. To figure how long it would take to pay this back, calculate your new monthly payment, using the table on pages 152 and 153. Subtract that amount from your current principal and interest payment to get your monthly pretax savings. Then, because the interest is tax-deductible, subtract 25 percent of the savings—or 15 percent or 28 percent, depending on your top tax rate—to get your approximate after-tax savings. Divide the total cost of obtaining the mortgage by those savings. The result is how long it will take to recoup refinancing expenses. The longer you expect to keep the loan beyond that point, the stronger the argument for refinancing.

What If You Have an ARM?

The problem with ARMs is that your current rate probably is below today's 30-year fixed rate. Should you keep it, trade to a fixed rate, or take advantage of low teaser rates on new ARMs?

Consider refinancing anytime there's a difference of two percentage points or more between your fixed-loan rate and current rates.

The longer you'll be in the home, the better off you'll be paying more points to get the lower rate.

SWITCHING TO A FIXED RATE. If you plan to stay in your house, it could make sense to lock in a fixed rate. You wouldn't necessarily save a lot of money compared with the ARM you trade in, but you'd get peace of mind knowing you wouldn't lose if rates rose.

AN ARM FOR AN ARM. When first year "teaser" rates are two to three percentage points lower than your current ARM, it's tempting to consider switching an old ARM for a new one. First-year payments would drop substantially. But after that, the interest rate would reach about what it would have been on your old ARM, assuming the index and margin were the same. You come out ahead only if your first-year savings exceed the cost of refinancing.

SWITCHING FROM A FIXED-RATE TO AN ARM. If you plan to sell within one to three years, you could cut your monthly principal and interest payments dramatically by switching to an ARM. Assume you have a $200,000, fixed-rate 30-year loan at 9.5 percent. You can refinance with a 5 percent ARM, cutting monthly payments in the first year from $1,682 to $1,074. If you paid $6,000 in closing costs, you'd be ahead by nearly $1,300 without taking taxes into account. Even if the ARM rate jumped to 7 percent (because of a two-point annual cap), you'd pocket an additional savings of $4,212 in year two.

Comparing Points and Rates

A point, which is 1 percent of the mortgage amount, is prepaid interest—you pay it up front. Paying more points lowers the note rate by some fraction of a percentage point, so you have to decide between a higher rate and fewer points or a lower rate and more points.

The longer you'll be in the home, the better off you'll be paying more points to get the lower rate. A three-step calculation can help you choose the best combination of rates and points.

1. Estimate the number of years you'll keep the loan.

2. Divide the years into the number of points.

3. Add that to the interest rate.

To see how this works out, see the examples in the box below.

Tax Concerns

When you're refinancing just the balance of your mortgage, interest on the entire amount is tax-deductible. If you borrow additional money, the interest on up to $100,000 extra is deductible as home-equity debt. Unlike points for the original mortgage, points for refinancing must be deducted over the life of the loan, whether you pay in cash or add them to the loan, unless you use the funds for improvements to your home. If you use all additional funds from the refinancing for home improvements, you can deduct all interest payments on the loan and the full amount of the points related to the improvement.

You can keep money in your pocket by folding the closing costs into the loan. This also has the effect of adding otherwise nondeductible charges, such as an appraisal fee, to the amount on which you pay deductible interest.

Shopping Tips

Check first with your current lender to see whether it offers lower rates to its customers. Lenders might be willing to lower the rate for a small fee to keep their customers satisfied. The key is whether the lender has

---

THE DIFFERENCE POINTS MAKE

The examples below assume that you'll keep your loan five years. In the first case, the interest rate is 6% with three points. Three points divided by five years equals 0.6. Add that to the interest rate for an effective rate—reflecting the points—of about 6.6%.

INTEREST RATE	NUMBER OF POINTS	EFFECTIVE RATE
6.00%	3.0	6.60%
6.25	2.0	6.65
6.375	1.5	6.675

Ask for the rate apart from the fees, and note which fees are nonrefundable.

held on to the original loan or sold it on the secondary market. If the loan was sold, then you'll have to go the traditional refinancing route.

To compare fixed-rate loans, look at the APR, even though it has limitations—it assumes you'll hold the loan to maturity, for instance. Some lenders include the application fee, while others do not. Ask for the rate apart from the fees, and note which fees are nonrefundable.

Property values can be a sticking point because refinancing takes more equity than buying a house. Some lenders won't lend more than 75 percent of a home's value when you refinance for more than the balance on your current mortgage. For example, if your home is valued at $300,000, and your loan balance is $160,000, you might be able to get a new mortgage for $225,000 (75 percent of $300,000). That would enable you to repay the existing $160,000 balance, and still tap $65,000 of your equity.

About one in four loan applications doesn't go through, and applicants lose hundreds of dollars in nonrefundable fees. Avoid that kind of disappointment and hassle by getting yourself preapproved. Check with local real estate agents to get an estimate of your property's value.

If you refinance with your current loan servicer, streamlined rules mean you could save $500 to $600 on the typical 3 percent to 5 percent of loan principal charged in refinancings, and possibly get your request processed and closed in weeks rather than months.

Because lenders want to sell the loans they originate, most now have policies that conform to Fannie Mae's guidelines.

You don't need a new home appraisal when refinancing into a fixed-rate loan with the same lender—provided the lender vouches that the property hasn't lost value since the original loan was made.

A full-blown credit report isn't necessary—just a check of your existing electronic credit file and a simplified income verification. Your mortgage-payment record must be good but not necessarily perfect.

You can roll up-front refinancing costs into the new loan, and you need not wait any minimum time before refinancing.

Borrower Protections

Under the Real Estate Settlement Procedures Act (RESPA), mortgage lenders must provide refinancers with "good-faith" estimates of settlement costs and other fees associated with the loan. You must be given these estimates within three business days after applying for a loan, whether you have applied directly to a lender or used a mortgage broker. If you request the information, the lender must show you a completed "HUD-1" statement setting out actual charges one business day before settlement.

While real estate agents can receive fees for referring buyers to lenders (they can charge you for mortgage advice or for accepting a loan application), consumer-protection laws require agents to tell you about fees up front and forbid them to require the use of a particular lender. They must also give you a special HUD form telling you in plain language that you might save money by contacting lenders on your own. It's a felony for real estate agents to accept cash or other rewards from a lender or title company just for sending business their way.

Special Help for Senior Citizens

If you find yourself in the awkward position of having too little income for a comfortable lifestyle, but plenty of equity in your paid-up home, you aren't alone. Three out of four Americans age 65 and older own their homes, and more than 80 percent of those people have paid off the mortgage. Total home equity held by America's senior citizens may be as much as $2 trillion.

But many of these elderly people have only modest incomes; they wouldn't benefit from conventional means of tapping home equity because they couldn't handle the monthly repayment schedule for a new

Reverse mortgages allow you to live off your nest egg and in it, too.

mortgage or home-equity loan. If you face such a dilemma, you may want to look into ways to unlock that equity and convert it to monthly income (see the box on page 268).

Special-Purpose Loans

A far simpler option is to take advantage of special-purpose loans available from many local government agencies, nonprofit organizations, and a few state governments. These loans are usually restricted to homeowners with limited incomes. The loans most often carry low or no interest, and can be used for property taxes or to pay for home repair, health-related modifications, or in-home services. They need not be repaid until the house is sold or you die or move away permanently.

The "loans" don't always involve cash. You might be able to defer paying your property tax by setting up a special account with a government agency. When you defer the tax, the account establishes a lien against your property for the amount of the tax, which will be payable when you sell the house or die. For information about how to apply for a special purpose loan, contact your city or county housing and neighborhood development agency.

Reverse Mortgages

These special mortgages allow you to live off your nest egg and in it, too. Like home-equity loans, reverse mortgages now come in several forms. You can choose between either fixed monthly payments, a lump sum, or a line of credit on which you can draw funds as you need them. You pay nothing back until the term is up, when the advances plus interest must be repaid, presumably from the proceeds from the sale of your home. Monthly income is tax-free. In addition, non-insured loans can be obtained from some state and local government agencies, nonprofit organizations, and private lenders.

INSURED LOANS. A program run by the Federal Housing Administration (FHA) provides government-backed insurance to local, private, and public lenders who make approved reverse mortgages to older homeowners. You are eligible if you own your home and are at least 62. If you are married, your spouse must also be at least 62.

The FHA sets the initial maximum payout that can be made through the reverse mortgage, basing its calculation on your age (or your spouse's age if younger), interest rates, and equity in the home—up to the limit set by the agency in your area.

Using that figure as a starting point and assuming a certain rate of appreciation on your home, the lender then calculates what you could take out in a lump sum at settlement and what you could obtain as regular monthly income or withdraw periodically as needed. As you receive payments from the lender, you create a debt of principal and interest that you must eventually repay. When the house is sold or when you move, your equity pays off the loan. (There are ways to structure the mortgage to ensure that you will always have some equity if you have to move in the future.)

The FHA pools the insurance premiums it collects on each reverse mortgage. The pooled funds can be tapped by lenders who lose money on their loans. This could occur when a borrower outlives his equity—that is, he lives so long or the home appreciates so little that the final loan balance exceeds the value of the house. Whatever happens, you or your heirs would never owe more than the proceeds from the sale of the home, minus sales expenses.

FHA-insured loans offer five payment options:

- **Tenure.** With this option, you get equal monthly checks for as long as the house is your principal residence.
- **Modified Tenure.** You can combine a line of credit with monthly payments for life or as long as you live in the home as a principal residence.
- **Term.** You receive equal monthly payments for a fixed term. You choose the term.
- **Modified Term.** You can combine a line of credit with monthly payments for a fixed period of months.

Whatever happens, you or your heirs would never owe more than the proceeds from the sale of the home, minus sales expenses.

FOR MORE INFORMATION

For free information on reverse mortgages, check out the following sources:

■ **AARP** publishes *Home-Made Money: A Consumer's Guide to Reverse Mortgages* (#D12894). You can read the booklet online at http://www.aarp.org/money/revmort. You can also order the booklet online or by calling 800-209-8085.

■ **The Department of Housing and Urban Development** (800-217-6970; http://www.hud.gov/buying/rvrsmort.cfm).

■ **Line of credit.** You determine when you need to borrow money and the amount. You may borrow up to the permitted limit.

Whichever option you choose, you can alter the payment pattern in the future should circumstances change. If you select a loan with a tenure or term-payment option, you may want to combine it with an agreed-upon line of credit that will permit you to tap a portion of the loan for unanticipated needs. Say you sign on for a tenure loan that pays $300 a month. A year later, you find you need to add a bath on the ground floor of your home for your husband, who has become too frail to use the only existing bath, on the second floor. You could contact your lender and request a lump-sum payment to make the improvement—as long as your request would not exceed the principal limit of the loan.

FHA-insured reverse mortgages can be fixed- or adjustable-rate loans. Lenders are permitted to offer reverse adjustable-rate mortgages with monthly interest-rate adjustments and no annual limitation on interest increases, providing they also offer annually capped loans, which must carry a lifetime interest-rate cap of no more than five percentage points and an annual limit on rate increases or decreases of no more than two points.

With a reverse ARM, the payments don't change when interest-rate adjustments are made to the loan, but adjustments have the effect of increasing or decreasing the rate at which your equity is used up.

THE FANNIE MAE "HOME KEEPER." Fannie Mae has developed the Home Keeper Mortgage, a reverse mortgage that allows you to tap your equity through a line of credit, fixed monthly payments, or a combination of the two. With this plan, borrowers choose a particular payment method at closing, but can change the method at any point.

To be eligible, you and your spouse must be at least 62 years old and own your home free of debt (or be able to pay off any note with money from the reverse mortgage at closing). You'll also receive counseling from the lender offering the reverse mortgage. The counseling program was developed by Fannie Mae.

Home Keeper offers a higher loan limit than the FHA mortgage as well as some different options. You can choose a revolving line of credit, which gives you the flexibility of borrowing against your line of credit, repaying the debt, and borrowing against the line of credit again. If you decide upon a fixed monthly payment, you can also choose to stop payments for whatever period of time you choose. All fees and interest on the debt will, of course, continue to accrue.

Rates for Home Keeper are variable and based on the one-month CD index published weekly by the Federal Reserve. There's a 12 percent lifetime cap on the loan, which can be adjusted monthly up to the full 12 percent. For more information about Home Keeper, call Fannie Mae at 800-732-6643.

BUYER BEWARE. Before you begin drawing on your equity, make sure you understand fully the costs, fees, and risks associated with a reverse mortgage. Standard fees you will come across include an origination fee, a service fee to cover monthly paperwork, a mortgage-insurance premium for FHA loans, and other closing

Before you begin drawing on your equity, make sure you understand fully the costs, fees, and risks associated with a reverse mortgage.

In a sale-leaseback, parents typically sell their house to a son or daughter, who immediately leases it back to them for life.

costs that vary by state. Most costs can be rolled into the loan (except origination fees on FHA loans).

Though the receipt of payments shouldn't affect your Social Security income or Medicare eligibility, you do need to be careful if you're receiving Medicaid or supplementary Social Security income. Discuss this with your state's Social Security or Medicaid office before you finalize any loan.

If you select a reverse-mortgage program that is not FHA-insured, find out if the loan amount can exceed the home's value. If this is the case, and you live in an area where home values are declining, you could be responsible for debt beyond the value of your home. With an FHA-insured loan, you can never owe more than your home's value or the loan limit, whichever is lower. You also can't be forced to sell or move if your loan exceeds the limit.

Sale and Leaseback

In a sale-leaseback, a homeowner gives up title to become a renter. Typically, parents sell their house to a son or daughter, who immediately leases it back to them for life. The parents, assuming they have owned and lived in the house for at least two of the five years leading up to the sale, can qualify to treat $250,000 (on a single return) or $500,000 (on a joint return) as tax-free. Because the child owns the house and rents it out, he or she can depreciate it and deduct the expenses that go with being a landlord.

Most sale-leasebacks are seller-financed. The parents receive a down payment and take back a note for the remainder of the sales price. Things can be arranged so that the buyer makes monthly payments, providing a steady income stream to the parents. Some advisers suggest that the parents use the down payment to purchase a deferred annuity, which ensures that the parents will continue to receive the same amount of income if they outlive the payments on the note.

Sale-leasebacks are designed for people who want to spend the rest of their lives in the house, and they are useful when the primary objective is to keep the house in the family. The main drawback is that these arrangements are complicated. Four separate contracts may be involved: a sales contract, a rental contract, a mortgage contract, and, usually, an annuity contract. Moreover, the terms of each contract are interrelated and open to negotiation.

Tax considerations should figure in choosing between a sale-leaseback and other options such as a reverse mortgage. The IRS requires that the landlord charge a market rate of rent, or it could decide the deal is a tax dodge and nullify some of the tax advantages. Charging the same rent for 12 years, for example, won't meet the test. It's advisable to put an inflation clause in the rental agreement—raising the rent annually according to a specified index.

Parents also generally want some assurance they can rent "their house" for as long as they live. You must accomplish this indirectly or the IRS may decide that no sale really took place. A lease term that exceeds the parents' life expectancies and a clause that guarantees the seller the right to renew the lease each year may fit the bill.

Tax Angles of Selling a Home

Chapter 15

Say what you will about campaign promises, but homeowners owe a debt of thanks to one set of escalating promises that punctuated the 1996 presidential contest.

First, Republican candidate Senator Bob Dole said that, if elected, he'd make the first $250,000 of profit on the sale of a home tax-free. President Bill Clinton quickly countered, doubling the offer: If re-elected, he promised, $500,000 of profit would be tax-free. Congressional candidates fell all over themselves jumping on the bandwagon and, when tax legislation was written in 1997, it included an almost unbelievable deal for homeowners: In almost all cases, Congress banned the taxation of profit from the sale of a home.

Generally, if you file a single income-tax return, up to $250,000 of profit will be tax-free; double that to a half a million if you file a joint return. The tax-free amounts are large enough that usually only owners of the most expensive homes, or those who remain in the same house for decades, are likely to pay tax on profit from the sale of a home. It gets even better: You can use this break over and over during your lifetime, too, protecting the profit from one home after another. There's no lifetime limit on how much profit you can claim tax-free and there's even a way to pull a vacation home under the tax shelter.

A pure ban on taxing home-sale profits would have been too simple to come out of Washington, of course, so the lawmakers concocted a slew of new rules: i's to be dotted; t's to be crossed. All the details are laid out here. But the bottom line is this: The majority of homeowners will not have to pay a dime of tax on their

The majority of homeowners will never again pay a dime of tax on their home-sale profits.

home-sale profits. (Unless, of course, future Congresses decide to change the rules.)

Tax-free profit is the cherry on top of the whipped cream on top of the frosting on top of the cake. Despite the long-ago ban on deduction of interest for debts, homeowners continue to enjoy a huge loophole: We get to deduct interest on our biggest debt: the home mortgage. And our homes give us entrée to the home-equity loan, to get around the ban on deducting the interest on the debt we take on to buy our cars or pay off our credit cards. There are all sorts of other benefits, too, not to mention a nice place to live and raise our families. Here, we'll discuss the tax angles of selling your home sweet home.

Keeping Uncle Sam's Hands Off Your Profit

In a nutshell, here are the rules:

- **Up to $250,000 of home-sale profit is tax-free;** $500,000 if you file a joint return.
- **To qualify,** you must own and live in the house for two of the five years before the sale.
- **Generally,** you can use this break only once every two years.

Now, the details:

Under the law, the first $250,000 of profit on the sale of your principal residence is excluded from taxable income. The exclusion is doubled to $500,000 if you are married and file a joint return. Very few homeowners rack up so much profit. A married couple who buys a home at today's median existing home price—about $219,000—could watch the home more than double in value before they'd have to begin worrying about taxes on the profit. If you happen to make so much profit that some of it falls outside the $250,000/$500,000 tax shelter, the excess would be taxed as a long-term capital gain—at 20 percent—assuming you owned the house for more than 12 months. (If you make more than a quarter of a million dollars of profit in less than a year, congratulations!)

To qualify for the break, you must own and live in the house for two of the five years leading up to the sale. In order for married couples to qualify for the $500,000 tax-free amount, only one spouse must have owned the home for two of five years, but both must have lived in the house for two of five years before the sale.

You can claim tax-free profit at any age and as often as once every two years, unless you acquired the home through a tax-free exchange. Then you must own it for five years (see page 278 for an explanation of tax-free exchanges). If you sell within two years, profit on the deal is not protected and will be taxed—well, it *might* be taxed.

Of course there are exceptions to the general rules.

If you sell your home for a good reason less than two years after you moved into it—defined by Congress as a move connected with a new job or a move mandated by health problems or other unforeseen circumstances to be set out by the IRS—you qualify for a partial exclusion.

Say, for example, that you have owned and lived in your house for just one year before you sell it to move cross-country for a new job. And, say it's also been one year since you sold your old house and took all the profit tax-free. In this scenario, you'd qualify to take up to one-half of the maximum tax-free amounts—the same ratio as your time in the house and the time since the previous sale bear to the regular two-year requirement. So, you could take up to $250,000 of profit tax-free if you file a joint return, $125,000 if you file a single return. (Again, if you score more profit than that in such a short time, congratulations.)

What if the time you've lived in the house and the time since you sold your previous home differ? Say you bought the new home a year before the sale but only unloaded the previous house six months before the sale of the second home. In that case, your maximum exclusion would be based on the shorter period. That's six months in this example, so you'd qualify to take

If you sell your home for a good reason (as defined by the IRS) less than two years after you moved into it, you qualify for a partial exclusion.

What if you used the old once-in-a-lifetime $125,000 exclusion under the pre-1997 tax law? You can still qualify for the new exclusion.

up to one-fourth of the tax-free amounts—the same ratio as six months is to two years. That means you could have up to $125,000 of profit tax-free if you file jointly or $62,500 if you file a single return.

Here are some other "what ifs":

What if you used the old once-in-a-lifetime $125,000 exclusion in the past (under the pre-1997 tax law)? No matter. You can still qualify for the new exclusion.

What if you and the person you marry each own a home and, after the wedding, one of you sells? What's the maximum exclusion on your joint return? Assuming the seller owned and lived in the house for two of five years before the sale, he or she can exclude up to $250,000. A similar rule holds that if you marry someone who has sold a home and excluded gain prior to the marriage, that sale doesn't prevent you from claiming a $250,000 exclusion if you sell your home within two years.

What if, following a divorce, you and your former spouse sell the family home? Assuming that both of you pass the two-out-of-five-year ownership and residency tests, you can each exclude up to $250,000 of gain on your individual returns. If ownership of a home is transferred to you in a divorce, the time your former spouse owned the place is added to your period of ownership before the sale for purposes of the two-year test.

What if your widowed mother has to go into a nursing home and her home is put up for sale? Your mother would qualify for the $250,000 exclusion, assuming she owned and lived in the house for at least one year and, when time spent in the nursing home is included, she meets the two-out-of-five-year tests.

What if your spouse dies and you sell your home the following year, when you don't qualify to file a joint return? Your maximum exclusion would be $250,000, not $500,000. But, if your spouse jointly owned the home, the tax on half of the profit built up before his or her death would be forgiven anyway, under the rules for inherited property.

Other events that might occur during your period of use and ownership of the residence that qualify as "unforeseen circumstances" by the IRS are:

■ **becoming eligible for unemployment compensation;**
■ **a change in employment** that leaves the taxpayer unable to pay the mortgage or reasonable basic living expenses;
■ **multiple births** resulting from the same pregnancy;
■ **damage to the residence** resulting from a natural or man-made disaster, or an act of war or terrorism; and
■ **condemnation, seizure,** or other involuntary conversion of the property.

A Tax-Free Vacation Home?

Although this dynamite tax break is designed only for your principal residence, there's a way to legally squeeze tax-free profit out of a vacation home. After you sell your main home and cash in on up to $500,000 of tax-free profit, move into your vacation place and make it your home for at least two years. As soon as you meet the two-years-out-of-five residency requirement, the profit—including appreciation during the time it was your vacation home— qualifies for tax-free treatment.

If you rent out the vacation home, however, the profit wouldn't be 100 percent tax-free. As explained later, profit attributable to depreciation allowable after May 6, 1997, is generally taxed at 25 percent. (If you are otherwise in the 15 percent bracket, that rate would apply.)

A Home-Office Trap

There's a catch to the new break if you claim home-office deductions for part of your home. The problem is that the part of your home you

> A tax-free exchange is a legal maneuver to defer capital-gains taxes that would otherwise be due on the sale of a piece of investment real estate.

treat as an office is considered a business property and not part of your home when it comes to figuring tax-free profit. If you claim that 10 percent of your home is a home office, for example, 10 percent of your profit wouldn't be tax-free. Also, any depreciation you claim for use of the home office after May 6, 1997, would generally be taxed at 25 percent.

If you stop claiming deductions for the home office at least two years before you sell your home, however, you can avoid this tax trap. In that case, the full house would qualify as your home for two of the five years before the sale and all profit—except that attributable to post–May 6 depreciation—would be tax-free.

Tax-Free Exchanges

Another possibility is to use a tax-free exchange for the office part of your home. You can defer taxes due on the profit—and on depreciation attributable to that space after May 6, 1997. But the only way to take advantage of this and the $500,000 exclusion is to swap your home and its office for a similar home and office by using what's called a tax-free or 1031 or Starker exchange.

A tax-free exchange is a legal maneuver to defer capital-gains taxes that would otherwise be due on the sale of a piece of investment real estate. Working through a third-party facilitator, the owner essentially swaps his or her property for a similar property of equal or greater value. Profits from the original property reduce the cost basis of the acquired property, thus increasing the taxable gain if that property is ever sold. Rental apartments and office buildings have long been the clearest examples of properties that qualify for such exchanges. Doing swaps of residences with home offices can get complicated.

THE RESIDENTIAL SPACE. The IRS says owners who swap homes in this manner can still use the home-sale exclusion on gains for the portion of the home they lived in. That's important because it is the most significant of the two tax breaks.

THE OFFICE SPACE. You should seriously consider a swap if your home office is large, your profits on the sale would exceed the capital-gains exclusion mentioned above, and you have claimed substantial depreciation deductions for the office space.

SELLING VERSUS SWAPPING. Let's say a single taxpayer has owned and lived in a house for five years and used a third of it for a home office. He claimed depreciation deductions totaling $30,000 for the office portion of his home, and the profit on a sale would be $300,000.

He's a good candidate for a tax-free exchange. If he sells: The tax rules say that because his office and residence are located within a single dwelling, any gain from the sale of the dwelling up to $250,000 would be tax-free. On the $50,000 excess profit, he'd owe a 15 percent capital-gains tax. In addition, there's a catch concerning the office space. His $30,000 in depreciation deductions served to increase his profit by the same amount, and that portion of his gain doesn't qualify for the exclusion. He has to carve that out and pay a 25 percent tax on it. So in our example, the taxpayer will have to pay taxes on the $50,000 excess profit and $30,000 attributable to the deductions, for a total tax bill of $15,000. If he swaps his home for another one: Things go better. He can claim the $250,000 exclusion and defer the taxes on the excess gain and the depreciation deductions he claimed for the office.

If your home office is a separate part of your property, such as a carriage house, you can still swap the entire residence and defer the taxes attributable to the office portion of it.

THE FINE PRINT. In the swap example above, the present tax bill is zero. But keep in mind that a tax-free exchange defers the tax; it doesn't eliminate it. Eventually you'll have to pay taxes on the deferred gains when you sell your new residence, unless you execute another tax-free exchange.

What's more, although the rules about swapping are a little clearer than before, they're still very tech-

> **Keep in mind that a tax-free exchange defers the tax; it doesn't eliminate it. Eventually you'll have to pay taxes on the deferred gains.**

But, if all profit is tax-free, who cares about figuring the tax basis? Maybe you.

nical. You must follow all the rules. The IRS keeps close tabs on these kinds of transactions because of the potential for fraud. You should hire an experienced real estate or tax lawyer to arrange a swap. A routine transaction may take five to ten hours of legal work—expensive hours that you'll have to weigh against the tax benefit.

For more details, see IRS Publication 523, *Selling Your Home*, and the IRS guidance on swaps, *Revenue Procedure 2005-14*. You can get copies of both documents by typing their titles in the search box at http://www.irs.gov, or by calling 800-829-1040.

Record Keeping

All this talk of tax-free profit demands a discussion on how you figure that profit. The tax-free profit rule is *almost* the emancipation proclamation for homeowners, declaring freedom forever from keeping records to track the tax basis of their homes. That's the home's value for tax purposes, something you had to know when you sold so you could figure your profit. But, if all profit is tax-free, who cares about the basis?

Good point. But, unfortunately, all profit is not tax-free. Who has to worry about the basis of their home? You do, if you answer yes to any of these questions:

Is it possible that you'll live in your home long enough for the profit to exceed $250,000, or $500,000 if you're sure you'll be married when you sell? (Remember, the profit on the home you live in now includes the profit from all previous homes that you may have "rolled over" under the old law. Under pre-1997 tax law, you could put off a tax bill on home sale profits by buying yourself a more expensive home.)

Do you now, or is possible that in the future you will, rent out part of your home or use part of it as a home office for which you'll claim tax deductions? As noted above, that can put the kibosh on 100 percent tax-free profit.

Is it possible that you'll sell your home before you have lived in it for two years?

In any of those situations, you'll need to know your basis—so you can figure out your depreciation deductions if you rent or have a home office and, in any case, to figure how much of any profit is taxable when you sell.

Your tax basis begins simply enough—as what it costs you to buy the house. But it changes, quickly and often.

For example, when you buy a home, costs that can be included in the basis include title-insurance premiums, transfer taxes, property-inspection fees, utility-connection charges, and amounts owned by the seller that you agree to pay.

Then, as you own the home, the cost of capital improvements adds to your basis, too. As has been discussed in Chapter 3, a capital improvement is something that adds value to your home, prolongs its life, or adapts it to new uses. To be sure, your basis includes what you pay for an addition to the house, a swimming pool, and a new central air-conditioning system. It's not restricted to big-buck items, though. A new water heater counts, as do an intercom or security system or new storm windows.

The cost of repairs, on the other hand, doesn't add to your basis. Fixing a gutter, painting a room, or replacing a window pane are considered repairs rather than improvements.

The best tax advice used to be to keep detailed records of any work done around the house, including receipts for items that might qualify as improvements. The pack-rat habit could pay off handsomely. Every dime you could add to your basis was a dime cut from the taxable profit when you sold.

But now, for most taxpayers, that would be overdoing it. Unless you're renting part of your home or using part of it as a home office, don't sweat the little things. Keep your closing papers to show what the place cost, but—unless you feel there's a good chance you'll bust through the $250,000/$500,000 tax-free

> **The cost of capital improvements (which add value to your home, prolong its life, or adapt it to new uses) adds to your basis, too.**

Recognizing that it has no financial stake in most home sales, the IRS doesn't even want to hear about them.

profit ceilings—set a minimum value for the records you'll keep of improvements that add to your basis.

As noted earlier, few homeowners will ever earn more than $250,000 profit on their homes. And, if you sense that you're about to run into that terrible fate you can always sell, cash in your tax-free profit, and buy another place to house future tax-free profits.

When you sell a home, your profit is basically the net proceeds of the sale (selling price minus expenses, such as the agent's commission) minus your adjusted basis. Adjusted basis is what you paid for the house plus the cost of improvements, minus any casualty losses on the property that you claimed while living there—for fire or storm damage, for example. The basis is also reduced by any gain from a previous home that you rolled over into the house under the old tax law.

If you wind up with a loss on the sale, you're out of luck. Home-sale losses are not deductible.

No News Is No News

Recognizing that it has no financial stake in most home sales, the IRS doesn't even want to hear about them. The deal doesn't have to be reported on your tax form if there is no chance for the IRS to share in your profit. When you sell, the settlement agent will ask you to sign a form certifying that your profit is tax-free—that is, that you meet the owner-ship and residency requirements, the profit is below the tax-free limits, and that you weren't renting out the place or using it as a home office. This relieves the settlement agency of its responsibility to report the sale to the IRS on a 1099-S form.

Owner Financing

Sometimes, particularly when mortgage rates are high, the sale of a home goes through only be-cause the seller helps finance the deal. If you wind up holding a note of some sort, your tax picture is more complicated.

The selling price of your home includes the face value of any mortgage or note you receive, as well as cash, and the total is the amount you use for figuring your profit on the deal.

Payments on the note may combine return of your basis (nontaxable), part of your profit (probably tax-free under the rules discussed earlier), and interest on the loan (taxable). You should report the interest as income on Schedule B, the same form you use to report interest on a bank account. There's even a special line for reporting interest on seller-financed mortgages, and you need to list the payer's Social Security number.

If you're having trouble selling your home and thinking of renting it, be careful. You could lose the tax-free advantages of the tax law.

What If You Can't Sell?

It's a homeowner's nightmare: You move to a new home but can't find a buyer for the old one. Not only might you have to get a bridge loan to finance the new house, you also face the prospect of making two mortgage payments month after month. Few family budgets can handle that financial burden. One solution is to rent your former residence to generate cash to help pay the bills. But that can lead you into a maze of tax complications.

The tax-free profit rules apply only to your principal residence. Can a house that's being rented to someone else when you finally sell it qualify as your home? The good news is that if you can show that the rental was temporary, the house still qualifies as your principal residence and you can claim the profit tax-free. There's no hard and fast rule for how long a "temporary" rental can last before it becomes permanent, meaning the house wouldn't qualify as your residence for purposes of the tax-free profit break. Clearly, though, the longer the rental, the more evidence you'll need showing that you were really trying to sell it.

Things get much more complicated when it comes to writing off your expenses on the temporary rental property.

Temporary or not, you become a landlord in the eyes the IRS. And, as you would expect, the IRS

The IRS says you can't have it both ways— you can't treat the house as a principal residence for tax-free-profit and as a rental property for tax-loss purposes.

demands that you treat the rent you receive as income, assuming you rent the place for more than 14 days during the year. (Rent the place for 14 days or less and you can pocket the rent payments tax-free.) You may be able to offset the tax bill on the rental income completely, however, with deductions for rental expenses including the continued mortgage interest and property-tax payments on the house, the cost of repairs, and even depreciation.

The big question is whether the arrangement can produce a tax loss if expenses exceed rental income— as they often will under these circumstances. Such a loss, of course, could shelter other income—such as part of your salary—from tax, assuming you actively manage the rental.

But the IRS says you can't have it both ways— you can't treat the house as a principal residence for tax-free-profit purposes and as a rental property for tax-loss purposes. According to the IRS position, you can deduct rental expenses up to the amount of your rental income, but no more.

The issue is up in the air, however, because courts have disagreed on that point. In a key case in which the taxpayers beat the IRS, the court ruled, basically, that because the taxpayers charged fair-market rent for their home they deserved the same write-offs available to other landlords, even if that meant they had a tax loss to shelter other income. At the same time, because the taxpayers continued their efforts to sell the place, they deserved the breaks bestowed on homeowners. (Of course, you'd have to sell in time to still meet the two-out-of-five-year residency test.)

The IRS is sticking to its position, though. If you find yourself in this situation and claim a rental loss, the IRS may challenge your deductions if it audits you.

Permanent Rental

If you're unable to sell your old house within two years, you may want to consider making the rental arrangement permanent. Some homeowners plan from the outset to hang on to their old homes, a move that can be among the easiest ways to become a real estate investor. However, this strategy will carry a heavy cost: forfeiting the right to tax-free profit on the place.

There's also another catch to converting your home to a rental property. The value of the house for figuring depreciation deductions—a key write-off for real estate investors—is your adjusted basis or the fair market value of the house, whichever is less. The basis may be far less than what the house is worth when you convert it, particularly if you have pushed the basis down by rolling over profit from previous homes under the pre-1997 law.

Assume, for example, that your house is worth $300,000. You bought it for $100,000 many years ago and, at that time rolled over $30,000 in profit from your previous home. If you convert the house to a rental property, your basis for depreciation purposes is a skimpy $70,000. Because you cannot depreciate the value of land, you must subtract its value to determine the amount on which to base your depreciation write-offs. (If someone else bought your home for $300,000 and turned it into a rental property, the new owner's basis for depreciation purposes would be $300,000—minus the value of the land—and he or she would enjoy depreciation deductions more than twice as large as you are allowed.)

Selling for a Loss

As noted earlier, if you have the misfortune to lose money when you sell a home, don't expect any help from Uncle Sam. Losses on home sales are not deductible. But you may have heard that there's a way to write off such losses. Often promoted as a great tax scheme, promoters say home-sale losses can be deducted if, prior to the sale, you convert your house to a rental property.

That's true, but there's a catch that makes the tactic worthless. The basis for figuring your loss begins as the lower of the adjusted basis or fair market value at the

> If you lose money when you sell a home, don't expect any help from Uncle Sam. Losses on the sale of a home are not deductible.

time of the conversion. (The basis is increased for any improvements after the conversion and reduced for any depreciation claimed.) In other words, any loss in fair market value that occurs while you're living in the house still can't be deducted.

Moving Expenses

Selling a home is often connected with a job switch, and that can give rise to special write-offs for part of your moving expenses. There are two basic tests you must pass to get this tax-saver:

- **Distance.** Your move must be connected with taking a new job that is at least 50 miles farther from your old home than your old job was. If your former job was ten miles away from your old home, for example, the new job has to be at least 60 miles away from that old home.
- **Full-time employment.** You must work full-time for at least 39 weeks during the 12 months after the move. If you're self-employed, in addition to working 39 weeks in the first 12 months, you also have to work full-time at the new location for at least 78 weeks out of the first 24 months.

To pass these tests you must work in the new area, not necessarily at the same job, for the required time.

You claim the deductions on your tax return for the year of the move even if you haven't yet met the 39- or 78-week test by the time you file. If it turns out you are not eligible, you should either file an amended return for that year or report as income on your next tax return the amount previously deducted as moving expenses.

Fewer expenses are deductible now than in the past. At one time, for example, you could deduct the cost of pre-move house-hunting trips and even some of the costs of selling your old home and buying a new one. Those write-offs are gone. But the law still allows what are probably the most common and the most valuable write-offs:

■ **The cost of moving your household goods** to the new location; and

■ **The cost of moving yourself and your family**—travel and lodging expenses but not the cost of meals—to the new hometown.

When toting up the cost of the move, include what you pay for packing your belongings and charges for connecting or disconnecting utilities to move appliances. You can also include the cost of moving household goods and personal effects from a place other than your own home—say, from your college student's dorm—up to the amount it would have cost to move them from your old home. You can even deduct the cost of moving your pets from the old home to the new one. If you drive your own car, you can deduct ten cents a mile, as well as any parking fees and tolls incurred along the way.

If your employer reimburses you for the move, you don't have to go through the rigmarole required in the past of reporting the reimbursement as taxable income and then offsetting it by claiming moving-expense deductions. When your employer pays just expenses that qualify for the deduction—so there's no tax to collect—the IRS doesn't want to hear about it.

When toting up the cost of the move, include what you pay for packing your belongings and any charges for connecting or disconnecting utilities to move appliances.

Polishing the Merchandise

Before you make any decision on how to sell your home—through an agent or by yourself—or even what price to ask for it, put your property in the finest possible condition to impress buyers, agents, appraisers, and inspectors.

The way your house looks and functions will affect your bargaining power as a seller. Nothing can help a sale more than a thorough spit-and-polish campaign and below-the-surface attention, so now is the time for cleaning, touch-ups, and postponed maintenance. Replace the torn screen in the basement window, reset the loose tile in the bathroom, repair leaking faucets, and repaint the scratched front door.

Any real estate agent can tell you that a home that is well maintained and nicely decorated "shows well." Other things being equal, this kind of home will sell faster and for a higher price than a comparable house that isn't as attractive.

Do not, however, undertake a major redecorating just to prepare it for selling. Why? Your tastes may not coincide with those of the buyer. Rather than crediting you with work already done, a would-be buyer is going to factor in the estimated cost of redecorating the premises his or her way when figuring how much to offer you.

So stay away from such things as expensive new curtains and wallpaper, and don't install wall-to-wall carpeting over otherwise good floors, such as plank hardwood or parquet.

Concentrate instead on the decorating you believe is needed to make your home look good—painting,

---

FOR MORE INFORMATION

Dress Your House for Success: 5 Fast, Easy Steps to Selling Your House, Apartment, or Condo for the Highest Possible Price! by Martha Webb, with Sarah Parsons Zackheim (Crown). This practical guide provides a five-step program—"Uncluttering, Cleaning, Repairing, Neutralizing, and Dynamizing." It includes tips on using color and aroma to advantage, and suggests which improvements will yield the highest returns on your money.

50 Simple Steps You Can Take to Sell Your Home Faster and for More Money in Any Market by Ilyce R. Glink (Three Rivers Press) offers tips and expert advice about how to get the most value from any house or apartment in the shortest time possible. It includes ways to avoid common mistakes homesellers make; ideas for keeping your house ultraclean and organized; and room-by-room improvements—including the basement, attic, garage, and the exterior—that will add instant value to your home.

---

replacing worn linoleum, or placing wall-to-wall carpet over unfinished flooring. Choose neutral colors and simple patterns that are likely to harmonize with the tastes of most prospective buyers; they'll view these improvements as savings to them in both money and time.

Also consider the ideas for faster ways to sell presented in Chapter 19.

First Impressions Count

Here are some simple things you can do to ensure that your home makes a great, overall first impression:

Start with a curb-to-door cleanup. Prune shrubs and tree branches, edge the lawn and keep it mowed, and, if the season permits, add a show of color with annual bedding plants. Paint the front door and put out a new welcome mat.

Inside, make your home look as spacious as possible. Get rid of everything extraneous, admit as much daylight as possible, and keep things shipshape. Inventory what you want to sell, give away, or throw away when you move. Then do so before you begin showing your home. Clutter turns buyers off, so empty out crammed closets, pack away extra books and rarely used china, and sort out attic and basement storage spaces to avoid the flea-market look. Put things in commercial storage if that's what it takes.

Depersonalize your space. Reduce distractions, and help would-be buyers visualize making themselves at home. Tuck away the family pictures covering your bedroom wall. The display of family roots may fascinate some shoppers and embarrass others. A home that appears to be stamped indelibly with your personality and style can be harder to sell.

Remove obvious clues to your political, religious, and social sentiments. Store away banners, bumper stickers, and partisan literature, including magazines.

Get the Place in Shape

Walk through every room of your home and make a list of everything that needs to be done. During your inspection, jot down problems and note what can be done to make each room attractive. Taking down dark curtains and opening a room to sunlight may change its character completely. So can repainting.

You can't anticipate what will catch the attention of a prospective buyer. Plaster walls and a new furnace may hardly elicit a comment—but the cracked toilet-tank top, that's another story. A buyer may spend hours

> **Walk through every room of your home and make a list of everything that needs to be done.**

(continued on page 294)

PREPARING TO SELL

Use this checklist to identify areas of your home that need work before you put it on the market.

INSIDE

Attic
- ❑ Check underside of roof for leaks, stains, or dampness.
- ❑ Look around chimney for condensation or signs of water.
- ❑ Clean and clear ventilation openings if necessary.
- ❑ Clean out stored junk.

Walls and Ceilings
- ❑ Check condition of paint and wallpaper.
- ❑ Repair cracks, holes, or damage to plaster or wallboard.

Windows and Doors
- ❑ Check for smooth operation.
- ❑ Replace broken or cracked panes.
- ❑ Repair glazing.
- ❑ Check condition of weather stripping and caulking.
- ❑ Examine paint.
- ❑ Test doorbell or chimes.
- ❑ Test burglar alarms.
- ❑ Wash windows and woodwork.

Floors
- ❑ Inspect for creaking boards, loose or missing tiles, worn areas.
- ❑ Check baseboards and moldings.
- ❑ Test the staircases for loose handrails, posts, treads.
- ❑ Clean carpets.

Bathrooms
- ❑ Check tile joints, grouting, and caulking.
- ❑ Remove mildew.
- ❑ Repair faucets and shower heads that are dripping.
- ❑ Check the condition of painted or papered walls.
- ❑ Test operation of toilet.

Kitchen
- ❑ Wash all appliances.
- ❑ Clean ventilator or exhaust fan.
- ❑ Remove accumulation of grease or dust from tiles, walls, cabinets, floors.
- ❑ Remove refrigerator "art" and magnets.
- ❑ Remove clutter from countertops.

Basement
- ❑ Remove clutter.
- ❑ Check for signs of dampness, cracked walls, or damaged floors.
- ❑ Inspect structural beams.
- ❑ Check pipes for leaks.

Electrical System
- ❑ Check exposed wiring and outlets for signs of wear or damage.
- ❑ Repair broken switches and outlets.
- ❑ Label each circuit or fuse.

Plumbing System
- ❑ Check water pressure when taps in bathroom(s) and kitchen are turned on.

❏ Look for leaks at faucets and
sink traps.

❏ Clear slow-running or clogged drains.

❏ Bleed air off radiators if needed, and
check for leaking valves.

Heating and Cooling Systems

❏ Change or clean filters from furnace
and air-conditioning equipment.

❏ Have equipment serviced if needed.

❏ Clear and clean area around heating
and cooling equipment.

OUTSIDE

Roof and Gutters

❏ Repair or replace loose, damaged, or
blistered shingles.

❏ Clean gutters and downspout
strainers.

❏ Check gutters for leaks and proper
alignment.

❏ Inspect flashings around roof stacks,
vents, skylights, and chimneys.

❏ Clear obstructions from vents,
louvers, and chimneys.

❏ Check fascias and soffits for decay and
peeling paint.

❏ Inspect chimney for any loose or
missing mortar.

Exterior Walls and Doors

❏ Renail loose siding and check for
warping or decay.

❏ Paint siding if necessary.

❏ Check masonry walls for cracks
or any other damage.

❏ Replace loose or missing caulking.

❏ Apply fresh coat of paint to front door.

Driveway

❏ Repair concrete or blacktop if necessary.

Garage

❏ Lubricate hinges and other
hardware on your garage door.

❏ Inspect doors and windows for
any peeling paint.

❏ Check condition of glazing
around all windows.

❏ Test electrical outlets.

Foundation

❏ Check walls, steps, retaining walls,
walkways, and patios for cracks,
heaving, or crumbling.

Yard

❏ Mow and edge lawn, reseed
or sod if necessary.

❏ Trim hedges, prune trees, and shrubs.

❏ Weed and mulch flowerbeds.

assessing the heating and plumbing systems and apparently ignore the fresh paint, refinished floors, and brand-new windows.

Use the inspection guide on pages 292 and 293 to see your home as buyers might.

Do Your Homework

Be prepared to answer questions. Get out heating, cooling, and water bills, and figure annual totals and monthly averages. Pull together appliance receipts, service records, and information on when major systems, such as the furnace, were installed. Collect warranties on siding, roof shingles, and so forth. Organize them in a folder for easy reference.

Are Disclosures Needed?

Many states require that owners who sell residential real estate disclose to all prospective buyers any material defect that the owner is aware of. Depending on the law in your state, you may be required to reveal known problems and defects in your home's roof, walls, foundation, basement, plumbing, heating and electrical systems, as well as past pest problems, and the presence of hazardous materials such as radon, lead-based paint, and asbestos.

The Radon Question

Radon wasn't a household word until a Pennsylvania nuclear-power-plant worker set off radiation alarms at work because he had been exposed to extraordinarily high levels of radon at home. A colorless, odorless radioactive gas produced by decaying uranium, radon exists naturally in soil and rock. But when it seeps into homes where it cannot diffuse as quickly as in open air, the gas can accumulate to unhealthy levels.

The Environmental Protection Agency (EPA) and private testing companies have detected unsafe levels of radon in nearly every state. But the EPA found unsafe levels in only about 20 percent of the homes tested

---

MORE ON RADON

You can request free copies of the following Environmental Protection Agency's booklets from your state's radon, radiation control, or radiological health office, order them online or by telephone from the EPA, or read them at the EPA's Web site (800-490-9198; http://www.epa.gov):

Home Buyer's and Seller's Guide to Radon

A Citizen's Guide to Radon: The Guide to Protecting Yourself and Your Family from Radon

Consumer's Guide to Radon Reduction

Your state's radon office can also provide an EPA report that includes a list of radon-testing companies.

---

in ten states, and of those, just 1 percent registered levels above 20 picocuries per liter, defined by the EPA as the equivalent of smoking two packs of cigarettes a day. The EPA says there is a definite link between indoor radon exposure and lung cancer.

Once you decide to sell your home, you may want to test for it, especially if there have been radon problems in your area. In some areas homebuyers are including contingency clauses in sales contracts that require a test for, and sometimes correction of, radon problems before they will buy. In most cases, unacceptable levels of indoor radon are handled by improving ventilation.

Check with your real estate agent about radon disclosure requirements and with your state or local environmental office about testing methods. If you're concerned, you may want to get a test done by an approved professional.

Lead Paint

Many states have lead-based paint disclosures as part of their mandatory property-condition reports. Federal law requires that when you sell a home built before 1978 you tell all prospective buyers about known lead-based paint used in and around the property.

Protect Yourself

Shift as much liability as you can from your shoulders to those of the professionals you are paying to assist you with the sale. If you are using an agent to help you sell your home, ask to be informed of your responsibilities. Make it clear that you want your agent to fully assume his or hers, as well. Use a home inspector who carries errors-and-omissions insurance. Discuss potential liability with your lawyer.

Sell Through an Agent or Go It Alone?

Chapter 17

The vast majority of homes are sold through a listing contract with a real estate agent, with the seller paying the typical 6 percent commission on the sales price. But what about the rest? Their owners apparently asked themselves, "Why pay someone thousands of dollars for doing something I can do myself, with the help of a few professionals whom I can compensate on a flat-fee or hourly basis?"

Saving $18,000 on a $300,000 home sale is plenty of motivation for a "fizzbo," or FSBO (For Sale by Owner)—a term real estate agents use somewhat disdainfully. The urge to try selling one's own home is especially strong in a seller's market, when qualified buyers are plentiful, listings are relatively few, and everything that's fairly priced gets snapped up.

Agents can reel off a dozen or more arguments against trying to sell your own home, among them that you could set the wrong price, accept an unqualified buyer or lose the help of agents, who won't bring their clients by to see your home. Sure, all of those things can happen—but some of them might happen even if you list your home with an agent.

An Agent's Strengths

The fact that most people do use an agent to sell their homes suggests that a lot of homeowners believe they get good value for the 6 percent commission. Selling a house by oneself is hard work, and it requires time, savvy, and a knack for selling.

The tasks involved in selling a house can be accomplished by an organized, determined seller aided by key professionals.

Good sales agents offer many benefits. They are experienced at the proper pricing of a property and writing of effective ads. They will advise you on sprucing up your home for an easy sale. In a slow market, they will beat the bushes for buyers. They can help screen buyers on financial qualifications. They'll review the buyers' offers and negotiate the best deal they can get for you. They'll help locate financing for your buyer and shepherd both parties through the twisting maze toward settlement.

Another important benefit of selling through an agent is getting your home listed in a multiple listing service (MLS)—the computerized clearinghouse of properties listed with professional brokers. Until recently, if you set out to sell your home yourself, your house couldn't be listed on the MLS. Now some brokers (mostly discount brokers) offer to list for-sale-by-owner homes on the service for a flat fee. This significantly improves your chances of finding a buyer. If you choose not to list on the MLS, then you'll need to really intensify your marketing efforts.

Finally, if the agent can get you a price at least 6 percent higher than you could get selling your home yourself without paying a commission, then the agent's skills cost your nothing, theoretically (see Chapter 19).

Going It Alone

Without denying real estate agents their due, the tasks involved in selling a house can be accomplished by an organized, determined seller aided by key professionals—appraiser, inspector, and real estate lawyer—who will charge on an hourly or flat-fee basis rather than on commission.

You don't need a license or official permission to sell your own property. But you will need the following resources:

TIME. If you are going to assume the task of selling your own home, then you will need to do as professional a job of it as any top real estate agent would do, and to do that will require time—and lots of it. You'll need time to prepare your home for sale, to study the market, to prepare professional-looking fact sheets and gather mortgage and financial data, and to show your home to prospective buyers. These are not particularly difficult jobs, but they will require that you devote hours to background work, preparation, and organization.

No matter how hard you work at selling your home, a house or condo may not move quickly if it is unusual in some way, in disrepair, in a deteriorating neighborhood, or equipped with expensive extras not every buyer wants, such as a swimming pool.

In today's real estate market, you need to show your home during the day, as well as at night. And be prepared to give up your weekends to running open houses. If you choose to show the house by appointment only, you will probably lose a lot of traffic and potential buyers.

If you can't arrange to be home during a showing, make sure that a responsible adult is there in your place who can answer questions and really show your home to prospects.

PATIENCE. Unless you are used to dealing with the public, it is easy to underestimate the amount of patience you will need to handle telephone calls, answer questions, give directions to your home, and show the property—over and over again.

INFORMATION. You will need to know all about your neighborhood, your property, your appliances, furnace, roof, plumbing and electrical systems. You must be willing to get the facts you need to assist prospects with financing. You should be thoroughly familiar with all comparable properties in your area.

KNACK FOR SELLING. If the prospect of displaying the merchandise, fielding questions, overcoming objections, and solving problems in order to make the sale impresses you as indelicate or undignified, reconsider handling this project without a real estate agent.

> In today's real estate market, you need to show your home during the day, as well as at night.

One idea to consider: Never show your home when you're alone.

INTUITION. Will you be able to tell a real candidate from a window-shopper? Time spent with individuals or couples who haven't really decided to buy is time not spent with those who have—and who only need to be sold on your home.

CASH UP FRONT. You'll need some cash up front for buying advertising in your local paper ($30 to $65 or more per week, depending on your area, the size of your ad, and whether it is a print or online ad), copying fact sheets, and buying contract and buyer-information forms. Most sale-by-owner Web sites (see page 306) will charge a small fee for their services. You might also be able to find a broker who, for a fee, will list your home on the multiple listing service and supply you with a sign and a lockbox. While an appraisal isn't required, it could be worth the $300 to $400 to have it on hand for interested buyers. You may also decide to have the home inspected for an additional $300 to $400 (but be sure to inquire into the scope of services included in the price). And, of course, you may need money to make repairs and spruce up the place.

SAFETY CONCERNS. Here's another issue you need to consider. Unlike a real estate agent, you probably won't have had the opportunity to meet and assess prospective buyers in a business setting before you let them into your home.

Some ideas you might want to consider include putting away all valuables (jewelry, credit cards, cash, or any small object that can be easily placed in a bag or pocket), keeping spare keys in a safe place, and, most important, never showing your home when you're alone.

PHONE ETIQUETTE. If you're placing ads in the paper and listing your phone number, you'll need an answering machine unless you're home 24 hours a day. Buyers will not keep calling back if they get no response. You may even wish to provide some information about the house in your message—such as number of bedrooms and baths or the fact that the backyard is fenced in or has a pond. And, above all, be sure to call back any prospective buyer promptly.

ELBOW GREASE. Make your place gleam, even if it means hiring a cleaning crew. Paint and make other improvements. Everything said in Chapter 16 about getting your home ready goes double if you're selling it yourself. A glib agent can talk a client past a plaster crack or dirty wallpaper, but you'll have a much harder time of it. (If you expect to reap taxable profit from the sale of your home—which won't be a concern for most homesellers—keep track of what you spend in getting the place in shape. Fixing-up expenses incurred in the 90 days before the sale can be used to shave the tax on any profit.)

INTERNET SAVVY. Check out the numerous sale-by-owner sites on the Internet. See the box on page 306.

Steps to Success for the Fizzbo

If you choose to act on your own behalf, then you'll want to take the following steps to sell your home efficiently and achieve the best result—a smooth sale at a satisfactory price.

Price It Right
The single most important task in the selling of a house is pricing it—right at the market value, neither too low nor too high. This requires either your own careful study of comparable transactions in your neighborhood or the services of a professional appraiser, who will do the same thing for you.

The owner must decide whether to price the house at full market value and try to pocket the commission savings, or to share these savings with the buyer, settling for a little less than the full asking price but more than he or she would get from an agent sale at asking price minus commission. (For a full discussion of pricing, see Chapter 19.)

The single most important task in the selling of a house is pricing it.

Prepare Fact Sheets

Prospects seldom take notes as they are being shown around. They may be reluctant to appear too interested, or they may find writing distracts them from looking. But they rarely refuse a printed fact sheet.

These fact sheets are important; they tell at a glance what you're selling, highlight the best points, and can later refresh the memories of lookers who may have seen a dozen other offerings. See the box below for a list of what to include.

In addition, inform potential buyers orally about known problems or defects (see the discussion in Chapter 16). You're legally obliged to, and failing to do so could cause you to lose a sale or become entangled in a lawsuit. Find out what disclosures and forms are required from sellers in your state. Make sure you know your responsibilities with regard to lead-based paint, radon, and asbestos. Make sure that professionals you hire, such as a home inspector or lawyer, carry errors-and-omissions or professional liability insurance.

WHAT THEY NEED TO KNOW

When preparing a fact sheet for prospective buyers, include the items described below and type it, preferably on a single page. Add a statement that the "information is not guaranteed but deemed accurate to the best of my knowledge." You may want to include the appraised value and a drawing of the layout. For added impact, attach a snapshot of the place—one that shows it to advantage in its best season of the year. Make copies of your fact sheet so you can give one to each prospect.

Relevant Information about the Property
- age
- construction
- square footage
- room dimensions
- mechanical systems (air-conditioning, heat, and so on)
- appliances that go with the home
- amenities
- lot size
- proximity to schools, public transportation, shopping, and such

Financial Information
- the price
- annual taxes
- annual maintenance and utility costs
- any relevant information about the current mortgage, if it's assumable, and seller-financing help, if any

---

Get Contract and Buyer-Qualification Forms

Preprinted contract forms, which vary from state to state, can be obtained from office-supply stores, stationers, discount brokers, real estate boards, or lawyers. Alternatively, you can ask the attorney who will represent you to draw up a contract to meet your requirements and protect your interests while conforming to state and local laws—particularly with regard to disclosures about your property's physical and structural condition. Some real estate lawyers may help clients negotiate a deal and assess the creditworthiness and financial abilities of prospective purchasers.

Qualification forms, which you can draw up yourself or with your lawyer's assistance, will help you decide whether a prospective buyer is financially able to follow through on his or her offer. When an offer is submitted, have the person fill out the form, listing annual income, debts, assets, place and length of employment, credit references, and any other relevant information.

VA AND FHA ANSWERS
Be prepared to answer questions about VA and FHA loans if your home is likely to attract veterans and first-time buyers. One reference is *All About Mortgages: Insider Tips for Financing and Refinancing Your Home* by Julie Garton-Good (Dearborn Publishing).

Gather Documents You May Need

Questions may come up that could be answered by a site plan or surveyor's report. If you're selling a condominium unit, be sure you have the declaration or plan of condominium ownership (also called the declaration of covenants or the master deed), the bylaws of the owners association, and the rules governing property use. Also have handy your actual stubs or photocopies of utility bills and recent tax bills.

Bone Up on Mortgage Financing

Offers usually are made contingent on the buyer's ability to get financing. It is in your interest to be helpful to buyers who find the prospect of getting a mortgage more intimidating than finding a home. Remember, this is the sort of service that a real estate agent provides to prospective buyers, and you must do the

THE MAKINGS OF AN EFFECTIVE AD

Read the Sunday paper and study the ads written by the professionals. You'll find that the best ads have full descriptions of the house, not sketchy write-ups with so much abbreviation that they're hard to decipher. The strong points are played up, the weak points omitted or put in the best possible light. A small house, for example, becomes "cozy" in a good ad. Avoid exaggeration and overly cute writing. In addition:

- **Always put in the price.**
- **If it's an ad for an open house,** list the address and some general directions.
- **Otherwise, you may wish to list only your phone number,** to get calls for appointments.
- **Run the ad in the Sunday paper.**
- **To ensure the most accurate ad,** fax or e-mail your ad copy to the newspaper rather than calling it in.

same if you are really serious about selling your house yourself.

Draw up a list of lenders and check weekly on financing rates and terms. Your local newspaper may publish such information (see Chapter 10 for other sources of mortgage-rate information). Bookmark a financial calculator on your Web browser (see http://www.kiplinger.com) or keep an interest-rate table and calculator handy so you can help a prospect calculate on the spot what monthly principal and interest payments would be.

You may be asked by some prospective buyers whether you are willing to assist them by taking back a second trust on your house. Before the issue arises, discuss the risks with your lawyer. Familiarize yourself with the various kinds of "creative financing" discussed in Chapter 9 and consider whether you'd want to get involved with it. See Chapter 20 for mistakes to avoid when offering seller financing.

Generally, when interest rates are not too high and there are many qualified buyers, you don't have to help the purchaser with financing. A sale that gives you cash for your property sets you free to invest as you wish, whether in your next house or in some other investment.

Put Up an Attractive Sign

Create a good impression by putting up a bright new sign in the front. Look in a hardware or sign shop for a "For Sale by Owner" sign that has a place below the main message for an add-on sign (or have one made professionally). During the week, you can hang out a phone number. And if you have an open house, you can remove that portion and hang an "Open" sign.

Signs are effective sources of clients for both amateur sellers and real estate firms. A response to a sign is a more valuable inquiry than a response to a newspaper ad. The sign caller is already in the neighborhood. He or she probably knows and likes the area and obviously likes the look of your home well enough to want to see the inside. You are two selling steps ahead of a classified-ad caller. That person is responding to general information, and may or may not like your area or the external appearance of your home when and if a viewing appointment is made and the prospect arrives.

Give Good Directions

All the good advertising money can buy won't get people into your home if they get lost trying to get there. Prepare easy-to-follow directions. Anticipate where prospects will be coming from, and route them along the simplest, most direct, and most attractive route you can devise. Keep a large map near your telephone to help you answer questions and redirect turned-about buyers who care enough to call.

Hold an Open House

Sunday open houses are a ritual among house hunters. You'll get a lot of serious buyers, a lot of lookers who are just curious, and a few neighbors who like to keep abreast of the local market. Any of these could lead to a successful contract, sooner or later.

> **A response to a sign is a more valuable inquiry than a response to a newspaper ad.**

Have a visitor register handy—a simple pad of paper or a notebook will suffice—so you can get names, phone numbers, and e-mail addresses. Some people will gladly sign it, while others will decline, preferring anonymity; be careful not to press the point.

Most buyers like to go through a house by themselves, so that they can discuss its strengths and weaknesses without embarrassing the owner. Station yourself in the front hall or the dining room, greet visitors warmly, and hand them a fact sheet that they can take through the house with them. But don't escort them unless they ask you to. (If you're worried about security, make sure any small objects of value are locked up or stashed out of sight.) Before they leave, ask them if they have any additional questions. Remember you're selling your house; try to engage visitors in conversation so you can make your best points.

If both spouses of a couple feel comfortable showing the house together, that's a good idea. If one gets into a deep discussion (or even an unexpected negotiation) with a serious prospect—in a private place, out of earshot of other visitors—the other spouse can continue to greet new visitors.

SELLING YOUR HOME ON THE INTERNET

If you are selling your home yourself, take advantage of one or more of the Internet sale-by-owner services. You will have to fill out an information form and usually provide a picture of your home. Before listing on a site, take the time to visit it and check the following:

- **Are enough homes listed to attract buyers?**
- **Would you use this site if you were a buyer?**
- **Is there a fee for listing?** Many sites are free but some charge fees for the listing or other services.

Two sites worth checking are:

- **http://www.fsbo.com** will run your ad, including eight photographs of the property for nine months on the Internet for $69.95. For more information, write to FSBO Inc., P.O. Box 500145, Atlanta, GA 31150, or call 800-690-5802.
- **http://www.allthelistings.com** will list your property for free, but its premium listing, for $59 a month, buys you a "front-page" ad that features up to six pictures of your house.

Be Ready to Negotiate

Some interested buyers will want to sleep on their first impressions and return to your house one or more times, ideally getting more comfortable with it each time they come.

But the highly prepared buyer—who knows just what he wants and thinks he has found it in your property—may want to get right into a negotiation, especially if the market is tight and he's afraid your house will go fast.

It isn't unheard of for a visitor to an open house to take one of your prepared contract forms, go home and fill it out, and then come back to submit it before the day is out.

If you have a "live wire" buyer in your midst, be ready to deal. There are some questions about your acceptable contract terms that are fine to discuss orally, such as an ideal settlement date, occupancy date (if different from settlement), and your willingness to finance part of the deal yourself.

But the most important element—price—should not be negotiated orally, nor your intentions telegraphed. While still in your home, some buyers will ask questions like, "Is your price firm?" or "What are you really willing to accept?"

Don't answer directly, but try to deflect these questions in a courteous, noncommittal way that keeps the buyer interested, with an answer like, "The house is fairly priced for the market right now, but all offers will be considered," or "The price, like other aspects of your offer, can be negotiated; please feel free to make us your best offer."

For a fuller discussion of seller negotiating strategies, see Chapter 20.

Anticipate Agents

As soon as you start advertising or hold your first open house, you'll get calls from agents asking for a listing. They will often tell you that your home is priced way too low, and if they help you sell it, they'll get you

> **If you're lucky enough to have a "live wire" buyer in your midst, be ready to deal.**

While you're holding firm to your own sales effort, don't allow agents to visit your property with prospects.

enough to more than cover the commission and net you more than you'll get selling by yourself.

They might be right; but then, their judgment isn't exactly objective. If you've proceeded on your course with care and have priced your house according to comparable values in the market, stand your ground—at least for a while. Tell inquiring agents you intend to try it yourself first.

Be wary of anyone who attempts to get a sales listing on your house by claiming to have a hot prospect who is looking for a home just like yours. If the agent's prospect is truly motivated, he or she probably checks out the Sunday real estate ads and will see your ad; at that point, you will get a direct inquiry from the buyer. (The main exception to this assumption, which makes the agent's claim more valid, is the out-of-town buyer who is relying totally on the agent to find houses.)

While you're holding firm to your own sales effort, don't allow agents to visit your property with prospects. If you allow the agent to bring a prospect without a written agreement, you may have in effect granted an open listing to the agent. And if the prospect buys, you may end up paying a commission. (Some states have tried to avoid misunderstandings—and suits—between fizzbo sellers and agents by enacting laws that effectively bar an agent from collecting a commission unless there was some sort of written agreement with the seller.)

While holding eager agents at bay, set a time limit on your own brokering, exactly as you would with a professional broker. Give yourself 30, 60, or 90 days, depending on the current selling climate and how quickly you must sell your house. Then, during your time period, be clear and firm with agents seeking a listing: "No listings until I've taken a crack at it myself." Do your best to sell the home, but if you don't succeed within your time limit, back off and turn the job over to an agent of your choice.

Getting Help

As we've already mentioned, you can get professional assistance from agents and discount brokers to help you sell your home more rapidly. Some require that you pay a partial commission, others set a flat fee. But before signing a listing contract or a contract with a buyer's broker, check for new "transaction fees" that some real estate brokerages are adding to their preprinted forms, ostensibly to cover paperwork. Although these fees are still the exception rather than the rule, remember that, by law, the agent is supposed to disclose any fees before you sign a listing or buyer-broker contract. If you don't want to pay the fee, ask the broker to strike it from the contract or find another company to work with. Depending on the kind of real estate market you're selling in, the help may be well worth every penny it costs you, but you shouldn't pay more than what you originally signed onto.

Temporary Listing Contract

If you think a particular agent has a buyer who might not see or buy your house without the agent's cooperation, you might be persuaded to give the agent a shot at selling your house, but for less than a 6 percent commission. This calls for a short-term, custom-tailored listing agreement.

Tell the agent to come alone to your house (even if the prospective buyer just waits in the car at the curb) and sign a temporary listing agreement that contains the name of the agent, the amount of the commission (generally just 2 percent or 3 percent, because you've done most of the work yourself), the name of the prospective buyer, and the asking price for this particular transaction. To cover the commission you're going to pay if the deal goes through, the price will probably be higher than what you've been asking for a fizzbo transaction.

Be professional and direct: You should limit the time an agent has to bring you a purchase offer from

Some situations may call for a short-term, custom-tailored listing agreement.

If you are willing to pay 3 percent to an agent who brings in the final buyer, you should let other agents know.

this buyer, so the agreement—covering only the specifically named buyer—should be valid for only one or two days at most.

Open Listing: 3 Percent Deal for All Agents

Because many house hunters do their searching with agents, who get compensated for those efforts only by sharing in the sales commissions, it's understandable that the agents will try to steer their clients away from fizzbo listings. A fizzbo who refuses to pay any commission will, in effect, be trying to split house hunters away from the agents who may have given them considerable help in the search.

If, as described above, you are willing to pay 3 percent to an agent who brings in the final buyer, you should let other agents know. They will probably be more than willing to cooperate—a 3 percent commission is about as much as they make on most home sales, because the 6 percent commission is usually split between the listing broker and the broker's agent. Agents will ask you to draw up a listing agreement—called an open listing—that guarantees them their commission if the deal goes through.

You should be willing to sign such a listing, one for each agent. Unlike the agreement above, it need not identify a particular buyer. It can cover as long a period as you wish, but writing in a finite expiration date is essential, because you may not legally sign an exclusive listing agreement with any agent while you have valid listings like these still floating around open.

If you decide to try this partial fizzbo method, make sure you put the words "sale by owner; brokers welcome at 3 percent" in your ads.

Discount Agents and Counselors

Some real estate brokers offer bare-bones service, charging flat fees or lower commissions in exchange for specific services that can run the gamut from the most basic—renting a sign—to service barely distinguishable from full-service brokerages. Most offer something in between. Some discount Realtors offer clients the option of a flat-fee listing for from $300 to $600. For this fee, an agent will come to your home to complete the MLS listing form, photograph your home's exterior, list your home on the MLS, list your home on the Internet with realtor.com and others, and supply you with a list of comparables in your area and price range along with copies of information sheets to supply prospective buyers. The MLS listing offers a 3 percent commission to the selling company, but if you sell the home yourself you pay no commission at all. For an additional charge of about $100 (refunded when all items are returned), you can get a lockbox and sign. Some will also assist you with preparing contracts and other documents for an hourly charge.

If you are considering a discount broker, apply all the same standards you would if you were selecting a full-service broker (see the next chapter). One service you probably shouldn't pass up is having your home advertised to other agents through the multiple listing service in your area. Make sure any discount broker you're considering can list your home with the service.

There also may be real estate counselors or broker-consultants in your community who help owner-sellers for a percentage of the selling price or work on an hourly basis. For names, check with large real estate firms in your area and watch for advertisements in the real estate section of the paper, or contact the Counselors of Real Estate (430 N. Michigan Ave., Chicago, IL 60611; 312-329-8427; http://www.cre.org). In some communities, title companies will help you close the deal once you have a contract with a buyer.

If you are considering a discount broker, apply all the same standards you would if you were selecting a full-service broker.

Picking a Broker, Listing Your Home

I f you're like most Americans, your home is your principal asset. If you want to turn the work of selling your home over to a broker, try to choose one who will help get the highest price (or the best deal) for you and perform the task honestly and effectively.

While any broker can list, advertise, and show your home, brokers and agents—like lawyers, doctors, and car dealers—come in every variety, bringing with them different economic backgrounds, personalities, resources, and levels of skill and integrity. Regardless of whom you hire, you're going to end up paying a broker and her agent thousands of dollars for their services. Despite the importance of the broker's job, two out of three sellers hire the first agent they contact. Needless to say, that's not the best way to do it.

Identify one or two brokerage firms in your area with a reputation for integrity and a proven track record selling homes comparable to yours. Then interview at least three of those firms' successful agents whose personalities and selling styles are compatible with yours.

Consider hiring a discount broker—a firm that will help you sell your house for less than a full 6 percent commission, in exchange for your doing some of the work that the listing agent normally does (see the discussion in Chapter 17).

Selecting the Firm

A real estate agency must support and set the standards for the agent with whom you will ultimately work, so you must shop for an agency, as well as the individual agent. Conversely, if you already have an agent in mind, is his or her agency likewise up to the task?

Find out how intensely the firm works your area. How many listings does it carry, both in and out of season? What percentage of those listings is sold by the firm's agents? One indicator is the frequency of the firm's name in the by-neighborhood listings in the Sunday paper and the number of the firm's signs you see in your area.

Check with lenders, lawyers, and former clients about the company's reputation and experience. When you sign a listing agreement, you are employing a firm or a broker to find a buyer for your property. If you pick a brokerage firm because you want to work with a particular agent, keep in mind that you are still relying on

---

ASSESSING A REFERRAL

Use this list of questions to help you assess the experience of your neighbors, friends, and co-workers with the agents they've worked with.

- **How long** was the house on the market?
- **Did the house sell for the original price,** or did you have to reduce the price substantially?
- **Do you think your agent got** you the best available deal in both price and terms, or did you accept the offer because you had to make a decision without any more delay?
- **Did the firm maintain** a strong selling push, or did you have to keep prodding?
- **Do you think the property could** have been sold faster? For more money?
- **Did they call** for appointments to show

your home and call to cancel when they had a change of plans?
- **Did the entire office** push your home, or did the job fall almost entirely to the listing agent?
- **Were the people** you dealt with courteous and pleasant to work with?
- **Did your agent** and her firm make it easy or hard for other firms to cooperate?
- **Did the agent** see you through closing?
- **With how many agents** did you have your home listed? If more than one, what happened to the other one(s)?
- **Did you refuse** to renew the listing, or did the agent withdraw voluntarily? Either way, why?
- **Knowing what you know now,** would you use the same agent again?

the firm's experience, contacts, and reputation. While most of your contact may be with the agent, satisfy yourself that behind that agent is strong supervision and plenty of expertise. To whom will the agent turn for advice should problems arise? In most firms the managing broker is responsible for resolving financial problems, supervising complex contract preparation, and counseling agents.

In your initial telephone contact, ask whether the 6 percent commission could be reduced under special circumstances—for example, if the buyer is found by the listing broker, with no sharing of commission with another firm. While brokerage commissions are officially negotiable, in practice most firms hold tight to their stated commission. Be sure to ask if there are additional fees not included in the commission. Review each firm's standard listing contract.

Find out how the firm is staffed. How many agents are full-time? How many are part-time? How experienced is the group as a whole? Do most agents concentrate on selling homes, or do they dabble in commercial real estate and property management as well? Do agents have access to administrative and secretarial help?

How will telephone queries about your property be handled? Call the firm as though you were a prospective buyer, and ask a few friends to do the same. When you call as a seller, you're almost assured of a warm welcome; the reception could be less enthusiastic for purchasers, especially in a seller's market when agents are busy. Does a would-be buyer get an alert and enthusiastic response? How long does it take to get a call returned? How carefully are messages and phone numbers taken? Does the answering agent have listing information available, and is he or she able to tell you what you want to know about the property?

Does the firm participate in the local multiple listing service? An MLS provides a computerized master list of all

> **Call the firm as though you were a prospective buyer. Does a would-be buyer get an alert and enthusiastic response?**

the homes for sale in a marketplace through its member real estate companies. Agents use this information extensively to match up buyers and sellers.

Is the firm hooked into a nationwide referral system? If your home could be attractive to corporate transferees, find out how many referrals the office received during the past 12 months. How many of those referrals resulted in sales and what was the average selling price?

Finding the Best Agent

Ask the head of the firm you select to give you the names of the agents in the office who have the most experience in your neighborhood and price range. An agent who does a lot of business with sellers in the area may work at developing a list of interested buyers or may maintain close contact with agents who have such clients. Select one who knows the community's price history and who has weathered bad years as well as profited during good

---

ELEMENTS OF A LISTING PRESENTATION

A prospective agent's listing presentation should include:

- **Information about the agent's experience,** education, and background.
- **Advice on repairs** and other improvements that would make your home more appealing.
- **Information about the housing market** in general and current activity in your neighborhood.
- **Market analysis** showing all recent comparable sales in your area and properties currently on the market. It should specify the selling price and date of sale for the sold homes, and the date of list-

ing for the unsold ones, along with detailed descriptions of each property.

- **Suggested asking price,** based on how quickly you wish to sell your home.
- **Discussion of the kind of advertising** and promotion to expect, including whether the firm lists homes on the Internet.
- **"Net proceeds" sheet,** illustrating what you might realize on the sale under varying financing arrangements and with various levels of commission.
- **Explanation of various kinds of listings** and listing agreements.

---

ones. Look for an agent who can not only answer a buyer's questions about recently sold homes, but who can also frequently say, "We made those sales."

As always, ask for referrals, especially from your former neighbors. Track down at least two who sold within the past six months to a year; ask them about the agent they used and those they chose not to use. See the box on page 314 for a list of suggested questions.

> **As always, ask for referrals, especially from your former neighbors.**

Interviewing the Agents

To save time, you may wish to hold an informal open house for agents, during which several will come to tour your home at the same time. Select two or three to give you a full "listing presentation" (see the box on the preceding page for what the presentation should include).

After all the presentations, select the one agent you want to do business with first. Your decision should be based on everything from professionalism and knowledge to personality.

After your interviews, you may find yourself looking at a pretty wide range of suggested asking prices. What then? Don't automatically jump to list your home with the agent who so confidently suggested the highest asking price. Make a couple of phone calls to other agents whose presentations impressed you. Ask for their reactions. Compare the high suggested price with comparable recent transactions.

Just as some agents will try to talk you into a low asking price to assure themselves a quick, easy sale (and sure commission), others will give you an inflated estimate of your house's value to get the initial listing. Only later, after your home has sat unsold for too long, will they suggest a price reduction.

Kinds of Listings

Once you've selected an agent, you'll need to work out an employment contract—called a real estate listing—with the agent's broker. The

Keep in mind that the standard contract can be modified to suit your needs.

listing contract appoints the broker (and his agents) as your agent for the specific purpose of locating a buyer for your home who meets the conditions set out in the listing. The agreement, whether oral or written, exclusive or nonexclusive, is a legally enforceable contract.

As you work through the listing contract with your chosen agent, keep in mind that the standard contract can be modified to suit your needs. With any kind of listing, if the agent brings you the deal that the listing calls for (full price and exact terms offered by a buyer who is ready, willing, and able to buy), you are obliged to pay a commission—whether you accept the deal or not.

These are the most frequently used arrangements:

Exclusive Right to Sell

This is the most common agreement. The listing agent is entitled to a commission no matter who sells the property, including you. If another agent produces the buyer, you still owe only the one commission, which will be split between the listing broker and the broker who found the buyer. This type of agreement usually assures you the most service. The agent is guaranteed a commission if he produces a sale, and you have an agent to hold responsible for making all "reasonable" or "diligent" efforts to find a purchaser.

If your employer has guaranteed to buy your home at a discount if you can't get a better offer on the open market (usually in cases of a transfer), be sure to amend an exclusive-right-to-sell agreement to prevent an agent from claiming a commission on your company's purchase. And remember to check for a new "transaction fee" before signing the contract, as discussed in Chapter 17.

Exclusive, or Exclusive Agency

You don't pay a commission if you find your own buyer without help from the agent. If you sign an agreement like this, in effect, you're competing with your own listing agent; if you get direct queries about your property, handle them yourself.

If you have a good prospect who expressed an interest in your home before you listed it with an agent, use this kind of agreement and add a clause that says you may sell the house to this named party—and any other whom you find yourself—without paying a commission to the agent.

Generally, the shorter the listing period the better.

Open

You agree to pay a commission to any agent as long as he or she is the first to produce an acceptable buyer. Again, you don't owe any commission if you are the first one to find a buyer.

This type of listing is most common when there is no multiple listing service. It's also the kind of listing often used by sellers who want to do most of the selling work themselves (see the preceding chapter for a discussion of fizzbos) but want the cooperation of agents in finding buyers.

The commission is typically half of the standard rate—say, 3 percent. The seller should notify agents of such an offer by putting the words "Brokers welcome at 3 percent" in newspaper ads and even on the "For Sale" sign. Then the seller signs a simple open-listing agreement with each agent who expresses an interest in bringing a buyer to see the home.

Make sure you specify an expiration date (not too distant) on every open listing, because you can't sign an exclusive listing with one agent if you have open listings still in force.

Elements of the Listing Contract

Here are all the essentials that you should expect to see in a good listing contract. Agents should provide you with the details of what they will and will not do to help you sell the house.

Expiration Date

Knowing the average and median length of time it takes for homes to sell in your neighborhood should influence your choice of a listing expiration

You can extend a listing beyond its original life, but don't inadvertently sign an agreement containing an automatic extension.

date. A period of three to six months is common. Generally, the shorter the better, but it isn't reasonable to insist on a three-month listing when homes like yours are taking six to nine months to sell.

A relatively short listing will give you the option of switching agents if friction develops with your first agent, or if you feel he or she isn't working hard enough to sell your home.

You can extend a listing beyond its original life, but don't inadvertently sign an agreement containing an automatic extension. If you wish, substitute a provision that extends the listing as much as 60 days if a buyer reneges on a signed sales contract.

You also may want to add a clause reinforcing your right to cancel the contract should the agent fail to do a good job. If you exercise that option, however, you may find that you are still liable for certain expenses that were incurred by the agent. Moreover, some listing contracts may even require you to pay a penalty for having canceled.

Protection Period

If, after the listing expires, you sell your home to someone your former agent had a hand in finding, there may be a clause in the contract that entitles the agent to a commission. Naturally, no agent wants to lose a commission because the listing agreement expires while he or she is still working with a prospective buyer.

Typically, protection clauses give commission rights to agents for 90 to 180 days after a contract ends. If a listing agreement contains such a provision, it also should provide, in fairness to the seller, that the agent give the seller the names of prospective buyers *before* the listing expires—and require written purchase offers from any such buyers within a reasonable time *after* the listing expires.

Commission

Commissions are negotiable. They are not set by law or by industry rules—something most sellers don't realize. A listing agent usually gets a commission based on a percentage of the final sale price of the property—typically 6 percent to 7 percent.

As a practical matter you won't get very far negotiating a lower rate unless you have special circumstances that make your property more economical to sell than others. You can make a strong argument for a lower commission or other concessions in the following cases:

EASY SALE. The property is fairly priced, and it's in a good location. Or the mortgage carries an attractive interest rate and is assumable, and the house is already in immaculate condition.

VOLUME DISCOUNT. You have other properties to put on the block along with your home.

DOUBLE SCORE. Another agent from the firm listing your property delivers a buyer, so the commission won't be shared with another broker.

SCALED-BACK SERVICE. You take on some of the burden of selling and lower the commission accordingly. You also may be able to find a "discount" real estate broker. In either case, be sure the listing contract is clear about what will be done for you in the way of advertising and promotion. Keep in mind that if the commission cut is too deep, cooperating brokers may not be interested in working for a share of an already small commission.

AGENT HAS A BUYER AT HAND. You pay less because the agent won't have to advertise, hold open houses at the property, or split the commission.

THE PURCHASE CONTRACT OR SETTLEMENT IS AT RISK. An agent may be willing to make concessions to hold on to a piece of a deal that's on the verge of getting away. Suppose the seller is dealing directly with a buyer he found himself; if that buyer's offer—which might net more for the seller—is accepted, the seller's listing agent won't get any commission on the sale. To com-

> Cooperating brokers may not be interested in working for a share of an already small commission.

Forget "buyer beware." The new philosophy is "seller beware."

pete, the agent may have to present a considerably higher contract from another buyer and also shave the sales commission, to make the second contract net at least as much as the first one.

Another reason for a shaved commission might be a problem that develops on the way to settlement— say, the seller finds out he has to pay more mortgage discount points than he expected. If the deal is at stake, the agent might offer to make up the difference out of his or her own commission.

Condition of Property and What's for Sale

The listing agreement should describe the general condition of the property. It should show what is being sold "as is" and what, if anything, will be repaired, removed, substituted, or altered prior to settlement. The agreement should list every fixture that will be sold with the house, and those that will not.

Make the agent aware of problems or defects in the property. If the listing agreement doesn't adequately spell out the current condition of the structure, the appliances and the electrical, mechanical, and plumbing systems, have it corrected or write a letter to the agent setting out the information. The old saying, "caveat emptor" (or buyer beware), doesn't stand anymore— the new philosophy, backed by court decisions, is "seller beware." Buyers have a right to know about the true condition of your house and property. If you don't disclose problems and the buyer later discovers them, in most states the buyer can sue you, your agent, and his or her broker—and often will win. (See the discussion in Chapter 16.)

Marketing Plan

Get the proposed marketing plan in writing as an addendum to the listing contract. It can serve as documentation should you feel that your agent is not fulfilling his or her commitments. (Some agents don't use formal marketing plans, so you may find they are unwilling to provide one. If that's the norm for your area, that's fine; but if it's not, you may want to consider an agent who can and will provide one.)

If your agent doesn't call you during the week to give you a progress report, then call the agent. Find out how effective the efforts have been, and whether there any good prospects. If not, are any changes being considered for the marketing plan, and what are they?

Know your target market. Ask the listing agent to give you a profile of your home's most likely buyer or buyers. Will they be first-time buyers, retirees, or corporate transferees? What kind of income will they have?

The marketing strategy your agent proposes should be designed to reach those potential buyers. A comprehensive plan should include these elements:

ADVERTISING. How often and where will your home be advertised? When your home is not being advertised, will the firm be advertising a comparable home so that interested buyers can also be referred to your property?

OPEN HOUSES. What efforts will the agent make to bring interested buyers to your home? For example, will agents who deal with likely clients be sent an information sheet describing the property and date of the open house? Will ads and signs be used?

MULTIPLE LISTING SERVICE. How promptly will an MLS list your property? Ideally, it should go into the computer very quickly, and you should specify a deadline in the listing contract; some multiple listing services require their members to enter new listings within 24 hours of the signing of the contract.

Some brokers will try to keep a new listing out of the MLS computer for several days or more; that gives their own agents a shot at selling the property "in house," so that the whole 6 percent commission is kept within the firm. Once agents at other firms see the listing in the computer and bring prospective buyers in to see the home, the odds increase that the listing broker will have to split the eventual commission with another broker (called the "co-op" broker or agent). You'll pay only the full commission in any event, and your interests are served by a fast sale.

The proposed marketing strategy should be designed to reach your home's most likely buyers.

Henceforth, your home has to be in tip-top condition and ready to show on a moment's notice.

AGENT TOURS. An organized tour for other agents in the office should be arranged soon after you sign the listing. An open house for agents from other firms is another useful sales tool.

SPREADING THE WORD. Will your agent inform your neighbors that you are selling? What other networks will he or she use?

FINANCING. Will your agent be able to work with interested buyers to locate financing?

Get Ready to Sell

Your agent will set about the task of selling your house as soon as the ink is dry on a listing contract, so you had better be ready, too.

Ideally, your home will be ready to show immediately, but if it isn't, do all the last-minute touch-ups and cleanups described in Chapter 16.

From now until a sales contract is accepted, your home has to be in tip-top condition and ready to show on a moment's notice. It's difficult and sometimes stressful living in a home that's for sale, but its tidiness during an appointment or open house will have a lot of bearing on how fast it sells and for how much.

Try to have everyone out of the house when your agent brings a prospect to inspect it, even if that means gathering up kids and parents on short notice. When you aren't there, the agent and house hunter can talk more candidly and the buyer can more easily imagine his or her own family living there comfortably.

Most important, you should be emotionally ready to deal with serious buyers. The signing of the listing contract and presentation of the first buyer's contract is not the time to discover that you have misgivings about selling or qualms about the asking price.

Setting the Right Price

Chapter 19

To set the right price on a home, you should combine an objective evaluation of your property with a realistic assessment of market conditions.

In good markets and bad, you are more likely to benefit by determining a fair value and sticking close to it than you are by asking an unrealistic figure and waiting for buyer response to sift out the "right" price. And in a buyer's market, setting the right price from the outset may be the only effective strategy.

Underpricing can deprive you of money that's rightfully yours. Unless you are in a frightful hurry, aim for full market value. Avoid overeager or unethical agents who suggest a price that will assure them a quick and easy sale—one that won't require an investment of time, effort, or money on their part.

The Dangers of Overpricing

You could set a fair price and then refuse to bargain. But that would deter all those people who hate to pay full price for anything and like to feel they're "getting a deal."

Better to leave a little room for negotiation by asking slightly more than you expect to get. How much more? Asking 5 percent to 10 percent above appraised value could be a good starting point. If sales are brisk in your area, you might just end up getting top dollar.

What many sellers don't realize is that overpricing can result in their getting less for their house than if they priced it right to begin with. The reason: Knowledgeable agents and buyers often won't bid on a

---

CONVERTING TAX TO SALES PRICE

In jurisdictions where there is a tax on the transfer of property, you can determine the sales price of a house by the tax paid. For example, if the tax or fee is 0.1% of the sales price and the transfer fee is $219, then the price paid was $219 divided by .001, or $219,000. You'll find the information you need at the courthouse or city real estate tax office.

---

severely overpriced house. By the time the seller wises up, many of his best prospects will have bought other houses, decreasing demand for the now properly priced property. An overpriced house can end up being sold for less than it would have a few months earlier.

Occasionally, an agent may agree to list a property for far more than it is worth—usually at the owner's insistence. The agent knows that, if the owner is serious about selling, the price will have to come down sooner or later. But sometimes an agent who is competing against other agents for a listing will give a seller an unrealistically high estimate of value, to ensure getting the listing. After the house sits on the market awhile, the agent will suggest a new, lower price more in line with what other agents suggested in the first place.

Some sellers who don't have a deadline for selling ("unmotivated sellers," they're called) will cling for a long time to their overly high asking price—say, 20 percent higher than it should be. They probably won't get their asking price, and even if they do manage to sell a year later for the original price, it will be because a rising market finally caught up with their price.

They might think that they were smart to hold firm, but in fact they were naive, ignoring the time value of money. In the year (or even six months) that they clung to their high price, the rest of the real estate market probably wasn't standing still. The next home they buy may have gone up in value by at least the same margin, and possibly more. Even if they don't buy a replacement home, they have lost the earnings they would have received on the invested proceeds of an earlier sale—say, 5 percent per year if conservatively invested and possibly much more if the money were invested in tax-free bonds or a rising stock market.

Study the Comparables

You run the risk of either overpricing or underpricing if you settle on a price based on less-than-solid information. Shop your competition. Whether you are using an agent or not, learn the offering and selling prices of similar properties. Find out how long each took to sell.

To be comparable, a house that sold has to be close to yours in age, style, size, condition, and location. You should also know the terms under which a house was sold. A $200,000 all-cash sale is very different from a $200,000 sale with $20,000 down and a $40,000 second mortgage taken back by the owner.

Timing is all-important, too. If you are offering your home when sales are brisk and demand is high, you should be able to add something to the price.

Try to find at least three comparables no more than six months old. Sale prices of homes are published in local or regional sections of newspapers. Information on home sales is available at the courthouse or city real estate tax office. You won't learn anything at the tax office about the terms of the sale, the style of the house, or how long it was on the market. If you are going it alone, your best bet is to copy the names and contact the buyers and sellers yourself.

If you are listing your home with an agent, this kind of market research should be prepared and presented to you. Nevertheless, ask questions. You owe it to yourself to be sure that properties being described as comparable to yours really are.

Seller Financing?

The market for mortgage money will play a major role in what you can ask—and what you can get—for your home.

A house that is overpriced can end up being sold for less than it would have a few months earlier.

An appraisal prepared by an experienced, licensed professional comes as close to an objective evaluation as you can get.

In the short run, mortgage interest rates and home prices usually move in opposite directions: When mortgage rates soar, it dampens demand for homes, and real estate prices typically level off or even decline. Not only are there fewer people out looking for houses, but also those qualified buyers will be able to drive hard bargains on price.

Conversely, the less a buyer has to pay in interest, the more house he or she can afford to buy—or to state it another way, the more the buyer will be able to pay for your property.

As a seller, getting the price you want when interest rates are high could depend on whether you've got something to offer in the way of financing help:

■ **Do you have a low-rate assumable mortgage?** That would be a big plus for the buyer and might justify a somewhat higher sales price. Look at your mortgage contract, or ask your lender if you're not sure. (Loans backed by the FHA and VA are assumable.)

■ **Are you willing to offer take-back financing to assist the buyer in making a deal?** If so, you should be able to command a higher price.

Most seller financing is, in effect, a discount on the sales price, so if you're offering a second mortgage (which would have to be discounted even further in order to be sold), you've got to get more from the buyer to make up for it. (For more on seller financing, see the next chapter.)

Get an Appraisal?

If your idea of what your property is worth and the listing broker's recommendation don't coincide, an appraisal may be in order. An appraisal is an especially good idea if you are attempting to sell your home yourself. The $250 to $500 it will cost is money well spent.

Real estate appraising is part art, part experience, and part science. As a result, opinions are subject to honest dispute. Nonetheless, an appraisal prepared by an experienced, licensed professional comes as close to an objective evaluation as you can get. Names of good appraisers should be available from real estate agents, mortgage lenders, and professional associations.

The value of your home falls within a range of prices. An appraiser uses education and judgment to determine that range, and should give you a market-value figure based on the most probable price which a property will bring. Appraisers should adjust the value of properties being used as comparables to reflect creative financing, sales concessions, and seller contributions or buydowns. (See Chapter 7 for more information on appraisal practices.)

With an appraisal report in hand, you and the listing agent should be able to come to an agreement. The asking price you ultimately choose may well be higher than the appraised value, but in most cases, it shouldn't be substantially higher. There's the rub. What is "substantially" higher in one community may be an accepted markup in another.

Go back to the comparables. How much of a spread was there between the original asking price and the actual selling price in each case? Is that the normal differential? Has anything occurred to warrant setting a higher margin?

Once you've done your analysis of all the variables that could justify your price, make your decision with confidence.

> **The asking price you ultimately choose may well be higher than the appraised value, but in most cases, it shouldn't be substantially higher.**

Special Advice for Fizzbos

If you plan to sell your house yourself, then setting the right price becomes imperative. Study your comparables closely. Get an appraisal. Use it to bolster your sales pitch when necessary.

Some fizzbo sellers solicit pricing opinions from real estate agents, even though they don't intend to list the house with an agent. That may strike you as a bit shady, but look at it this way: If you don't make a sale within your time frame, you'll probably turn the job over to a professional. Agents may be willing to

Agents may be willing to prepare market analyses for fizzbo sellers because it gives them a chance to introduce themselves.

prepare market analyses for fizzbo sellers because it gives them a chance to introduce themselves and an opportunity to persuade sellers to use their services for a commission.

At the heart of any fizzbo pricing decision is motivation. Do you want a fast, easy sale? Then set the price lower than you would if you were selling it through an agent. Remember that in a fizzbo sale, the buyer also assumes that she is getting a better deal than if she bought through an agent. Do you want to sell for top dollar and still keep the saved commission for yourself? Then be prepared to bargain on other aspects of the deal.

In most cases, the best deal is one that's good for both parties. You keep some of the saved commission, but you don't hog it all. Aim to show a prospective buyer that:

1. the asking price is consistent with the market,

2. he'll save because there's no commission involved, and

3. you'll net more for the same reason.

Faster Ways to Sell

You need to sell your home and you know it's not the best of times. Cheer up. There are more steps you can take to add luster to your home.

In a slow market, sellers often list their houses at what they believe is a realistic price but assume they'll have to lop off several thousand dollars. Would you do better by lopping that money off the top and listing your home for less? Probably not. Price cuts may be taken for granted in bad markets, and the buyer will probably offer you less than your asking price, anyway.

Instead, look for ways to help the buyer. Don't automatically shy away from unconventional deals. Perhaps you can get your new dream house by selling your home to the builder, or save a hurried buyer time by having your home inspected and repaired before putting it on the market.

The key to success is to start with inexpensive and risk-free enticements, then follow up as you need to with more complex strategies to custom-design an approach that will sell your house. Get your house really ready. Go beyond fresh paint, spotless floors, and a well-groomed yard (see Chapter 16) by offering warranties, inspections, and, in some cases, fix-ups.

Get Your Home Inspected

Having your property inspected before you list it can pay off because you have time to decide what to do about a problem before a buyer finds it. Ask the inspector for repair recommendations on these big-ticket items: roof structure, shingles, foundation, basement or crawl space, heating and air-conditioning systems, and electrical and plumbing systems. Should you fix the problem or cut the price? Find out what it would cost to do the repair. Compare that with the price cut a buyer might ask. Keep in mind that buyers often insist on a discount that's more than the cost of a fix-up. If you offer to pay for the repair, your motives may be suspect. You may get a green light, but with conditions if a buyer believes you'd have the work done on the cheap.

Your agent should be able to give you the names of home inspectors in your area, or you can look in the *Yellow Pages* under "Building Inspection Services," "Engineers (Inspection or Foundation)," or "Real Estate Inspectors." Inspectors who are members of the American Society of Home Inspectors (ASHI) have agreed to abide by a written code of ethics and by prescribed standards of practice. The National Institute of Building Inspectors, the training arm of House-Master, also trains and certifies its inspectors by ASHI standards. Both organizations have continuing education requirements (see the box on page 133).

Expect to pay $300 to $400. You may be able to defer payment until closing, even if you hire an inspector on your own. Some real estate firms can also arrange for deferred-payment inspections (see Chapter 8 for more information on home inspections).

Offer a Decorating Allowance

Say you've spruced up the place along the lines suggested in Chapter 16, but along comes a couple who

Keep in mind that buyers often insist on a discount that's more than the cost of a fix-up.

> A buydown, in which you pay to reduce the buyer's interest rate, can be a powerful selling tool.

love the house but hate the carpet and can't stand your wallpaper. You can offer a decorating allowance—to be paid at settlement—covering agreed-on redecorating expenses.

Consider a Home Warranty Policy

This protects the buyer by paying for certain repairs and costs of replacing heating and air-conditioning systems and major appliances—less deductibles—for up to a year as specified in the warranty contract. The cost: $350 to $600. Ask your agent for names of companies that offer home warranties.

Target Your Buyer

Ordinary ads are of little use when buyers are scarce. So are flyers and the other scattershot approaches. What you need is something to catch the buyer's eye—something that makes your house stand out. That might be as simple as paying for a larger classified ad, for example (for more information about sales tools like signs and ads, see Chapter 17).

Offer Help with Financing

Here's where things get more complex. You'll want to consider how you can offer a financial package that appeals to more than one type of prospective buyer. Just make sure your choices work to your advantage by obtaining good advice from an agent and lawyer who represent your interests.

Buy Down the Mortgage Rate

A buydown, in which you pay to reduce the buyer's interest rate, can be a powerful selling tool. It isn't complicated, and it lets you avoid the risks of lending directly. Sellers who buy down the purchaser's rate by one percentage point for the full term of the mortgage get roughly 2 percent more for their homes than do homeowners who don't offer buydowns.

The amount you pay to buy down the interest rate for the life of your purchaser's mortgage loan depends on the size of the loan. The lower the buyer's down payment, the bigger the loan and the higher your cost. The lender, for example, may charge 4.75 percent of the loan amount for a 1 percent permanent buydown. Short-term or temporary buydowns—two percentage points off the rate the first year and one point the second year, for example—are cheaper; they cost about 2⅜ percent. At closing, as part of the closing costs, you write a check to the lender that covers the agreed-on portion of the interest charges. The lender holds the money in escrow and credits the interest monthly as the payments come due.

A buydown can work better than a cut in your asking price because buyers get a double benefit: a cheaper mortgage and the ability to qualify for a larger loan. For example, on a 30-year, 6 percent fixed-rate, $200,000 loan, a buyer would have to make monthly principal and interest payments of $1,199. A one-percentage-point buydown—to 5 percent—would cut the monthly principal and interest payments by $125, to $1,074. And because lenders use the reduced interest rate to qualify the buyer, you make it possible for the buyer to afford 8 percent to 10 percent more house.

Lowering your sales price—and the amount the buyer will need to borrow—by the cost of the buydown ($9,500, or 4.75 percent of $200,000) won't accomplish the same thing for a buyer who is struggling to meet lender qualifications. At that amount ($190,500), the buyer would make principal and interest payments of $1,142 a month, $68 more than with the buydown.

Treat the cost of the buydown as a drop in sale price. This should reduce the commission you pay to the real estate agent (your contract should specify a fee based on the net sales price) and any taxable gain on the house.

Pick Up Some Payments

You can draw buyers—especially first-timers strapped for cash—by offering to pay their principal and interest for several months.

A buydown gives buyers a double benefit: a cheaper mortgage and the ability to qualify for a larger loan.

Have the contract worded so that you write a check at closing for the amount you've agreed on. Specify that the money be put in an escrow account with the lender and applied monthly to pay for principal and interest. It helps the buyer's cash flow and, more important, it has tremendous psychological appeal. Buyers like the idea of getting to live for free while you pick up the tab. You treat it as a reduction in price for tax purposes.

Offer Help at Closing

Maybe your buyer isn't concerned about the monthly payment. Maybe he or she has a good salary but not much in savings. In that case, during negotiations you can offer to pick up some closing expenses. But be aware that lenders place a limit on seller contributions. If you exceed that limit, the additional assistance will reduce the amount the lender is willing to finance.

A simple and effective tactic is to offer to pay one or more of the points the buyer would have to pay to get a mortgage. You may also offer to prepay taxes or, for a condo or town house, to pay the first year's common charges. As the seller, you treat these concessions as a reduction in price. Even prepaid taxes get taken off the price, except any prorated share for the time during the year that you still lived in the house.

> ### THE REAL DEAL
>
> If you agree to pay some of your buyer's points, do not overlook the full value of your concession—including its tax deductibility to the buyer. Say that you agree to pay 1.5 points on a $300,000 mortgage. That will save the buyer $4,500 (1.5 percent of $300,000), plus another $1,125 in tax savings for one who is in the 25 percent bracket (25 percent of $4,500). That extra contribution from Uncle Sam might make it easier for you to get your price.

Consider Becoming a Lender

Helping the buyer at closing is attractive because you don't take on the risks of becoming a lender. But if your buyer can't qualify for an institutional mortgage (because she's self-employed, for example, or already owns a number of investment properties), offering financing is your next choice.

Becoming a lender is riskier to you, so read Chapters 9 and 20 for tips and traps. You should require

---

HIRE A SITTER

If you move into your new home before you can sell the old one, you're at a considerable disadvantage. You're saddled with two mortgages. An empty house is harder to market, and if it sits vacant for too long, your homeowners insurance could be canceled. You could rent the place, but that can have unhappy tax consequences. And the delay in selling could be costly if your market heads south.

In such a situation, consider hiring a sitter, or home manager. Begin your search for such service by asking for leads from the agency with which your home is listed.

Another option may be: **Caretakers of America** (303-832-2313; http://www.caretakersforamerica.com), which operates in about 25 cities. Caretakers hires subcontractors to live in your home at no cost to you. While living in your home, the subcontractor pays a reduced rent to Caretakers as well as all utility costs.

---

one to two percentage points above the going rate on any loan you make and terms that meet your particular needs. Limit the length of the loan if you can—three to eight years is preferred. Have your agent check the borrower's credit, financial condition, and employment status carefully. Work with an experienced and knowledgeable real estate lawyer (and perhaps a real estate agent as well) on contract terms and financial safeguards. Make final approval contingent on a legal review. Then record a lien to protect your interest.

Lend Part of the Down Payment

The trade-off is more risk. Be very cautious about making a loan so large that it reduces the buyer's equity in the property below 20 percent. The lower the new owner's stake, the more likely a drop in property value could trigger a default on the loan. A second mortgage puts you second in line, behind the primary lender, if the buyer defaults. For your protection, include language in the note and the contract to the effect that should the buyer default on any mortgage lien against the property, you have the right to declare him in default on all of them.

Consider selling the borrower's note to a private investor and look into what you would be paid for it.

In lousy markets, sellers must come up with innovative strategies custom-made for the deal.

Expect to accept a discount—based on yields that could go as high as 20 percent or more—because investors want to be compensated for factors such as risk and the time value of money. If you intend to sell the note, make final acceptance of the purchase offer contingent on locating someone who will buy the note at closing. Your real estate agent should be able to help you locate an investor. Or check your local paper's classified ads under "loans" or "money available."

Hire a real estate lawyer to draw up the loan papers. Use legally acceptable terminology that mirrors, whenever possible, standard mortgage documents and terms.

Treat the discount as a capital loss, which can offset capital gains and up to $3,000 per year of other types of income for tax purposes.

Provide an Interim Mortgage

You could also offer to become the primary or sole lender for a limited period of time. Say a couple has cash for the down payment but they can't qualify for a mortgage while still paying on their old house. As a seller, you could offer them a loan at 8 percent for one year, with interest-only payments due quarterly and the full principal due as a balloon payment either when the old home sells or at the end of the year, whichever occurs first. (You would treat the interest as taxable income.)

Get Creative

In lousy markets, sellers must come up with innovative strategies custom-made for the deal.

SUBSTITUTE THE DOWN PAYMENT. Consider taking a note or equity in place of a cash down payment. You may have a buyer who has a note carried back on the sale of another property. He or she may be willing to assign this note to you in lieu of all or part of a down payment. A couple may have considerable equity in a property they want to keep and may be willing to write a note secured by a deed of trust or mortgage on their property in your favor. This could become part or all of the down payment on your home.

LOOK FOR A TRADE. If you've found a home you like and your own place isn't selling, talk to the other owner about a trade. Trades can be tricky because there's seldom an even exchange. Builders, for example, often insist on taking a steep discount for the traded house. Get expert advice.

PROPOSE A DEAL IN WHICH EVERYONE WINS. The dream house one couple and their three children wanted was a new Cape Cod–style home with a bowed roof and details not often found in houses today. The builder had dropped the price by $50,000, to $450,000. But all offers for the couple's own house—listed for $289,900 and reduced to $284,900—fell through when prospective buyers couldn't sell their own houses.

Finally, the builder offered $263,200 (the equivalent of $280,000 minus the agent's commission) for their old house. That was a little less than they had hoped for, but "we figured we would trade the risk of losing a few thousand dollars of profit for the certainty of closing and getting the house we wanted." The builder ended up selling the old house six months later for $280,000.

Take the Lease-Option Route

When homebuyers are so scarce that cutting the price of the house isn't the answer, think about leasing instead, and turn the lease into a sale. The easiest but least-effective option does nothing more than give the renter the right of first refusal to buy the house. A better offer is a lease-option. This lets you tap into a wider pool of people: buyers who could handle the monthly mortgage payments but don't have enough cash for a down payment.

HOW A LEASE-OPTION WORKS: A potential buyer agrees to two things: to lease your house for a specific monthly rent, and to pay you for an option that gives him or her the right to buy the place at a set price within the option period—typically six months to two years. Payment for the option (called option consideration) gen-

> If cutting the price of the house isn't the answer, think about leasing instead, and turn the lease into a sale.

Critics say lease-options are no better than renting because they take your house off the market.

erally comes in two parts. First is a one-time, up-front nonrefundable payment, which can range from 1 percent to 5 percent of the price of the house. Second is an amount—typically 10 percent and up monthly—that is paid in addition to rent. Both are credited toward the purchase price when the option is exercised and should act as a powerful incentive to buy. If the renter chooses not to exercise the option, the money is yours to keep.

Lease-option sellers often get their sales price, even in slow markets. For example, in one slow Florida market, where nearby houses were going for 15 percent discounts and averaging 160 days on the market, a lease-optioned house stayed on the market for only 16 days before going for asking price.

IS IT BETTER THAN RENTING? Critics say lease-options are no better than renting because they take your house off the market. But proponents believe tenants who consider themselves potential owners are better caretakers. They are also financially strong enough to make the up-front option payment and write big monthly rental checks.

A greater concern is that if home values drop, your renters may not exercise the option. You can always renegotiate at the end of the option period. But even if your home appreciates, you can't be sure they'll buy—which can cause real problems if you've already bought a new, more expensive home: You must sell your old home within two years of the time you buy the new one or you'll owe tax on the profit when you finally sell.

CHECK OUT THE BUYER. You want to be certain your lease-option renter will qualify for a mortgage when the option term is up. Lenders will generally require that the buyer come up with a 5 percent down payment in addition to any part of the option consideration credited to the down payment. Your buyer must also have the income to qualify for the mortgage loan.

CONSIDER THE TAX CONSEQUENCES. The money you receive as option consideration is not taxable, at least not right away. If the option is exercised, that money is considered part of the purchase price; and that means it affects your gain or loss on the sale. If the option expires, however, you must report that amount as taxable income in the year the option expires.

The part of the monthly payments not attributed to the option is rental income. It's taxable, but you also get to deduct rental expenses.

Make sure the lease-option contract is properly drawn up by a lawyer. Also, check with your lender before you set up a lease-option arrangement. You don't want your lender to treat the arrangement as a sale during the lease period because that could prematurely force you to pay off your mortgage.

Boost the Incentives

Real estate agents hit by hard times are sometimes more willing to negotiate lower commission fees. But in the same climate, others dare to ask for more—and get it—by arguing that homeowners need more help when buyers are scarce. When times are tough, you don't have to buy the argument that paying more is the way to go. But if you're willing to pay up and that's what it takes to sell, use the following guidelines:

■ **Get the best.** If you agree to pay a larger-than-normal commission, make sure you get a top-selling agent with a track record of moving homes even in a bad market. Ask for extra services such as inspections, appraisals, warranties, and decorating help.

■ **Insist on a short listing period (60 to 90 days).** If the broker doesn't get the job done in that time, then find someone who will.

■ **Get a written marketing plan,** including concrete commitments on when the agent will show the house and on the placement, type, and frequency of ads. Look for innovative marketing, such as a no-cost, ten-day "red hot summer sale" with extra advertising.

> **Real estate agents hit by hard times are sometimes more willing to negotiate lower commission fees.**

■ **Insist that your house be listed in the multiple listing service quickly,** no later than within 24 or 48 hours.

■ **Make sure the broker is knowledgeable about financing options,** including take-back mortgages.

Negotiating with Buyers

Tension between buyer and seller is inevitable. A buyer wants the most house for his money; a seller wants the most money for his house.

If you've employed an agent to represent only you, rely on this professional to direct events toward a satisfactory conclusion. If you are selling on your own, consider hiring a lawyer or agent (acting as a real estate consultant) to help with negotiations; alternatively, brush up on basic aspects of the art when you hang out the "for sale" sign.

Read the chapters meant for buyers. They'll give you a sense of how an informed, well-prepared buyer might go about selecting a home, making an offer, and negotiating the best deal.

Negotiating Through an Agent

Buyers and sellers usually find bargaining awkward and uncomfortable. Both are likely to be more frank and open when talking to a third party. For these reasons, an experienced agent often is successful when two-party, face-to-face negotiations fail. You should be comfortable being utterly frank with your agent. Agents know sellers sometimes take positions they don't mean to hold to the end. Let your agent know what is most important to you. Be precise about what is and isn't acceptable. Make sure the agent has satisfied himself—and you—that the buyer is financially qualified to fulfill the contract offer; this can be done only by checking all the facts the buyer has submitted on a written financial-qualifications form.

Early contracts on a well-priced house are usually submitted by the most serious, well-qualified buyers.

If a cooperating agent brings in a serious buyer, have your agent (usually the listing agent) brief him on your requirements as soon as possible. Cooperating agents should be firmly instructed not to reveal any confidential information about you or your situation to the buyer. If for some reason your agent cannot do this, impress it on the co-op agent yourself before sending him back to the would-be buyer.

As your agent should know, all negotiating should be done in writing, not orally. Be careful not to react to trial balloons the buyer sends up hoping to discover your bottom-line price and other terms. Ask for a written offer.

Don't feel you must commit to the first contract presented, particularly when it's below your expectations. Remain confident. You've priced your home properly and it's competitive with other houses on the market, so hang tight.

On the other hand, don't disregard a good offer just because it's the first or second one you receive. As experienced agents know, early contracts on a well-priced house are usually submitted by the most serious, well-qualified buyers—people who know their own needs and resources and who have studied the market carefully. A reasonable offer from such a prospect is worth serious consideration and probably a counteroffer from you.

Considering the Contract

Money, people, and the law are primary elements in any real estate sales contract. A valid real estate contract must be in writing and must have been freely offered by the buyer and accepted by the seller. All parties to the contract must be legally competent to do business (for example, of legal age and mental competence). Money or other valuable consideration must be exchanged for title to the property.

Assuming you are using a specific-performance contract—the most common form of contract used in home sales—keep in mind that if things go wrong the buyer could require you to sell your home to him or pay damages. Obviously, you should be familiar with the terms of any contract form you give to a would-be purchaser. But when a buyer presents you with an offer set out in an unfamiliar document, take time to study it before responding.

Once a contract offer passes your preliminary review and becomes a candidate for acceptance, it should be reviewed by your lawyer or be made contingent on that review, especially if you are selling your home yourself. (See Chapter 7 for a discussion of contingencies that are commonly sought by purchasers; decide in advance how you want to respond to these conditions.)

Consider the contract as a whole. Is it slanted in favor of the buyer? If so, consult with your lawyer about making changes. Analyze the document as a series of paragraphs or clauses, each written to benefit one party or the other. Evaluate them one by one.

Don't be overly impressed by a large earnest-money deposit—it doesn't automatically cement a contract. Most offers contain language that makes it likely such deposits will ultimately be returned to their offerers if a deal doesn't go through. Look for other signs—contractual and psychological—as evidence of a buyer's serious intentions.

Beware of the contract that binds only you. Getting a seller to accept an offer that nails down the price and terms but leaves the buyer free to escape through any number of clauses is a perennially favorite buyer strategy. Avoid such a pitfall by examining each contingency. Is each clear and precise? Is it reasonable?

Price and Terms

If you receive what you consider an insultingly low offer, don't give in to an emotional response. Now is the time to be realistic, objective, and, above all, cool. Examine the offer. Was the price based on an independent appraisal or a broker's market analysis? How long has your property been on the market? How many

> **Beware of the contract that binds only you. Examine each contingency. Is each clear and precise? Is it reasonable?**

A first offer, even a low one, may reveal what's most important— price or terms— to this buyer.

written offers have you received? What kind of market are you in—buyer's or seller's?

If you're considering financing part of the sale, you must look beyond the price alone and consider the terms offered. Such things as the amount of the down payment, the number and amount of payments, length of the loan period, interest rate, and other terms have a dramatic impact on the value of the offer.

Most properties don't bring full price, after all. Don't use price alone as a reason not to counter or negotiate. A first offer may reveal what's most important—price or terms—to this particular buyer and thus give you the key you need to begin the bargaining.

Condition of Home and Inspection

It is fair that the purchaser should have the opportunity to have your home inspected for soundness of construction and state of repair. Keep the process fair by insisting that the person or firm to be used is named in the contract by professional designation, and be sure to set a time limit for the removal of the contingency—five or so working days.

Include all mandatory and voluntary disclosure statements about the condition of the property and known defects in the body of the contract. If radon or lead-based paint is a problem in your area, having test results available will save everyone time. The same goes for other required or desired tests.

Watch what you guarantee. Occasionally, a purchaser asks a seller to guarantee that the roof won't leak, the heating system won't go out, or any number of other such assurances. Don't do it. If you do, you are not making a sale, you are taking on a partner. Do not undertake to remain responsible for your property once you have sold it.

As a rule, contract language determines what must be in working order at settlement. Make sure everything is clearly spelled out; otherwise, local law and custom may prevail. Suppose that only three of the four burners on your stove work and you don't want to pay for repairs. Unless your contract specifically states that the stove is being sold with three working burners, not four, you may end up paying for the repair at the settlement table.

Buyers often are willing to negotiate on the condition of the house. For example, if your home is a candidate for extensive upgrading, a prospective buyer who is planning renovations that include installing central air-conditioning may be happy to bargain over the broken window unit because it would be discarded anyway once work begins.

Financing

If the contract is contingent on a buyer's ability to obtain an acceptable loan, does the clause spell out what actions are required by the buyer? What interest rate and number of discount points does the buyer consider "acceptable"? Is there a time limit? What will happen if no loan is secured by the agreed-on deadline? How will you know when the buyer gets a loan commitment? How can the contingency be removed? Generally, you'll want to leave the buyer as few escape hatches as possible.

Response Deadline

You'll be asked to respond to a contract offer within a specified period of time—say, one or two days. Try to get as long a response time as possible. If you are presented with a desirable contract containing a deadline you are unable to meet—perhaps because your lawyer or spouse is out of town—counter promptly with a more suitable time frame—and an explanation.

If you think you'll have other offers coming in, you'll want to buy as much time as possible to review them and perhaps use one offer to jack up another. Tell other interested parties (or have your agent tell them) that you've got a good offer on the table and that if they want a shot at this purchase, they had better move fast with an attractive offer.

What if you receive multiple offers at the same time? You have two choices: Either respond in exactly the same manner and with exactly the same wording

> **You'll be asked to respond to a contract offer within a specified period of time—say, one or two days.**

When you accept a contract offer contingent on the sale of the buyer's house, you are shouldering a great deal of risk.

to each, or examine and respond to each in the precise order in which you received it.

While you are studying the offer, keep the buyer informed of your progress. A buyer left hanging for too long may have second thoughts and may even withdraw before you have a chance to accept or to produce a counteroffer.

Sale of Buyer's Home

Should you cooperate with a prospective purchaser who must sell a home before buying yours? Maybe. But when you accept a contract offer contingent on the sale of the buyer's house, you are linking the sale of a property you know—yours—to the sale of one you don't know—his. You'll be taking your house off the market until the buyer's house is sold and closed. If things go awry, you could end up weeks later just where you started—hanging up a "for sale" sign. You are shouldering a great deal of risk when you agree to this kind of contingent sale. George Rosenberg and Bill Broadbent, authors of *Owner Will Carry* (see box on page 348), suggest it may be desirable to counter such an offer in the following way:

Inquire about equity in the buyer's house. If there is enough equity (in terms of loan to value) to safely create a note secured by the buyer's house, then you can complete the sale of your house. The note created by your prospective buyer is made payable to you, the seller, whose house he wants to buy. The note could be due in a year or so and bear interest at any mutually agreeable rate. You could agree to allow interest (if any) to accumulate and not be payable until the note is due or the buyer's home sells, whichever event occurs first. You could also agree to accept the created note in lieu of a down payment. When the house sells, the note is paid off.

This kind of agreement works only when the buyer has substantial equity in her house. The combination of the new note plus old mortgage(s) should add up to no more than 85 percent to 90 percent of the current market value of the buyer's home. It puts buyer and seller on more equal footing and ensures that the buyer will be motivated to sell.

Nevertheless, if you believe accepting an offer contingent on the sale of the buyer's home is the best you can hope for under the circumstances, seek the advice of a broker familiar with the market in the area of your potential buyer's home. Assure yourself that the property is salable and reasonably priced. Get marketing plans set out in the contract. For example, it should be clear what the owner proposes to do if the home doesn't sell after one month, after two, and so on.

Consider asking for an up-front nonrefundable option (in lieu of an earnest-money deposit), which you will retain if the deal fails to close within a specified time. Have the contingency sale clause reviewed by your lawyer. Better still, have her write it.

Settlement Date and Occupancy

If you're selling your home because you already have another house under contract, seek a settlement date that will enable you to take your sales proceeds to the next closing. Be realistic; the buyer of your home will probably need at least 30 to 50 days to arrange financing and come to closing.

Most sold homes are delivered to the buyer empty and clean on settlement day. If you need a temporary place to live after settlement, resist the path of least resistance. Our best advice: If at all possible, avoid staying in your old home even one night after closing. And don't accept the new owner's offer—no matter how friendly—to accommodate you with a short-term lease.

Other Conditions

Other contingencies address problems or events that may happen between the time the contract is signed and the time title is passed to the buyer. If your house burns down or a natural disaster strikes, what happens? Does the buyer have to buy and pay the agreed-on price? Can the whole deal be called off? Can a lower price be offered? What about insurance proceeds?

If you need a temporary place to live after settlement, don't consider staying in your old home even one more night.

Take Back a Mortgage?

High interest rates and shortages of available mortgage money are always bad news for both homebuyers and sellers. Be sure any solution suggested to you—by whatever name and by either buyer or agent—doesn't just shift the problem from their shoulders to yours.

First of all, do you really belong in the mortgage-lending business? If you need your equity to make a down payment on another home, you shouldn't take back a mortgage. And even if you can afford to help your buyer with financing, you may not want to. Mortgage lending is complicated. It involves both originating and servicing the loan. Origination is setting up the loan—screening applicants, appraising the property, and drawing up papers. Servicing is collecting monthly payments, dunning for delinquencies, sending annual statements, and foreclosing when necessary.

Tempted by the possibility of earning a high return from taking back a first or second mortgage?

A properly drawn and executed first deed of trust or first mortgage would put you in the most secure position, assuming you required a large down payment as an equity cushion should the value of the home drop. Once recorded, the house generally can't be sold without your permission. A second deed of trust or second mortgage, however, puts you second in line behind the lender holding the first. Should the buyer default, forcing the first-trust holder to foreclose, you could be wiped out unless there is enough equity left after paying off the first to pay you.

There are rewards, but they don't come easily or cheaply. Take-back financing is never without risk. Your biggest danger is ending up with a deadbeat buyer and a contract that doesn't give you the legal protection you need. Close behind is financial risk. Because seller

---

TAKE BACK OR TAKEN?

For a discussion of what you will—and should—go through to get a deal you can live with, read *Owner Will Carry* by Bill Broadbent and George Rosenberg (Creative Solutions Inc., 1380 Broad St., San Luis Obispo, CA 93401; 800-366-6037; http://www.arrnettbroadbent.com/ownerwillcarry.html; $39.95, plus $4.40 shipping and handling. A $7 discount to readers who mention this Kiplinger book). The book includes a CD-ROM.

take-back mortgages are usually worth less than sellers realize, they are the equivalent of cutting the price. And when interest rates and other terms of seller take-back mortgages are too generous to buyers, holding such paper can be distinctly inferior to alternative investments you could obtain with cash.

How to Protect Yourself

Avoid making these all-too-common mistakes:

AMATEUR LOAN DOCUMENTS. Generally speaking, the best-drawn documents are the ones prepared by lawyers and used by professional lenders. Don't settle for less. Hire a lawyer who specializes in real estate loans and an attorney who has experience writing mortgage-loan documents. Ask professional mortgage lenders, mortgage loan brokers, and agents for names of the lawyers they use.

TOO LITTLE DOWN PAYMENT. Don't take back a mortgage when a buyer wants to put down less than 20 percent. Professional mortgage lenders demand at least that much equity when there is no mortgage insurance, and so should you. This gives you an adequate buffer in the event of foreclosure because it increases the probability that the property can be sold for enough to cover your loan. It also gives the borrower a big incentive to avoid foreclosure in the first place.

TOO LOW AN INTEREST RATE. Sellers rarely ask enough, even on second mortgages. A lower-than-market interest rate reduces your return if you keep the note and reduces what you will be paid if you sell it. In addition, the Internal Revenue Service requires that a minimum interest rate be charged. Check with your lawyer or tax accountant for information on how much or how little interest you can charge the buyer without running afoul of either state law or the IRS.

TOO LONG A TERM. Keep the length of the loan as short as possible—one or two years, if you can get it. Resist

> Professional lenders demand at least 20 percent down when there's no mortgage insurance; so should you.

Avoid getting involved with anyone who proposes that you take back a note and deed of trust without recording it.

going over three years. The longer the term, the deeper the discount when you sell the loan. (Because one to three years isn't a long loan term, find out how the buyer proposes to pay off the note. If it's by refinancing, you'd be wise to provide the buyer with a reasonable way to extend the note.)

SKIMPY CREDIT CHECK. Too often, laymen tend to rely on appearances. If the buyer to whom they intend to extend a mortgage seems okay, they make the loan. Prospective buyers of that mortgage, however, are likely to ask for the credit report on the borrower. A credit report is inexpensive and relatively easy to obtain by sending your request along with the buyer's authorization, name, address, and Social Security number to a national or local credit bureau (see Chapter 2).

ALLOWING LATE PAYMENT. Pros have learned that failure to crack down on first-time delinquents often leads to costly problems. Make sure your loan documents include a late charge, and enforce it to the letter.

LACK OF RECORDATION. Avoid getting involved with anyone (buyer, broker, agent, or investor) who proposes that you take back a note and deed of trust without recording it. It could happen like this: A buyer offers you $4,000 down on your $200,000 home. The buyer will obtain a bank loan for $160,000 and wants to give you, in lieu of cash, a note for $36,000 secured by a second deed of trust on the house—providing you agree that instructions to the escrow officer or settlement lawyer will reflect only the new $160,000 loan and that you received $40,000 outside of escrow. You are asked to hold the $36,000 note for several months without recording it so that the bank won't be aware of the additional lien on the property.

This is illegal. If you go along with it, you are essentially participating in a scheme to defraud the lender. There is nothing to keep the new owner of your home from further encumbering the property without your knowledge. You also have no way of knowing whether any judgment was attached to the owner that would take first priority over your unrecorded second deed of trust.

Forging an Agreement

If you're selling through an agent, contracts will be presented to you through that agent, and you will counter all offers through the same agent.

Everything in the offering contract is negotiable. Decide what you don't want to give in on and what doesn't matter that much to you. Changes can be inked in over or next to language on the contract, or a new contract can be drawn up from scratch. A draft contract can go back and forth between buyer and seller any number of times, but you'll both want to avoid an interminable negotiation, where fatigue and disgust could jeopardize the whole deal.

When everyone has agreed to the terms, initialed the changes, and signed the contracts, you've got an agreement binding on all parties. All that remains is the removal of contingency clauses, arranging of financing, clearing of title, and other steps to settlement.

> ## STRATEGY FOR NEGOTIATION
>
> If you are a for-sale-by-owner seller, you will probably be doing your own negotiating with prospective buyers. In that case, a little book worth its weight in gold is *Getting Past No, Negotiating Your Way from Confrontation to Cooperation* by William Ury (Bantam Books).

Selling on Your Own

If you're on your own, keep your dealings as professional and courteous as possible. Don't take anything personally; remember, the buyer has a right to try to pay as little as possible and get the best terms. It's a business deal, so try not to be offended by a low initial offer or overly generous terms or any other initial offer the buyer may make.

If a sale is to be made, both parties must be willing to ask for what they want, voice their objections, and offer alternatives. Begin negotiations by seeking out

BEFORE A BUYER ASSUMES YOUR MORTGAGE

If a prospective buyer wants to assume your current mortgage, ask the following questions. You have the right to know:

- **How does** the buyer intend to pay for the property?
- **Has he or she** been preapproved by a lender?

- **Where will** the down payment come from?
- **How knowledgeable** is the buyer about market value, the neighborhood, and so forth?
- **Are the terms** of the sale understood?
- **Has the property** been examined thoroughly?

areas of agreement. Find out what is attractive about your property, and build on that. Move on to issues that don't involve anyone's ego, such as the desired date of possession. (Normally, that's not a touchy issue, but, like everything else in a real estate sale, it can be.) Get the buyer thinking about moving in; it makes the whole purchase seem more real.

You could hire an experienced real estate lawyer to negotiate for you, paying the lawyer a flat fee or hourly rate. When you consult a lawyer to have your sample contract drawn up or to review a contract presented by a buyer, find out whether he or she would consider negotiating on your behalf.

Check the Buyer's Credentials

If the buyer intends to assume your current mortgage, you must be even more careful than usual about verifying his or her financial stability and credit record. Under some circumstances, if the new owner defaults on the mortgage he assumes from you, you could be held liable.

All the legal fine print in the world can't make a good deal with a bad buyer. You could be back to square one if an impulsive or unprepared buyer is derailed by the first negative comment from a home inspector or mortgage lender. To repeat: Make a judgment about a prospective buyer's commitment and financial capability before proceeding into a nitty-gritty examination of the purchase offer. Ask your prospect for a net-worth statement and get answers to the questions that are outlined in the box on the preceding page.

Keep Selling

When you sense your prospect is getting close to the contract-writing stage, keep selling. Now is not the time suddenly to begin acting the role of pleasant host or hostess, assuming the buyer will take it upon herself to do the rest. Avoid these common mistakes:

- **Appearing too eager.** If the buyer feels you are overly eager, or too anxious to make a deal, you may lose a sale. He may become suspicious, or he may pressure you into making major concessions.
- **Appearing too tough.** A good deal can slip through your hands if you are too rigid or unpleasant to work with. Try to be flexible and objective. If you can't agree over one point, keep pushing toward agreement in areas where you do see eye to eye. Try not to close the door on any one point completely; just put the matter off until later.
- **Failing to empathize.** Try to see the buyer's side of things. Never become defensive. Be ready with all the information needed; be confident and patient.

If you reach a point where you recognize you must compromise or concede, get everything else agreed on in writing. Then, when you do concede the point, the deal essentially is locked in.

Once you have an accepted contract—fully signed and with all changes initialed—stop talking! Stand up, shake hands, and change the subject.

Now you have a contract and are on your way to the settlement table.

A good deal can slip through your hands if you are too rigid or unpleasant to work with.

Preparing for Settlement

Buyers may dread the arrival of closing day and the huge outlay of cash, yet still be eager to get on with it so they can move into their new home. Sellers look forward to collecting their bounty, but their anticipation may be tinged with anxiety and sadness about giving up their home for good.

The bulk of the work between contract signing and closing falls on the buyer, who must arrange for a home inspection, financing, and homeowners- and title-insurance policies.

As the seller, you have relatively little to do at this point. If you agreed to have something repaired, do it now. If a problem arises with the title, you could become involved with paperwork, legal bills, and delicate diplomacy (see Chapter 11). If a title problem is so complicated it threatens to delay settlement, your buyer may want to void the contract. Your lawyer may be able to smooth things over for a time, but if the deal seems headed for the rocks you'll need to determine what your rights and options are.

Keep Yourself Informed

Keep abreast of progress on both sides. If your buyer is having trouble getting a loan on the terms specified in the contract, you should know it; if she is turned down, it could jeopardize the whole deal, and you could end up putting the house back on the market. A day or so before closing, make sure all the necessary papers and documents have been gathered and are in the hands of the right players. The settle-

IF YOU HOLD AN FHA LOAN

Federal Housing Administration (FHA) rules permit mortgage lenders to charge sellers a month's worth of interest no matter how early in the month settlement occurs. A seller paying off an FHA loan who agrees to settle on June 5 will pay May interest on June 1, and then pay nonprorated interest on June 5 for the month of June. This practice is allowed because these loans are pooled and sold to investors in the secondary market. Investors are promised an entire month of interest income no matter when in the month they buy Ginnie Mae mortgage securities. A lender who waives the right to charge sellers a full month's interest must pay the difference to investors out of its own funds.

ment agent was probably selected by the buyer, but you are free to bring your own lawyer to the closing.

Nothing is more tedious than sitting around a settlement table while the escrow officer or settlement lawyer telephones lenders, insurance companies, contractors, and others for figures that should be at hand. A process that should take an hour instead drags on for half a day.

At this stage, there should be no arguing over who pays what because everything should have been spelled out in the contract. You don't want any surprises, either. Your agent should have kept you up-to-date on what you should expect to net from the transaction. You should have received an estimated-net sheet when you signed the listing agreement, and another along with each contract presentation. Prior to settlement, the escrow officer or settlement lawyer should have provided you with a copy of the settlement sheet (see Chapter 12).

If you are handling your own settlement, you can get an estimate at the time you arrange for closing, or "open escrow," whether it is with a title or abstract company or an abstract lawyer.

Can things go wrong? Sure. Documents can be misplaced, delayed, or lost. Some of the common last-minute glitches can be avoided.

People who should be present at closing need to be kept informed of any change in the date, time, or place. They should be reminded a week before closing, and again the day before. If closing is being conducted by the buyer's lawyer, and you want your lawyer to be there, too, you should have cleared the initial date before signing the contract. However, if closing is delayed or changed for any reason, you'll need to clear it with your lawyer again. Follow up with each individual on whom you are depending.

Anyone named on the deed under which you hold title must sign the new deed by which you grant title. In many jurisdictions, if you have married since acquiring title, your spouse also will have to sign the deed. If a co-owner doesn't live nearby, allow time to have the deed signed and returned before settlement.

You should know when you will be paid. Don't expect to walk away from the settlement table with a check in hand, but don't leave the question of when and how you will be paid undetermined. Most settlement lawyers do not disburse checks until all the necessary documents have been recorded. If that's the procedure, when will the recording take place, and how often are checks made up? Most likely, the buyer's lender will want to review settlement papers and wait for the deed to be recorded before disbursing any funds.

If you are buying another property, consider having both settlements at the same office, scheduled back-to-back. That way, the timing of the disbursement is not a problem. You sign a paper authorizing the title company or lawyer to assign the funds from your sale to your purchase.

The Papers You'll Need

For more details on the settlement process, see Chapter 12, "Get Ready for Settlement." Here's a checklist of what will be needed for closing:

> At this stage, there should be no arguing over who pays what because everything should have been spelled out in the contract.

- **A copy of the sales contract** and documentation showing that any contingencies have been removed or satisfied.
- **All documents needed to complete the transfer** of title. These usually are handled by the title insurance or abstract company and your lawyer or closing officer. They may include: certificate of title, deed, correcting affidavits, quitclaim deeds, survey, and title insurance policy or binder. Be sure the closing officer has the necessary papers showing that all judgments, liens, and mortgages have been removed or satisfied.
- **Homeowners insurance policy.** When the buyer plans to take over the unused portion of your hazard insurance, you'll need to make arrangements in advance so that all the paperwork will be completed on time.
- **Prorations for ongoing expenses** such as insurance premiums, property taxes, accrued interest on assumed loans, and utilities (if not shut off between owners). The proration date usually is determined by local custom but can be different if the contract so specifies.
- **Receipts showing payment of the latest water, electric, and gas bills.** Escrow accounts are set up in some areas to cover the final water bill. If the final bill is not paid and the water service is provided by the community, a lien would be placed against the property.
- **A certificate from your lender** indicating the mortgage balance and the date to which interest has been prepaid. The closing officer usually obtains these figures calculated to the day of settlement.
- **Photo ID** such as a driver's license.

Index

Share the message!

Bulk discounts
Discounts start at only 10 copies and range from 30% to 55% off retail price based on quantity.

Custom publishing
Private label a cover with your organization's name and logo. Or, tailor information to your needs with a custom pamphlet that highlights specific chapters.

Ancillaries
Workshop outlines, videos, and other products are available on select titles.

Dynamic speakers
Engaging authors are available to share their expertise and insight at your event.

Call Kaplan Publishing Corporate Sales at
1-800-621-9621, ext. 4444,
or e-mail kaplanpubsales@kaplan.com